D0904782

Oil Booms

by Roger M. Olien &
Diana Davids Olien

OIL
BOOMS

Social Change
in Five
Texas Towns

University of Nebraska Press
Lincoln & London

Library of Congress Cataloging in Publication Data
Olien, Roger M., 1938-
Oil Booms.
Bibliography: p.
Includes index
1. Company towns – Social aspects – Texas –
Case studies. 2. Social change – Case studies.
3. Petroleum industry and trade – Social aspects –
Texas – Case studies. I. Olien, Diana Davids, 1943-
II. Title.
HT123.5.T4Q46 307.7'6 81-11686
AACR2

For Conrad and Kathleen
who have shared our
interest and excitement

Contents

Illustrations

Tables

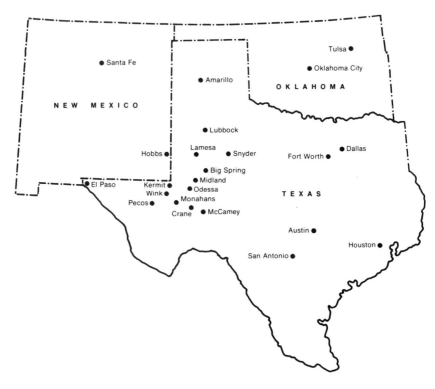

Oil boom country: the Permian Basin and the Southwest.

Preface

FOR SEVEN YEARS we have lived in a booming oil community. As we watched Midland, Odessa, and neighboring towns prosper from oil activity, we became deeply interested in oil booms and in their effect upon community development. Bibliographical search turned up few serious studies of booms in general, let alone of oil booms in particular. Urban historians have apparently assumed that spectacular growth in population has occurred universally in American cities and that one boom is pretty much like another. Writers in business history have written only scanty accounts of the social consequences of business activity. A third group of historians, specialists in the American West, have shown little interest in business operations and in related phenomena. Thus, these three major fields contained little reliable information on oil booms, and the few careful studies of related phenomena were generally far removed from us in place and time.

But if oil booms have thus far escaped scholarly scrutiny, they have never failed to attract popular notice. Literature touching on the subject has generally followed the shopworn clichés popularized by the journalists of the twenties. Walter Rundell, for example, found little more than folklore, journalism, and a handful of master's theses on which to base his introduction to a striking collection of photographs, published in 1977. His predecessors in popular literature were content to let colorful anecdote and lurid exaggeration sum up the subject of the social and economic impact of oil.

Rather than retell tall tales, *Oil Booms* shifts the focus on petroleum development from folklore to social and economic history. We have approached the effects of oil activity through the research techniques of the social sciences. This has meant that we have also worked within the unavoidable constraints imposed by limitations of the surviving record. We have gathered and tested abundant interview material against firmer information; in the few instances where corroboration was not available, we have used interview material only if it met the test of general congruity with other sources.

On the basis of this evidence, we have undertaken to show what happens in an oil town through description and analysis of five communities. We do not intend our story to be local histories of these communities, however, and we have limited our consideration of them to specific problems in community growth. Our focus, in short, is the effect of petroleum activity on community life, a subject of both historical and contemporary importance.

Many persons have given us most generous assistance in carrying out this project. Our research was made far easier by the full cooperation of public officials in Ector, Midland, Scurry, Upton, and Winkler counties. County clerks Lucille Wolz, Rosenelle Cherry, Beverly Ainsworth, Buena R. Coffee, and Ruth Godwin were especially helpful. School district and municipal employees in McCamey, Midland, Odessa, Snyder, and Wink also greatly assisted our work in public records. We are also grateful for the help and suggestions of personnel at the Department of Human Resources in Austin, of the inter-library loan staff of the University of Texas of the Permian Basin, and of our interviewees, who shared their best recollections with us. Mrs. Willsie Lee McKinney, Mrs. Severo Hinojosa, Clyde Barton, and George Mitchell were of special help in arranging and assisting in interviews. Our typists, Myra Grimes and Mary Porter, have been skilled and expeditious. Research and writing of the manuscript were supported in part by fellowships awarded by the Permian Basin Petroleum Museum, Library, and Hall of Fame in Midland, Texas. Its archivist, Mrs. Betty Orbeck; Sharon L. Sutton, director of the Scurry County Museum; and Mrs. Bobbi Jean Klepper, archivist of the Permian Historical Society, are due special thanks for their help and efficiency.

We have exercised full control of this study; the observations and conclusions within it are our own.

BRINGING IN THE WESTBROOK & CO. WELL N° 1
ON T. G. HENDRICKS RANCH, WINKLER COUNTY JULY 22 1926.

An Endless Trek of Teams and Trucks
To West Texas Oil Fields

*Top: Drilling crew at the discovery well of
the Hendrick Field, Winkler County, Texas, 1926.*

Bottom: Hauling pipe in the late 1920s.

Introduction

MENTION THE WORDS "oil boom" and a vivid image comes to mind, a popular picture perfectly summed up for moviegoers of 1940 in *Boom Town*. What *Gone with the Wind* did for the antebellum South in cinematic popular history, *Boom Town* did for the oil patch, with Clark Gable providing the romantic swashbuckling for both films. Through the adventures of Gable, the hard-working and equally hard-living entrepreneur, and Spencer Tracy, his rough-cut sidekick, *Boom Town* distilled the essence of the popular notion of a raw, new oiltown: a place where feisty, hard-driving, and hell-bent oil hands were surrounded by conniving promoters, profiteering merchants, and steadfast lawmen. As the moviegoer saw it, the boomtown was a turbulent, bloody place where shootings, fires, explosions, and random violence were commonplace in everyday life. With a full array of gushing oil wells and flaming derricks, *Boom Town* immortalized the stereotype of the oil community.

This popular vision of oil booms was not mere cinematic fantasy. Like many of Hollywood's vivid tapestries, it was woven from real material—the fast-paced activity and occasional high drama of oil booms. Booms were, in fact, well suited for dramatic treatment through the exaggeration of real people and the condensation of actual events. Their bustle and commotion have, over a dozen decades, prompted scores of magazine articles, novels, and popular books, as well as a handful of more serious monographs. Nevertheless, the captivating drama of oil booms, far from prompting closer study of the social realities of oil-field life, has discouraged examination of actual conditions.

The heightened romantic view of oil booms in popular writing has been so predominant—and profitable to its promoters—that the most basic questions about oil towns and the people who lived in them have neither been raised nor answered. Who were the people who came to oil boomtowns? Where did they come from and why did they move on? While they were in boomtowns, how did housing and public services meet their needs? What part did women and members of racial and ethnic minority groups play in the boomtown? Were boomtowns really as lawless as their stereotype paints them? To pose some even more basic questions, what is an oil boom, and how has it changed in nature over time? Why should an oil boom differ from any other sort of boom? To these most simple and straightforward questions existing literature has had no reply. In all that has been written about oil booms, no one has tried to explain what they are.

In the most general of contexts, an oil boom might be described as an extreme variety of a familiar modern phenomenon, rapid urban growth. Fast-paced urban expansion has been one of the most common and consequential trends of modern times. During the first half of the nineteenth century, industrial development brought floods of new residents to London and Manchester, in England, and to Pittsburgh and Lowell in the United States, as well as to hundreds of other cities in the Western world. During the latter half of the century, the creation of industrial centers and transportation systems prompted sizable immigrations to Chicago and Omaha. On occasion, modern warfare has brought about massive shifts of population; American mobilization for defense during World War II, for example, caused migrations to new manufacturing centers like Willow Run, Michigan; Seneca, Illinois; and Pascagoula, Mississippi. More recently, the decline of rural economies and the contraction of economic opportunity in the countryside have unleashed what seem like human tidal waves on Mexico City, Calcutta, Hong Kong, and other Third World centers. At the present time, the extension of oil exploration and the possible expansion of oil, oil shale, and coal production in the American Rocky Mountain states has created both the expectation and fear of new booms.

This evocative word, "boom," which conveys images of teeming crowds and hectic activity, is commonly taken, in the context of extractive industrial activity, to describe the sequence of sharp increase and rapid decrease in the population of a town or region, change caused by the exploitation and depletion of a natural resource. During the nineteenth century, writers applied the term to the famous gold and silver towns of the American West; more recent observers have used it to describe the rise and decline of oil-field towns.[1]

Though western, urban, and business historians have shown increasing interest in the boom phenomena, they have given relatively little serious thought to the particular nature of mineral booms in general and to oil booms in particular. Booms, in the general sense, have occurred under a wide variety of conditions, with common delimiting aspects, but mineral booms have a distinctive character. Mineral booms relate directly to the nature, extent, and market value of an unrenewable natural resource. The natural resource determines where they take place and how long they last. During Colorado mining booms, for example, numerous observers saw towns appear and vanish within the span of a few months between the discovery of gold and the "tailing out" of the vein. The camps of placer miners in California were just as evanescent, because miners could work pockets of gold-bearing gravel thoroughly during single seasons. By contrast, the rich Comstock lode of Nevada remained in production for decades; sustained extraction and processing of silver-bearing quartz supported a relatively stable community in Virginia City. In the early years of the American oil industry, dozens of Pennsylvania towns, such as Pithole, Shamburg, and Pleasantville, waxed and waned with the flood and ebb of the tide of oil. The common element in all mineral booms is an invariable occurrence: when the natural resource is gone, or appears to be, most of the people who extracted it leave. Few permanent residents have lingered amid the debris mineral booms leave behind them.[2]

That the extent of natural resources directly influences mineral booms is not their sole distinguishing feature. Unlike the booms associated with real estate and manufacturing, most mineral booms have taken place in thinly-settled areas, far removed from the main lines of transportation and communication: a phenomenon as obvious in Kiruna, Sweden, as in the Alaskan Klondike or in the Wyoming oil fields. Even the oil region of Pennsylvania was a relative backwater in 1859, when Edwin L. Drake made the first significant discovery of oil in the United States. A century later, discoveries in Ohio, Kentucky, and Tennessee occurred in the more remote and less prosperous parts of those states.[3] The few instances in which oil fields were discovered in population centers, as in California, are exceptional in the general history of American petroleum development. Booms caused by the exploitation of minerals, then, are more pronounced, often shorter lived, and usually located in more remote places than those that grow from other forms of economic activity.

Oil booms, as a distinctive type of mineral boom, must be understood within the context of their specific economic cause. They have special characteristics which stem from conditions and methods of operation peculiar to the petroleum industry. Unlike hard-mineral mining, for example, oil activity is labor and capital intensive during its exploration phase: it has taken more men and money to find oil than it has to produce it, a situation as true in Pennsylvania during the nineteenth century as it was in Texas in more recent times. Moreover, a special phenomenon, flush production, is unique to oil among the extractive industries; it has impelled developers to take the greatest possible quantity of oil in the shortest time, thereby shortening the various oil booms.[4] As a flowing mineral, moving through porous rock and sand formations under the pressure of water or gas, oil moves to wellheads, the points of least pressure, sometimes rising over derricks and rigs in great black columns—the familiar gushers of films and novels. According to the common law of capture, established as a precedent in law during the nineteenth century, the rising oil belongs to the man who produces it, even if his well draws from a mineral formation that lies under adjoining and undrilled areas belonging to other landowners and leaseholders. Oil operators were often hell-bent to drill and produce oil on proven territory as soon as possible—before wells on adjoining and neighboring tracts drained oil from the deposit underlying their leases. To take the other man's oil was the object, and the practice was strictly legal.

The laws of property and of physics thus spurred operators to fast action. Whenever commercial oil production was confirmed, most operators rushed into production quickly in order to recoup their investments and to maximize the recovery of crude oil from their wells. Oil men also hurried to produce as much oil as possible from free-flowing wells before the reduction of pressure in the oil-bearing formation required "going on the pump," a practice necessary to the recovery of oil that was not free flowing, but one which increased operating costs and cut into profits. Drilling took place at a flat-out pace; oil was produced in as great a volume as transportation and storage facilities would allow. Among oil men, the race was to the swift. Its course was familiar to all of the competitors.[5]

In some instances, reward for initiative was denied when a massive increase in production exceeded demand for crude oil, and the price of

the commodity fell so sharply that only the biggest wells were profitable. Low domestic prices discouraged exploration in Oklahoma at
various times during the early decades of the twentieth century; cheap
imported Arabian oil had a similar dampening effect on activity in the
Permian Basin of Texas and New Mexico during the 1960s. Though
the development of hard minerals also responds to market conditions,
the producers of gold, silver, and copper have not encountered the
problem of overproduction, a recurring difficulty in the history of the
petroleum industry. Petroleum exploration responded quickly to market conditions, and sharp drops in the price of crude oil ended booms
just as decisively as the depletion of the mineral. From beginning to
end, an oil boom has a precarious dependency on supply, individual
initiative, and price.

The sequence of events characteristic of an oil boom has followed a
pattern recognizable since the earliest years of oil-field development.
Most commonly, onshore development has begun with lease and land
speculation in advance of the discovery of commercial production,
speculation based on rumor, promotion, low lease costs, and current
scientific theories. Early lease action, like that which follows the actual
discovery of oil, has moved relatively fast in the United States; leasing
campaigns have often covered large regions in short periods, with little
impact on the populations of the areas involved. For example, an active
leasing campaign began in Winkler County, Texas, in 1919, in response to discoveries in distant areas; lease agents negotiated more
than one hundred oil and gas leases in 1919, most of them for pennies
per acre. Thereafter, there were few lease transactions in the county
until 1924, when major oil companies began to buy "protection leases"
against the day of possible discovery. Such an accumulation of leases by
major companies was common. The Roxana Petroleum Corporation
(Shell), for example, had purchased protection leases in Upton County
before the discovery of the McCamey field, and it continued the practice in Ward and Pecos counties in Texas and in Lea County, New
Mexico. When the discovery well in Winkler County came in in 1926,
the Roxana, Gulf, Humble, Pure, and Sun oil companies held substantial blocks of leases. By the time the Hendrick Number Two well
confirmed the presence of oil in commercial quantities, Atlantic, Standard Oil of California, Magnolia, Marland, Prairie, and the Texas
Company had also collected leases in the county. Prediscovery leasing
activity produced no significant growth in the relatively permanent
population of Winkler County, or elsewhere; leasing agents were

highly transient, and the early comers usually moved on even before a townsite was platted. Before they passed on, however, they gave local ranchers lease money, and their activity gave rise to hopes and anticipations of boom and riches.[6]

The opening of an oil field meant the arrival of certain kinds of oil-field workers. With the drillers and their assistants came rig builders, roustabouts, and teamsters. Rig builders usually worked in four- or five-man crews; ordinarily, it took them slightly less than six work days to construct a cable-tool rig, complete with bull wheel, derrick, and machinery housing. Roustabouts did whatever heavy work was needed on the job, and teamsters kept a constant supply of materials flowing into the field. Once production was established, large crews of tank builders and pipeliners arrived. Tank builders usually worked in groups of a dozen men, including a foreman, his assistant, carpenters (later replaced by metal workers and welders), laborers, riveters, and caulkers. Pipeliners dug trenches and laid pipe in crews of 100 to 150 men, until the use of ditching machines in the twenties and the introduction of lap welding in the thirties cut labor requirements. Accompanying all these workers were supply workers, oil operators, oil scouts, and those who provided the necessities of oil-field life in stores, cafés, boardinghouses, saloons, hotels, and drugstores. This large and miscellaneous assortment of persons made up the most numerous part of the population of an oil boom.[7]

The population buildup that followed oil discovery was often intense. Within a few days of completion of the confirmation well in the Burkburnett area, for example, thirty rigs were running and eighty additional derricks were under construction, each requiring the labor of fifteen to twenty men. In other instances, the increase of population was more gradual. The massive influx of workers to the Cushing field of Oklahoma did not begin until the fall of 1912, nearly half a year after the discovery well came in. In the Hendrick field of Winkler County, post-discovery drilling was delayed nearly a year because the field was far removed from existing pipeline and railroad connections, and storage facilities were lacking. As long a delay as a year was atypical; the general historical pattern in petroleum development is that of rapid drilling and a rush to flush production.[8]

The rapidity of drilling campaigns accounts for both the flood effect of incoming population and the relatively short duration of oil booms. In the McCamey and McElroy fields, most drilling took place during a twelve-month period, in 1926 and 1927, giving McCamey its boomers, as the first wave of workers were called. Development of the Yates pool, in adjoining Pecos County, occurred during 1927 and 1928; the drilling of wells in that field sustained McCamey's boom. In the Hendrick field, 438 wells were drilled during 1928, 130 in 1929, and none the following year. This highly concentrated activity generated Wink's first and only real boom.[9] The peculiarities of drilling formation and depth have also affected population levels. The amount of time required for the completion of a well has varied widely, from ten to twenty days in the early days of the industry to nearly two and one-half years on a recent 25,000-foot gas test well in the Permian Basin. Since World War II, deeper drilling and related improvements in technology have required increased numbers of better educated and better trained workers, thereby adding to the initial flood of exploration workers and extending the impact of exploration on local economies. Thus, a decrease in drilling, measured by the number of wells completed, has not always produced corresponding drops in drilling-related employment nor in the twenty-five to thirty jobs per well in service and supply.[10]

Because boom growth depends more upon the exploration for oil than on production of it, the intensity and extent of drilling activity are of great consequence in an oil boom—unlike coal mining, for example, which maintains its highest employment levels during production. After the commercial production of oil has been established and wells are flowing into pipeline and storage facilities, a lesser number of production workers operate and service the wells, pipelines, and tank farms. The pumpers, who tend to the production and maintenance of producing wells, have always been the most numerous group in this category during the twentieth century. Pipeline operations also employed relatively large numbers of workers as engineers, firemen, and line walkers, until the automation of operations, a process completed during the 1960s.

The succession of speculators, explorers, and workers, appearing in all oil fields has little in common with the orderly change of shift at an industrial plant; the various development phases of an oil field are rather more like a casually organized parade. There was never an even and orderly exchange of exploration workers with those engaged in production work. Not only were there far more of the former, but significant numbers of exploration workers also often settled in the various oil centers with their families and took production jobs. Moreover, until drilling fell off sharply in a field, both production and exploration work went on simultaneously. In fact, the population peak of an oil boom occurred when both activities were intensive. In the Cushing field of Oklahoma, for example, the maximum labor force was on hand during October, November, and December, 1914, when 900 wells had been completed, drilling had not slackened, and the field had achieved more than two-thirds of its maximum production level. The Hendrick field, Winkler County, Texas, had its maximum impact in development from mid-1927 to late 1928, when three pipeline systems, several large tank farms, three large oil camps, and more than 500 wells were completed. Thereafter, for the next three years, a third as many wells were drilled, the number of producing wells declined, and labor requirements of production work fell off. By 1929, the population of Wink had declined from the high point reached a year earlier. Similarly, the Yates field reached its maximum point of exploration by October, 1928, when about 250 wells had been completed. Unlike Cushing, Hendrick, and most other fields, however, the Yates field, in Pecos County, Texas, did not experience a rapid decline of production because the major oil companies controlling it agreed to limit the field's rate of production. A major field in 1980, Yates continued to provide significant quantities of oil and to support production-related employment.[11]

In numerous oil fields, a further phase of activity followed the establishment of substantial production, the construction of refineries and other related manufacturing plants near sources of supply. As long as the capital requirements for building a rudimentary refinery were relatively low, they sprang up during the booms; entrepreneurs sought to seize the advantages of low prices, available to the buyers of crude oil during flush production. There were fifteen-barrel refineries and other small operations scattered throughout the oil region of Pennsylvania by 1897. The rich Cushing field in Oklahoma was the site of ten refineries by 1915, and numerous inexpensive natural gasoline skimmer operations were in business in the East Texas field during the 1930s. In some oil fields, large corporations built refineries near substantial sources of supply. The Humble Oil and Refining Company, for example, built a refinery near McCamey, in Upton County, Texas, in 1927. Its labor force and Humble's divisional management staff in McCamey were large enough to "replace" the exploration workers in the local economy when drilling declined. In this instance, manufacturing operation worked to sustain near boom-level populations.[12]

Lacking manufacturing facilities, the towns that boomed in response to activity in a single field normally built to a peak and began to decline in a two- to three-year period. Flush production, achieved through rapid drilling and the fastest possible natural flow of oil from the wells, doomed most towns to a brief period of hectic activity followed by a longer period of decline. Occasionally the whole process was complete in little more than one year. Nevertheless, so rapid a rise and fall was not inevitable. Because it escaped flush production, the Yates field has sustained segments of the population of McCamey and other towns for more than a half century.[13] Not all oil towns that boomed, however, were tied to production alone. In most instances, mineral booms have supported large commercial, financial, service, and management centers, often at some distance from the areas of production. Mining activity in California and Nevada, for example, underlay the growth of San Francisco, much as Denver grew on the shorter-lived mining towns and camps of Colorado. In the oil industry, Titusville lived beyond its nearby oil boom as an operational center, just as Tulsa, Wichita Falls, Tyler, Longview, Midland, and Odessa have done during the twentieth century. Less directly reliant on drilling and production in a single field than on area-wide development, the oil-center towns have responded more to regional than to local activity. Their gains are less dramatic and their declines, when they occur, are less precipitous.

Though many oil towns outlived their local booms by becoming regional centers, when Permian Basin residents saw oil development take place around them in the twenties, they were familiar with the popular vision of boom followed by calamitous bust. The popular notion seemed like simple common sense, for surely exploitation of a finite resource had to cease at a future date. Residents of both Odessa and Midland were skeptical about the long-term benefits of oil. In 1927, leading Odessans feared that their town would wax and wane like older and better known oil towns in Oklahoma. Thinking on similar lines in 1929, Midland old-timers dismissed oil man Thomas S. Hogan's twelve-story Petroleum Building as "Hogan's Folly"; they were certain that oil people would be long gone before the building could be paid for. So deeply engrained was the conventional wisdom that bust would follow boom that Snyder civic leaders, less than a year into that town's boom, were more preoccupied with realizing permanent gains from hectic activity in Scurry County than with day to day problems. As community after community in the Permian Basin prospered from oil, residents continually tempered their perception of the bustling present with the vision of a future when only abandoned rigs and a few pumping wells would dot the wind-scoured plains.[14]

Yet conventional wisdom erred. The experience of the Permian Basin demonstrated that oil booms are not necessarily followed by economic disaster, as the dark view of the twenties held and as Permian Basin residents at first believed. When the first oil fields were discovered in the Permian Basin, oil-field science was in its infancy. The surface geology used in scientific exploration was not even usable in some areas of the Basin, most notably the sand dunes of Ward and Winkler counties, and it did not indicate the presence of oil in multiple pay zones, a common phenomenon in the Permian Basin. Great gains in scientific understanding of oil, in geology and geophysics, however, led to new and greater discoveries of oil and gas. Similar advances in recovery techniques, the domain of petroleum engineers, sustained production and employment in production and service operations. These developments, beyond the vision of an observer of the late twenties, meant that Permian Basin prosperity did not vanish with the Model T Ford.

Some Permian Basin towns like McCamey and Wink have greatly declined in size since their first hectic years, but the continual progress of oil development has kept towns in the area from the desolation of places like Pithole, Pennsylvania. Though the Permian Basin experience can be taken as a strong corrective for the boom and bust presentation of oil development, most literature on oil has not passed beyond the sensationalism of the twenties, a school of colorful exaggeration best popularized by the journalist Boyce House, who was technical adviser during the production of the film *Boom Town*. Indeed, folklorists have been most active in writing about oil booms, and such newfangled items as multiple pay-zones and secondary recovery have held little glamour for the folklore collector. Revision of the dark boom-to-bust view of oil booms is long overdue.

The Permian Basin offers a useful context for a reexamination of oil development and oil booms for a number of reasons. Oil has been and remains of primary economic importance; on the discovery of oil in the twenties, the region was economically static. The economic stimulus provided by construction of the Texas and Pacific and Santa Fe railroads had dissipated and various promotions of farm and ranch settlements had long since run their course. Throughout the area, agriculture suffered from prolonged drought in 1917 and 1918. When oil came in, there was no other significant stimulus to economic growth. The development of the region has thus been squarely linked to oil.

Though developed later than other major producing regions, the Permian Basin has had experience with oil booms that spans more than half a century. It is still highly significant in the petroleum industry, since more than one-fifth of domestic production and a similar proportion of domestic reserves are located in the region. Dating from 1920 to the present, the relatively long period of strong production furnishes a chronological series of useful examples, drawn from McCamey during the 1920s to Snyder during the 1950s. The recent experience of the region is likely to be valuable in future oil development planning, more so than the fully chronicled history of Pithole, Pennsylvania, during 1865. The absence of broadly significant geographical and economic variation within the region also recommends it as an area for comparative study of the experiences of five oil boomtowns: Midland, Odessa, McCamey, Wink, and Snyder.

Midland received its name because the site of the town was midway between Fort Worth and El Paso on the Texas and Pacific Railroad. As in the other parts of the central Permian Basin, permanent settlers came to Midland during the 1880s. The county, comprising 887 square miles, was formally organized in 1885.[15] From its beginning as a townsite promotion, Midland grew slowly and erratically during the late nineteenth and early twentieth centuries because the vagaries of rainfall—not more than sixteen inches in an average year, and half that amount or less during a drought—made farming and ranching risky ventures. "I've spent half of my life praying for rain" was a common local saying. The central Permian Basin was, nonetheless, the scene of widespread agricultural promotion between 1900 and 1910, and one hundred new farms were established in Midland County alone during the decade. Many farms relied on irrigation even during relatively wet years. The post–World War I drought thinned ranks of farmers in Midland, as it did in Ector, Upton, and Winkler counties, and both city and county lost about one-third of their inhabitants.[16]

As the dusty croplands reverted to native grasses, ranching replaced farming. Ranch land in Midland County supported nearly thirty-five thousand head of cattle in 1919, more than in Ector, Upton, and Winkler counties combined. Midland became a pleasant backwater cow town. It was a supply and residential center for the substantial ranchers who operated throughout the entire region, which included eastern New Mexico. Ranchers built comfortable town houses for their families, who lived in Midland during the school term and migrated to ranch headquarters during the summer. Ranchers' trade sustained the modest mercantile community, which also served the occasional needs of settlers in adjoining counties.[17]

By 1920, then, Midland had settled into a fixed character, a close-knit community led by white ranchers and businessmen. There was a small Mexican-American community, and there were sixteen black residents, employed as domestic or farm workers. Local life was pacific, and even small-town politics proceeded without major dustups. The town of Midland lacked sufficient inhabitants to warrant incorporation until 1911. In the meantime, the county commissioners oversaw roads and bridges—though there were few of the former and none of the latter—and the meager county budget. The town more or less ran itself, which was just as well because three out of four commissioners represented the rural precincts and were elected by a combined total of about 13 percent of the electorate, a situation that was largely unchanged until the 1960s.[18]

Midland began to feel the effect of oil activity in 1926, when independent operators arrived from San Angelo, Colorado City, and other places farther away. A five-year growth period ballooned the town's boundaries; new residential and commercial construction sprang up at a rate beyond precedent in the community. The city's function as the management center for the region was secured by John B. Thomas, a local doctor, who built a six-story office building in 1926, the first in town; Clarence Scharbauer, a local rancher, completed his handsome 150-room Scharbauer Hotel in 1928; and Hogan built his million-dollar Petroleum Building the following year. By providing the office and hotel accommodations needed by independent oil men and larger corporations, these and other farsighted entrepreneurs laid the foundations for Midland's future. From 1931 to 1934, their gambles appeared to be poorly placed, for activity in the region decreased, population moved away, and occupancy rates and revenues plummeted.[19]

The downturn predicted by the old-timers on the courthouse lawn, however, proved to be brief. Following the decline of the early thirties, Midland entered its second growth period, spurred initially by the resumption of oil activity and by an influx of the dependents of airmen who were stationed at neighboring Sloan Field during World War II. After the war, increased oil-field activity supported modest but constant growth in Midland, until its third boom, which began in 1948 and extended through 1953. Expansion of the city during this period rested on discoveries in Andrews, Ector, and Scurry counties and on the opening of the half-million-acre Spraberry trend, which extended roughly north and south through Midland County. Development of this field was rapid, increasing the number of producing wells in Midland County from 4, on January 1, 1950, to 170, one year later. Midland's visible affluence was the object of interest throughout the country. The *Baltimore Sun* reported on Midland's booming activity: "New cars, expensive homes, several impressively tall buildings, a newly refurbished and very social country club, more than $4,000,000 worth of building last year, all testify to the snowballing prosperity of this sprawling, new, oil-rich town." Though not exactly new, there was no denying the prosperity of the city, at least until the shutdown of the Spraberry trend broke the fortunes of numerous oil men and interrupted the postwar boom. Activity picked up again in 1956 and lasted into the 1960s, when rising costs, fixed prices, and cheap foreign crude slowed and reversed the trend of development. When the rising price of Venezuelan, Arabian, and Iranian oil stimulated activity in the Permian Basin in 1973, Midland launched into its most recent boom.[20]

Oil transformed Midland from a sleepy ranching town to a bustling city with more than sixty thousand inhabitants—a story with a direct parallel in Odessa, some twenty miles to the west. Odessa, like Midland, began as a townsite promotion in 1884. The northeastern businessmen who owned the townsite company carried their booster approach as far as their choice of name for the townsite; by adopting the name of the great Russian wheat market, they implied that the area would soon become a great agribusiness center like its namesake. Unfortunately for the farmers who speculated in the cheap land, the townsite company could not promote rain, and the drought of 1917–20 led to a substantial out-migration. By 1920 Odessa had lost 36 percent of its 1910 population: the entire county contained only 760 inhabitants.[21]

Odessa's decline continued during the early 1920s, ending only in 1927; in that year, oil activity in adjoining Crane County initiated a four-year population boom. Though one visitor described it as "nothing much but a turn in the road," by 1930 Odessa had outgrown its one-horse-town days. The town's relatively limited growth during this period was the result of reined-in enthusiasm by outside creditors. Though the county commissioners wisely built roads to the oil fields to the south, securing Odessa's status as an oil-field labor and supply center, according to the *Odessa News-Times,* ". . . it was the opinion of many local sages that it would slowly dwindle back to the sleepy cow town of some 300 population." This gloomy prophecy seemed to be working out between 1931 and 1933, when low crude-oil prices, the opening of the giant East Texas field, and slow development of the Judkins field in Ector County brought about a substantial exodus of population. As one resident recalled, "It was like the morning after the storm. Penwell and Odessa were cleaned out, and everybody who had come left."[22] It was not yet apparent that Odessa's location in the center of major fields and the farsighted construction of county roads would ensure the future of the blue-collar city. The shape of the future began to emerge in 1935, when activity in Ector and neighboring counties stimulated a second boom, which continued until World War II disrupted supplies of both pipe and oil-field workers. Growth resumed at the war's end and lasted until 1954, when the temporary shut-in of the Spraberry trend led to a net out-migration. The next year brought a strong revival of development, which continued unabated until 1960. As with Midland, Odessa's most recent boom began in 1973.

Both Midland and Odessa were established population centers at the time of their initial population boom during the late 1920s. They had, at least, limited public services, functional legal systems, and recognized community leaders. By contrast, McCamey and Wink were entirely the creatures of their respective booms, lacking established facilities, leaders, and traditions.

McCamey grew up around a railroad siding on the Orient (Santa Fe) Railroad, where oil operator George B. McCamey erected a crudely scrawled sign to indicate the proper delivery point for his goods. Settlement followed the onset of drilling in 1925, in "the oil Klondike" of America, as the *El Paso Evening Post* described the area. By the time McCamey was incorporated at the end of 1926, town-lot sales had been recorded for more than a year, and a rag-town collection of timber and plasterboard stores and houses and of war surplus tents clustered on that bare spot of the dry plain. McCamey's first boom brought new life to Upton County, which had been losing population since the drought of 1904. Four-section farmers began to sell out their holdings in 1911 and 1912; most of the remaining agriculturalists left after drought and killing frosts in 1917 and 1918. By the beginning of the McCamey boom, then, Upton County's population had dropped to half of its 1910 level. McCamey's rise reversed the decline of the county.[23]

Like Midland and Odessa, McCamey boomed during the peak years of area exploration, receiving additional impetus in late 1927 when "the Humble" completed a large refinery, a company camp, and its regional offices on the outer edge of the city. Like the other Permian Basin boomtowns, McCamey lost residents during the early 1930s, especially after Humble closed the refinery and moved its offices to Midland in 1932. Thereafter, McCamey gradually declined, with intermittent revivals in 1937 and 1938, and in 1943 and 1944, created by drilling in extensions of proven fields, and in 1952 by the discovery of new pay-zones. By 1960 McCamey was no larger than it was in 1931; the natural growth of the population was equal to the strong out-migration.

If McCamey's story was one of rapid growth and gradual decline, Wink's was more surely one of explosive growth, precipitous decline, and lingering death, interrupted only by the comic entrance of the federal government with an urban renewal program long after the disappearance of a renewable city. The rise of Wink hit Winkler county like a bolt of lightning. Like the other counties in the region, only more so, it came upon hard days following the postwar droughts. It had lost 82 percent of its 1910 population by 1920. Most of the local ranchers—there were barely half a dozen—were land poor, borrowing money from banks and each other from roundup to roundup and from crop to foreclosure. By the beginning of the decade, nearly everyone had borrowed on every possible asset: twenty-three of the twenty-four owner-occupied houses were mortgaged, and the average mortgage was for more than one-third of the presumed market value, the upper limit for prudent lenders. Life was tough and relatively rough: the best road in the county in 1919 was an unimproved dirt road, which local ranchers covered with dried bear grass. Kermit, the county seat, contained the courthouse, half a dozen houses, and as many graves in its cemetery as there would be in 1926, when oil was discovered on the Hendrick ranch.[24]

The boom got underway the next year, following the discovery of a second strong-producing well and the construction of storage and transportation facilities for the new oil. By mid-1927, the Wink town-site company was selling lots; newcomers moved in tents and built sheetrock and metal buildings. Wink soon outstripped Tulsa, Westbrook, and Cheyenne, other promotional townsites near the Hendrick field. With more of the drilling done by independent operators in Winkler county than in Upton, Pecos, and Crane counties, develop-

Snyder was a modern boomtown. Though the growth of its population was as dramatic as that of Wink and McCamey, it did not suffer the same debilitating out-migrations. Its development occurred over a longer period, in large measure because there were fewer operators in the field. The owners of large spreads in Scurry County, moreover, were more inclined to look for long-term income than to short-term windfalls: most of them were already reasonably prosperous. Fewer leaseowners meant fewer offset wells, less uneconomical drilling and developmental drilling over a longer period of time, through the 1950s and 1960s. Control of production by a small number of companies and conservation regulations of the Texas Railroad Commission tended to hold down the tendency to flush production, thereby maintaining a fairly constant level of production employment. In short, Snyder never went into a tailspin; even during its declining years, the natural increase in the population frequently offset the loss of population through net out-migration. Snyder, like Midland and Odessa, stayed on the map, while the future of McCamey grew dimmer, and Wink nearly disappeared altogether.

All five of these towns faced a similar set of problems during their oil booms. To a considerable extent, those problems were common to most, if not all, oil boomtowns. Examining the successes and failures of communities which had to face problems of boom growth makes it easier to see guidelines for future development, as the increasingly eager search for new sources of energy produces the boomtowns of our own time. Just as important as this uncommon opportunity to learn from experience, study of the day-to-day lives, backgrounds, and motivations of boom participants provides a positive context for a general view of oil booms: for despite hectic and occasionally rugged conditions of life, to the boomers, drifters, workers, and their families, oil booms offered economic opportunities that outweighed the attendant hardships of boom life. It was the chance to get ahead, rather than the "social chaos" so shocking to nonparticipant commentators on oil booms, that meant the most to those who took part in petroleum development. Difficulties were temporary: economic advancement, whether for communities or individuals, was real.

Top: Downtown McCamey, Texas, in 1926.

Bottom: Crane, Texas, on January 7, 1927,
when it was fifteen days old.

1.
Population

MOBILITY WAS the first and dominant impression to strike observers of the oil field. From the oil regions of Pennsylvania during the 1860s to Alaska more than a century later, the human part of an oil field scene was in constant motion. Teamsters and truckers hauled pipe and other supplies to rigs; pipeline crews moved across the countryside; drilling crews rushed to and from their rigs at the changes of "towers" or shifts; and overloaded wagons, trains, and automobiles carried thrill seekers, tramps, and workers who were either following jobs or seeking them.

With the daily coming and going in the oil field there were also migrations produced by frequent shifts of oil-field activity and sharp variations in drilling and related oil-field business. In response to prices and patterns of discovery, drilling in the United States has fluctuated wildly during relatively short periods. Between 1910 and 1913, for example, it nearly doubled, while during the next two years, by contrast, it fell by nearly half. Increased drilling attracted new labor to the oil field; its subsequent decline, in effect, drove many newcomers to alternative employment. It was still possible to find work in drilling and related employment in 1914 and 1915, but those who sought it left Pennsylvania, West Virginia, and Illinois, where the decline was precipitous, and moved on to Oklahoma, Texas, and Louisiana, where new discoveries produced new jobs. Thus, North Texas went through three successive drilling booms between 1910 and 1916, before drilling activity increased by more than 600 percent from 1917 to 1920. During the initial year of the following decade, drilling declined 55 percent. Following the decline in North Texas, fields in Lousiana, Arkansas, the Texas Panhandle, and the Permian Basin opened up and drilling activity shifted to these regions. In later years fluctuations within the Permian Basin were nearly as dramatic. Following World War II, there was a veritable rush to the region, a reflection of several rapid increases in drilling activity, which rose by 50 percent from 1947 to 1948 and again from 1949 to 1950. Both surges in drilling spurred the growth of Midland and Odessa; the latter marked the onset of the boom in Scurry County and the beginning of boom times in Snyder.[1] As the drilling data indicate, oil-field workers experienced sharp fluctuations of the demand for their labor and continual regional shifts in work sites.

Among workers, three groups—boomers, mobile workers, and drifters—followed jobs or the prospect of them in the twenties and thirties. Many of them moved from El Dorado, Arkansas, to Borger, from Borger to Wink, from Wink to East Texas, and from East Texas back to the Permian Basin with little more than they could tie on their cars or carry on their backs.

After the confirmation of substantial production, the earliest arrivals in a new oil-field were the boomers. This colorful group included speculators who sought to buy and sell leases before prices and production stabilized, townsite promoters, businessmen, camp followers, and men seeking work in the oil field. Many colorful stories—some of them true—have been told about the boomers. Workers in this group rarely moved to new areas with the assurance of employment, but they nonetheless pulled up stakes and moved in the vanguard of oil-field traffic. Both living and working conditions in their new locations were more primitive than those they had previously had, but that did not discourage them.

The boomers' impetus to keep moving on was both economic and psychological. Boomers could hope that workers first on the scene would be better paid: at least until the number of incoming workers swelled the labor force sufficiently to bring wages down to levels that prevailed in the wider region. In 1926, for example, the opening of fields near McCamey drew in rig builders and drillers from the Texas Panhandle; they sought wages which were about one-third higher than the going rate in other areas. As the *Oil Weekly* observed, "Boom attractions and higher wages always prove a great drawing card to field men." The quest for the top dollar kept many men on the road.[2]

While most boomers looked for higher wages, they had little choice but to move along with the action, because of the brief term of employment. For drillers, tool dressers, and roustabouts, the job frequently ended with the completion of the well; rig builders faced unemployment with the completion of construction contracts. That most boomers liked to specialize in a particular type of work, whether pipelining, rig building or other jobs, helped keep them moving. The first job completed, the boomer found that news of high wages attracted so many newcomers that the labor supply exceeded demand and that work he preferred to do was no longer available. When wages declined and jobs were of short duration, the boomer moved on. He might move only a short distance if he were located in a region that was developing, perhaps from McCamey to Crane or Crane to Wink, but he did have to move.

For all the economic inducements to mobility, there was another important aspect of the boomer's constant movement, and that was the urge to be where events were breaking, where the action was, where the gambles were still big and the living was still loose. As one self-identified boomer from San Angelo recalled: "I'd go to the booms just in order to be with the action. I just liked to be where the action was. And though I never got into scrapes myself, I liked to go watch them guys get drunk and somebody get whipped real good. I guess you'd call me a boomer."[3] The boomer was an individual who relished the excitement and rough life of a new field.

Just behind the boomers, were the more conventional oil-field workers, often traveling with their families. These people moved entirely out of necessity; the intermittent and dispersed character of oil-field work required that the large numbers of workers who preferred oil-field employment to other work be willing to relocate in order to follow employment. Throughout the history of the oil industry, from California to New York, a large proportion of mobile workers came from farms or ranches. During the numerous downturns in agriculture, farmers' sons, and sometimes their fathers, turned to oil-field work, particularly if it could be found close at hand. They took up jobs as teamsters, tool dressers, and roustabouts, using some of the skills they acquired on the farm, and applying them in the oil field under conditions already familiar to farm workers—long hours, hard work, and occasionally unpleasant weather. The appealing difference between farm and oil-field work was that the latter paid much better, usually better than the other work available in the vicinity.

Once in the industry, farm boys preferred to stay in it, but when no oil work could be had, they often returned to the farm. J.S. Peebles, now in retirement in Wink, Texas, came off the farm in Tahlequah, Oklahoma, in 1914 and went to work laying pipeline in Nowata, eighty miles to the north, where his grandfather had a small farm. When oil work gave out, he returned to the farm, keeping an ear open for a good lead on a job back in oil. It came in 1920, and he drove to Shidler, in Osage County, to work on a connection gang for Carter Oil, a Standard company. When that job was completed, he found work as a tool dresser on a cable-tool rig, thanks to the fact that he had learned smithing on the farm. After work shut down at Nowata, he went to Wyoming to dress tools. From Wyoming, Peebles moved to Borger, from there to McCamey, and finally to Wink, where he located a job in production, which he held until he retired several years ago.[4] Similarly, Peebles's neighbor in Wink, L.V. Gill, left the family farm in Arkansas in 1917, to take up roustabout's work in Oklahoma; during the next two years, he did two more stints on the farm and worked in a sawmill, before he found work on a connection gang in Ranger in 1919. Thereafter, he made half a dozen oil fields and returned to the farm several times, before 1928, when he arrived in Wink, which was to be his home for the next fifty years; there he found a permanent job in pipeline operations.[5]

The frequency of their moves required that mobile workers and their families travel light. A third man, Hoke Tehee, a full-blood Cherokee, quit his job on a farm and took a job dressing tools at Nowata; thereafter he moved through six states to follow work before settling in Monahans, Texas, during the Great Depression. He recalled: "We didn't move anything. We just packed a suitcase and sold everything we had in the house to get rid of it. We'd take what we could in the car. Then we'd buy things new the next place we went."[6] Other workers traveled with one or two prized possessions, most often a Victrola, a sewing machine, or a radio. A driller's wife who traveled with her husband's work in the forties could pack all her housekeeping gear in a foot locker: she was ready to move on one hour's notice.[7]

The mobile workers and their families were hard-working, rural conservatives, not nomads by choice. During the 1920s, many of them talked about eventually buying a farm and raising chickens; after World War II, their goal was a two-bedroom home in an oil town. They always aimed to settle down. Tenancy, endemic rural depression, and hard times forced them off the farm; the shifting of oil activity kept them moving in pursuit of work.

The more fortunate mobile workers had jobs with major oil companies and moved across the Mid-Continent and Gulf Coast regions according to their employers' needs. Both Humble and Gulf, for example, moved supervisory personnel from the Texas coast to McCamey and on to Crane and Wink during the late 1920s. One

Humble employee recalled: "I moved so many times, the moving men knew my furniture better than I did." Companies did not give employees much notice of a move. Then as now, middle management and technical personnel must still be prepared to move on, if they want to move up in the corporate structure.[8]

Educated and specialized workers, however, were not the only persons to move with company employment. In oil-field construction, unskilled workers frequently moved to continue their employment. On the ten spreads of Lock Construction in Texas, Oklahoma, and Louisiana, from 1935 to 1938, workers tended to stick with their jobs through constant relocations. Thus, the spread that operated out of Pawnee, Oklahoma, composed of Indians, moved through Oklahoma and Kansas; the fifty-man Mexican-American crew that operated from Dumas, Texas, worked South Texas, the Permian Basin, and the Texas Panhandle. The Midland spread, also crewed by Mexican Americans, for the most part, stuck with the company through numerous jobs in Texas and Oklahoma. All of the crews moved along the routes of the pipelines as they were completed. Between jobs, they generally returned to their bases of operation, where many had located their families. In the meantime, steady employment required great toleration for suitcase living and long absences from their loved ones.[9]

A third group, the drifters, did more than tolerate living out of a suitcase and being away from family: they preferred it. Typically, the drifter was older than the farm boys; he was often a hard drinker and a loner. Most drifters were known by no more than a nickname, commonly a personal physical reference, such as Shorty, Slim, Heavy, Pinky, Red, or Blackie; or perhaps by character traits, such as Cry-Baby, Hot Shot, or Water Tank (a heavy drinker). In many instances the nicknames referred to tastes and habits. One old hand in Wink was called Buttermilk, while one of his friends, who had particularly revolting table manners, even by the less than fastidious standards of the drifters, was known as Tea Cake. Most oil fields had old-timers with geographical names—Tex, Kentucky, or Tulsa. Other workers seldom knew much more about them. As a retired pipeliner described an especially tough drifter, "He was all he said he was. He covered all the ground he stood on. You couldn't question him too much." But in the days when no one checked a man's references, if any were given, it was not necessary to know more than that a worker was willing to work for at least the day.[10]

One thing was certain about the drifter: even if he were a good worker, he would not make a steady hand. Typically, the drifter worked until he had earned a stake or until the next payday; then he moved on. If the stake were spent on a mind-boggling binge, he returned to the job until he earned another stake. Wise to the ways of drifters, employers put off payday until the completion of the job, in order to forestall the impromptu disappearance of their crews.[11]

Apart from their penchant for casual labor and their desire for anonymity, little is known about drifters. They were seldom counted in census reports. Most of them gave away few bits of personal information, and what they did provide—mainly tales about old girl friends—was usually rejected as low-grade intelligence by the more stable hands. Recollections of the drifters, a handful of studies of transient workers, and current observations of present-day drifters suggest a dominant characteristic: most of the drifters were trying to lose themselves. Often drifters were married men who had abandoned families in distant places; most of them suffered from personal problems such as alcoholism, drug addiction, homosexuality, or serious personality disorders.[12] Supervisors and employers recall that drifters were occasionally arrested on the job on fugitive warrants, commonly for violent crimes; more often, lawmen stopped by after the drifter had moved along and the trail was cold. More than a few of the drifters had served sentences in jails or at "Uncle Bud's Place," as they called the Texas State Prison at Huntsville.[13] Yet some of these men made good hands, if they stayed around long enough to learn work routines. A few settled down and raised families, but many more degenerated physically and socially, visibly seedier on every return visit. Mounds of liquor bottles and empty Sterno cans identified the tents and cot houses drifters inhabited. Not surprisingly, older drifters often show up in death records as suicides or as victims of liver diseases. The drifter's life-style undermined his health. In all of these regards, oil-field drifters resembled other transient workers; they were much like the hobos identified in Chicago from 1910 to 1921, the transients who were studied by the U.S. Industrial Commission in California in 1915, and the older inmates of migratory labor camps that Eric Hoffer observed in California during the Great Depression. Drifters were not unique to the oil industry, nor did they work exclusively in oil or in any other single pursuit. The drifter turned his hand to whatever work he could find, whether in oil camps, on farms, in lumber camps, or at a variety of unskilled jobs in cities. Unlike the boomers and mobile workers, drifters took oil work by chance rather than by preference.[14]

After 1930, the mobility of boomers, mobile workers, and drifters alike changed considerably. The Great Depression was one influence behind this change, for it threw many workers out of the oil-field work force. Unemployed oil-field hands often turned to work outside the industry, to jobs on county construction or utility crews, and settled down in towns; others worked through a variety of jobs until a renewal of activity in production during wartime gave them the chance to reenter oil. Walter Wingo, for example, worked for the Texas Electric Service Company and an ice company before resuming oil-field work; he and his family settled in Midland, where his wife also found employment. As communities built more miles of better highways, oil workers had additional reason to settle down; they could live in town and commute to various worksites rather than live on leases and move with rigs. With the exception of offshore fields from the thirties onward, most new production was within commuting distance of settled places. In the fifties a growing shortage of oil-field labor meant that workers in a town like Odessa could find steady work whenever they wanted it, without uprooting themselves or their families.[15]

The position of mobile workers and drifters within the oil industry changed considerably with the advance of mechanization in the oil field. Mechanization, particularly in pipelining, both speeded the pace of work and diminished job opportunities for these workers. By the 1950s, their ranks had thinned, though pipeline superintendents could still round up crews for jobs by combing the cheap hotels near the Fort Worth stockyards where drifters settled between jobs. At the same time, mechanization cut the number of jobs available in pipelining; however, another development in the oil industry kept some types of work open to transient labor. The Great Depression brought major oil companies to adopt the financial expedient of contracting out drilling and service work. Contracting out offered new opportunities for independent drillers and small service companies, who hired workers without much concern for formal personnel practices. Particularly in the booming postwar decade, these employers hired hands as they could find them and when they came along. Returning veterans found oil-field jobs, just as the doughboys had in 1918 and 1919, and wandering misfits located day-labor jobs with well-service contractors. Many of the new mobile workers moved out to jobs in Latin America and the Middle East; others put money aside, bought houses, and settled down.[16]

Though drifters remained an important part of the oil-field labor force, even smaller contractors gradually came to prefer more settled

TABLE 1   Percent of the Population 45 Years Old and Over

1920	Eastland County	12.8	Texas	16.4
1930	Winkler County	8.1	Texas	18.4
1940	Ector County	12.1	Texas	22.2
1950	Scurry County	17.4	Texas	24.8

SOURCE: United States Department of Commerce, Bureau of the Census, *Fourteenth Census of the United States, 1920: Population*, vol. 3, pp. 985, 996; *Fifteenth Census of the United States, 1930: Population*, vol. 3, part 2, pp. 942, 971; *Sixteenth Census of the United States, 1940: Population*, vol. 2, part 6, pp. 760, 795; *Seventeenth Census of the United States, 1950: Population*, vol. 2, part 43 (Texas), pp. 67, 94.

employees. As oil-field drilling became ever more expensive, technical, and fast-paced, unseasoned hands new to their work crews cost employers money in lost time. Accordingly, employers gradually followed major companies in trying to keep steady employees rather than recruit drifters as needed. With a view to keeping workers from quitting to avoid moves or long drives to work, some drilling firms decentralized operations or limited geographical areas where they would take contracts; workers that were once mobile were thus able to settle down and keep jobs that might otherwise have opened up for drifters.[17]

Boomers, mobile workers, and drifters all swelled the populations of the oil boomtowns and then moved on. They left scant records of themselves, either in public documents or personal recollections. They appear in the aggregate in the data of the United States Bureau of the Census, which indicates that like migrations to gold and silver booms, migration to oil fields drew large numbers of late adolescents and young adults. Oil-field labor was young men's work. Thus, in Eastland County, men between the ages of eighteen and twenty-four made up one-third of the population, while they accounted for only about one-fifth of the whole population of Texas. Roughly the same proportions held in Winkler County in 1930, in Ector County in 1940, and in Scurry County in 1950. It was twice as likely that one would have met middle-aged or elderly men and women on the streets of Dallas or Abilene than on the streets of Wink in 1930 or in the shops of Odessa in 1940.

McCamey, as Bessie Leonard recalled it, was like scores of other oil towns in this regard: "We were practically all young people. The only real older man I can remember [was] in his seventies. [He] had a young wife, grown children, and his son was working there. His young wife had two babies. And that's the only real older man I can remember."[18]

TABLE 2   Sex Ratios in Selected Counties, 1920–50

1920	Eastland County	143.7	Texas	106.8
1930	Winkler County	131.7	Texas	103.6
1940	Ector County	108.8	Texas	100.9
1950	Scurry County	120.3	Texas	100.4

SOURCE: United States Department of Commerce, Bureau of the Census, *Fourteenth Census of the United States, 1920: Population,* vol. 3, pp. 985, 996; *Fifteenth Census of the United States, 1930: Population,* vol. 3, part 2, pp. 942, 971; *Sixteenth Census of the United States, 1940: Population,* vol. 2, part 6, pp. 763, 1000; *Seventeenth Census of the United States, 1950: Population,* vol. 2, part 43 (Texas), pp. 63, 104.

Before the Great Depression most unskilled work in the oil patch was done by young men just off the farm; but married men who had come off the farms at earlier times and in other oil fields were also tied to the fields, as semiskilled workers and roughnecks. They usually left their families on farms, at past work sites until they found housing, or in relatively permanent quarters to which they returned between jobs. To some extent the personnel policies of major oil companies generated the disproportionate numbers of young, unmarried men who came to boomtowns. Oil companies preferred them, even among their technical employees. George Abell, who worked as an instrument man for a major oil company in more than a half dozen states before he settled down in Midland, recalled that the companies preferred young men like him "because they could live under circumstances that were a little rougher."[19]

There were fewer women in oil towns than there were in more settled areas. In Eastland County, for example, there were about 144 men for every 100 women, a ratio that is even greater for the eighteen through forty-four age group, which had 163 men for every 100 women; the state as a whole had 104 men for every 100 women in the same age category. In Ector County, twenty years later, the greatest differences occurred in the thirty-five to thirty-nine and forty to forty-five age groups, which had ratios of 128.6 and 165.3, respectively, though there were more women than men in the twenty to twenty-nine age group. For Snyder, the 1950 Census disclosed an imbalance closer to the traditional pattern, with a high ratio of 135.5 among persons twenty-five years and older. Among single people fourteen years old and over, there were 3 men for every woman, while the married, widowed, and divorced people were about evenly matched by gender.

TABLE 3 The Black Population of Selected Counties, 1920–50

1920	Eastland County	1.1%	Texas	15.9%
1930	Winkler County	4.0	Texas	14.7
	Upton County	4.2		
1940	Ector	3.4	Texas	14.4
1950	Scurry	0.4	Texas	12.7
	Ector	3.4		

SOURCE: United States Department of Commerce, Bureau of the Census, *Fourteenth Census of the United States, 1920: Population*, vol. 3, pp. 985, 996; *Fifteenth Census of the United States, 1930:* Population, vol. 3, part 2, pp. 942, 971; *Sixteenth Census of the United States, 1940: Population*, vol. 2, part 6, pp. 763, 1000; *Seventeenth Census of the United States, 1950: Population*, vol. 2, part 43 (Texas), pp. 63, 104.

Though women found work in oil towns, they did not work at oil-field labor, an employment pattern reflected in the imbalance in sex ratios.[20]

Ethnic and racial minorities were also underrepresented in the populations of oil-field towns in the Permian Basin. Actually, there were few blacks in the relatively stable oil population. Agriculture in the Permian Basin attracted black farm workers on a limited seasonal basis, but few remained after crops had been harvested. The oil industry provided little direct employment for blacks, though transient teamster crews occasionally included black laborers. The greatest number of permanent jobs for blacks came from expanded service operations, especially in Midland, where hotels, offices, and private homes employed such service personnel as doormen, bellboys, janitors, maids, and cooks.[21]

Among Permian Basin towns, Midland had the largest permanent settlement of Mexican Americans; in 1930, Mexicanos comprised 14 percent of Midland's population. Most of the Mexicano workers had been drawn to the area by construction and maintenance work with the railroads. When oil development stimulated the economy of the area, they found alternative employment on road crews, in hotel kitchens, and in private homes. Like blacks, Mexicanos rarely occupied industrial positions in the oil industry in either drilling or production. Native-born white Americans were thus the preponderant majority in both the oil industry and in the Permian Basin before and after the discovery of oil. Though both minority communities grew during the period under consideration, they did so as the indirect consequence of

TABLE 4   European-Born Whites as Percent of
the Whole Population of Selected Counties, 1920–50

1920	Eastland County	4.9%	Texas	7.7%
1930	Winkler County	1.1	Texas	6.7
1940	Ector County	0.5	Texas	4.2
1950	Scurry County	0.4	Texas	3.6

SOURCE: United States Department of Commerce, Bureau of the Census, *Fourteenth Census of the United States, 1920: Population*, vol. 3, pp. 984, 996; *Fifteenth Census of the United States, 1930: Population*, vol. 3, part 2, pp. 763, 941; *Sixteenth Census of the United States, 1940: Population*, vol. 2, part 6, pp. 762, 1000; *Seventeenth Census of the United States, 1950: Population*, vol. 2, part 43 (Texas), pp. 63, 104.

oil activity. There were more blacks and Mexican Americans in the Permian Basin oil towns after petroleum activity began, but the growth of the Anglo community far outstripped that of the minority groups. Minority population grew both from natural increase and from limited in-migration after the onset of oil activity, but it was smaller and more constant than that of the Anglos, whose ranks swelled and thinned in direct and short-term response to the level of exploration.[22]

Native-born white Americans were in a large majority in the West Texas oil counties; the area attracted relatively few immigrants. The greatest numbers of foreign-born whites in both 1920 and 1930 came from Russia; in 1940 and 1950, natives of Germany were the single largest group. Neither group was numerous. In Wink, during boom days, the largest group of naturalized Americans consisted of two families of Russians, both of them headed by managers of retail stores. Throughout the Permian Basin, European-born whites were less significant numerically than either Mexican Americans or blacks.

Despite several decades of oil activity in Oklahoma, relatively few American Indians joined the oil-field labor force. In 1930, census takers located a handful of American Indians in the West Texas oil towns. Ector and Upton counties both reported four, though neither had any in 1920, and one Indian lived in Midland. Scurry County contained seven Indians in 1920 and three in 1930, but oil activity was not significant at either date, and there is no apparent relationship between petroleum developments in other parts of the region and the North American Indian population of that agricultural county.[23]

To sum up, the population of oil boomtowns was largely young, male, white, and native-born, a profile that is related to the geographical origins of oil-field workers. When asked where those who followed oil came from, residents of former boomtowns often answer, "From everywhere, all over." But though it may have seemed as if the fame of a boomtown like Wink had drawn in newcomers from all over the world, most Permian Basin workers tended to come from relatively few geographical areas. Nearly all of the older oil workers in West Texas recall that the early day cable-tool drillers in the region migrated from the older oil regions, especially from Pennsylvania and West Virginia, and that the less-skilled workers were from Texas and adjoining states. Interviews with oil men and newspaper articles tend to bear out these generalizations: drillers Bill Chancellor, Orville Myers, and Burton F. Weekley were all born in West Virginia; W.A. Black, who drilled the first oil well in Ector County, was born in Pennsylvania and moved to Texas from Ohio in 1929. The identification of the migrant population through birth and death records permits an expansion of these individual examples, but it also discloses a chronological change in the origins of the oil-field population.[24]

During the twenties there was a strong geographical mix of the total work force in the Permian Basin oil towns. Among twenty-eight job classifications, Texans made up a majority in only ten. With regard to two groups, bankers and lawyers, familiarity with Texas law and business conditions, and the informal connections that are necessary to success in either field, made the majority of these professionals native sons. Merchants, clerks, and salesmen, all of whom tended to follow boom activity, were more often from Texas than from any other state, as were other boom riders such as waiters, waitresses, cooks, barbers, laundrymen, most construction and maintenance workers, and truckers. The publisher of the *Penwell News* in 1930 had operated earlier in Barstow, Texas, Hobbs, New Mexico, in Cushing and Drumright, Oklahoma, and in Smackover, Arkansas: journalists, too, joined the ranks of the boomers.[25]

As Appendix A "The Origins of Labor, 1927–30," indicates, most of the oil-field workers—roustabouts, roughnecks, pipeliners, tank builders, and connection gangs—came from Texas and the contiguous states during the early period of petroleum development in the region. Dramatic changes during the following decades appear, however, with regard to both drillers and unskilled labor. During the early period more than one-third of the drillers came from Pennsylvania, while only one-fifth came from the Southwest. Two decades later, nearly nine out of ten drillers were natives of Texas and adjoining states. Even sharper changes occurred with regard to unskilled labor, where the proportion native to the Southwest nearly doubled during the latter period, reflecting the entry of Texas-born Mexicanos into the labor force and the diminished importance of Mexican nationals, particularly among the ranks of railroad employees. It is probable, overall, that the increasing proportion of Texans and other southwesterners reflects both the tendency of children born in the region to follow their fathers' lead in taking up oil-field work and the general expansion of the oil-field labor force after World War II; the latter development drew strongly on local populations for less skilled jobs, much as the petroleum industry had done since 1859. The relatively high proportion of tool dressers from the region, 88 percent, reflects the semiskilled nature of the work, between roustabouting and drilling. Tool dressing was not always an entry-level job, but an alert and ambitious roustabout could learn some of the skills through observation, acquiring the rest if he were hired on in the position. If a roustabout proved to be an able tool dresser, he might well move up to driller. Interview responses indicate that a significant number of those who were operators by 1949 had been roustabouts or tool dressers in 1927–30.[26]

Like tool dressers, a major proportion of oil management employees, some 65 percent, were born in the region. This employment category, which includes geologists, drew heavily on the Southwest, in part because regional differences in geological structures led companies to hire those whose experience could be directly applied to local problems. The hiring of technically-trained personnel, moreover, was often done on the basis of recommendations by professors known to headquarters and divisional personnel. Over time this informal regional employment network of educators and company management developed to the point that in at least one area, geology, professionals who were not trained in either Texas or Oklahoma were a decided minority in West Texas.[27]

Medical doctors and dentists, many of whom received their training in Texas, were frequently among the oil-field boomers who moved from town to town. By the late twenties, major oil companies regularly retained physicians to treat their employees. In communities like Midland, which had been the medical center for a large portion of the Permian Basin before the coming of oil, local physicians became company doctors. In remote areas, however, companies sent out their own doctors to live in and serve oil camps. Thus, in McCamey, Humble had its own doctor at its camp; many McCamey residents reckoned his abilities to be superior to those in town. Indeed, one McCamey resident recalled being told by a town doctor, "We're here because we're failures somewhere else," not a reassuring comment to a prospective patient.[28] Boomtowns attracted young men fresh from medical school, as well as those doctors who traveled from boom to boom. That doctors were among the boomers is indicated by the Upton County Medical Register. The two physicians to arrive in the county in 1926 both had offices in Eastland County when it boomed a half a dozen years before. Some seven physicians registered in Upton County in 1927; three of them had come directly from Texas and Arkansas oil fields.[29] Oil brought perhaps as many as a dozen physicians to Winkler County, and several of them set up small hospitals in Wink. Doctors also arrived in Snyder in 1949 and 1950, establishing substantial practices among newcomers. As one local doctor put it, they moved to Snyder "for the money, of course." Few remained in town by 1955. When oil activity dwindled, oil-town doctors often moved on with the population, leaving the residents of towns like Wink to find medical care in places with more enduring prosperity.[30]

Though the census data can establish, to a great degree, the demographic characteristics and the geographical origins of oil boomtown population, the rare coincidences of peak oil activity and census-taking has made estimates of boomtown population highly variable and generally unreliable. For the most part, observers have responded to visual impressions that testified to the social reality of the boom. Apparently half the population might be found on the dusty main street, day or night; there were many more people than one could possibly count in the commercial district of a town. Such tumultuous growth did show up when census takers reported rates of mobility. The census recorded that Scurry County, site of the vast Canyon Reef field, had the highest migration rate (52.9) reported in the 1950 Census of Population. More than half of the people who were counted there in 1950 had lived somewhere else in 1949! Even locations of major defense installations, such as Chattahoochee County, Georgia, the site of Fort Benning, had a lesser proportion of population coming and going. Among the top ten mobility areas of 1950, eight were in Texas, and seven of this number were in West Texas. The mobility rate for the general area of the Permian Basin, excluding Scurry County, was about 25 percent from 1949 to 1950, with 14.4 percent of the 1950 population having arrived during that year; out-migration from 1949 to April, 1950, amounted to 11 percent of the population in the latter year. Nearly two-thirds of those who had changed houses from 1949 to 1950 also moved into or out of Texas as well. Moreover, most of the moves were long distance: nine of ten were from noncontiguous states. It was employment, above all, which brought nearly fifty thousand newcomers to this area of West Texas in 1950.[31] No wonder all the world seemed to be strolling in the Snyder courthouse square.

Impressions, however current and vivid, were highly unreliable clues to the number of people in boomtowns, for a number of reasons. The wood-framed and false-fronted business districts, usually no more than four to six blocks long, filled up readily, particularly at the end of shifts. Though the rough-sawed board walks and dirt streets were nearly deserted between tours, for a few hours every day they swarmed with off-duty workers who bought meals, sought diversion, and provided for their ordinary needs, before they retired to the cot houses, bunkhouses, and tents of the settlement. Wives and children of workers often joined the crush during rush hours to indulge in the cheapest form of local entertainment, people watching. Of such amusement, Alice Keene, a housewife during the Wink boom, recalls that "it was just like going to a movie." One family of Ector County ranchers would eat their evening meal and "then drive into town and park and see all the people that were around." For good reason, then, one could not hope to arrive at a realistic estimate of boomtown population by observing street crowds and making mental comparisons to streets in conventional cities.[32]

Not every observer, moreover, was particularly concerned with furnishing a fair assessment of the population. Journalists, oil promoters, and real estate speculators alike benefited from the general acceptance of inflated population figures. Milling crowds contributed credibility to the unvarying pitch of promotion: vast fortunes could be made by imaginative investors willing to take risks. Where so many were willing to come there must surely be the chance for great wealth. Writing of Desdemona in 1919, A. H. Blackiston, for example, wrote of wild life and vast profits, of one oil company that returned $120 for every $1.00 invested, and mused: "While contemplating the vast stores of wealth uncovered there today one cannot but revert to the early Spanish conquerors and their vain search for the hidden treasures of Cibola, which all the time lay beneath their feet in vastly greater amounts than they ever fancied in their wildest dreams." The exploitation of oil was not so much a chance for investment as a hunt for treasure.[33]

Boom promotion by journalists served the interests not only of oil promoters but also of real estate speculators, whose principal asset was often widespread public belief in the boom. The latter were quick to emphasize sky-rocketing population. The promoters of the Wink townsite, for example, estimated the 1927 population at 3,500 inhabitants, a higher figure than can be reached except through flights of imagination. The *Pecos Enterprise and Gusher* added the booster's finale: " . . . it has all the appearance of a modern oil city, reminding one of Goose Creek, Burkburnett, and Borger in their palmiest days." Even a reader who believed that Borger had had palmy days might well have been skeptical. When the newspaper article was written, Wink still lacked schools, churches, hospitals, electric lights, and clean water, and Hendrick Boulevard was either clouded by driving dust or covered with muddy muck.[34]

Estimates by relatively disinterested participants tended to be more reliable. The Midland, Texas, City Council asserted that the local population was 46,465 in 1955, a figure they lowered by about 5 percent twelve months later. In Odessa, the Council guessed that the city contained 50,807 people in 1954, though the *San Angelo Standard-Times* set the figure higher by more than 3,000. In more recent times, estimates and predictions of population were based on formulae derived from reports of utility connections, indicating the number of water, gas, electric, and telephone accounts. Though certainly more accurate than visual impressions and promoters' assurances, this method was unnecessarily imprecise. The high level of variation possible with its use was made clear in Snyder in 1950, when the mayor calculated the city's population at 15,000 and the city manager placed it at 18,000; in fact, the number of utility connections could have supported estimates ranging from 6,000 to nearly 20,000. Estimates based on utility connections, moreover, tended to underestimate the social and economic effects of the nearby company camps and of the "rag towns." Such settlements existed near most oil communities. Corsicana had Juarez, Wildcat, Tudartown, and half a dozen other spots nearby; the Ranger area included Jakehamon, Leeray, and Edhobby, while McCamey had Crossett and the Humble and Gulf Oil camps. Ector County contained Hilton, Badger, and Penwell in addition to Odessa; and Wink's nearby settlements included Tulsa, Brookfield, Westbrook, and the Roxana, Humble, and Southern Crude camps. All of these settlements were tied to exploration and production in the immediate area of major towns, and they contributed to the growth of the economy and social life of the larger settlements. Though they were not necessarily reflected in official estimates of population, and they did not always tie into the public utilities of the towns, the camps and settlements furnished trade for town businesses, members for voluntary organizations, and children for local schools. In the last instance, camps and other settlements can be included in estimates because inhabitants were included in the scholastic populations of the independent school districts.[35]

The most reliable basis for estimation of oil-town population is school data. Every fall, all public schools in Texas must report the school-age population to authorities in Austin, a practice which began in the nineteenth century. This data, used by the United States Census Bureau to study mobility, is also a more accurate guide to population increases in the five oil towns than utility connections, when allowance is made for the variation in ratio between the scholastic population and the population as enumerated in the reports of the decennial census. Use of school-age population figures produces systematic and much reduced estimates of oil-field populations, which can be taken as reliable within prescribed limits. School data does not, for example, reflect settlement and migration that preceded the creation of the school district, and it probably misses a substantial part of the drifting population which was often underenumerated in the U.S. Census. The school data, however, provides a more reliable long-term view of population than those estimates based on other information; it is the best basis for estimating population for the forty-year period of this study.[36]

The estimates for both McCamey and Wink, contained in Appendix B, "Estimates of the Relatively Permanent Population and of Gain or Loss through Migration," are far below the most frequent guesses, which place five to fifteen thousand people in McCamey in 1927 and ten to fifteen thousand settlers in Wink in 1929. Even when an allowance is made for the possibility that at least half of the relatively nontransient workers and their families might have lived in company camps and in other settlements outside the city limits, it is difficult to justify the higher figures that are usually offered, especially for Wink. However, if one assumes a high level of mobility during booms, it is possible that the high estimates might approximate the cumulative number of residents during a particular period, though as great a number were never in residence at any one time. Thus, it is possible that about seventy-five hundred people were in and around Wink during 1928, and about seven thousand in and out of the area at some time during the following year. Additional guesses could support any number of figures at highly varying levels, but these exercises would be less useful than careful consideration of the coming and going that seems to have been the principal characteristic of boomtown populations. One unpublished study of population turnover in Midland between 1945 and 1960, for example, suggested that the total turnover was roughly four times the net gain or loss in a particular year.[37]

A rough calculation of in-migration can be made by subtracting the natural increase of the population—the excess of births over deaths—from the total increase. This data, along with the estimates of population, will support a year-by-year description of the populations of the various towns, and it leads to a number of useful observations relating to the duration of oil booms in the selected towns and cities.

The initial phase of petroleum activity, including primary exploration, the construction of transportation and storage facilities, and the development of crude-oil production, tended to last about two years. McCamey, Wink, and Snyder followed this general pattern, as did Midland during the development of production in the Spraberry trend, from 1951 into 1952. Odessa presents less clear-cut data, because it tended to respond strongly to activity in adjoining fields, often during the same years in which fields were opened and developed in Ector County. Thus, oil-field workers and oil industry supply and service companies found work in the Keystone field in Winkler County in the period 1935–38 as well as in areas within Ector County. The same situation existed during the years 1945–48, when Odessa grew from oil activity in Ward and Andrews counties as well as from production in its immediate vicinity. To an even greater extent, Midland's booms were compounded by activity in the region. Though significant quantities of oil and gas were not produced in Midland County until late 1950, it expanded in response to developments in Upton and Winkler counties during the 1920s; in Ector, Winkler, and Andrews counties during the 1930s; and in Ector, Upton, Andrews, Gaines, Scurry, and other counties during the late 1940s and 1950s. The counties in which exploration and production alone sustained population growth tended to enjoy one-year revivals of activity with the geographic and stratigraphic extensions of earlier fields, as took place in both McCamey and Wink from time to time during the 1930s, 1940s, and 1950s. Snyder, its population cresting in 1950, did not boom again until the 1970s.

Contrary to the popular assumption, close study of population levels of five Permian Basin towns clearly shows that the boom-and-bust sequence did not hold in relatively recent oil booms. Wink, alone on the fringe of area developments and limited by water flooding in the Hendrick field, declined sharply during the decade following its establishment, but it did not vanish. McCamey's population fell when Humble relocated to Midland, but production employment and the natural increase in the population sustained McCamey's size, as they did Snyder's several decades later. Both Midland and Odessa continued to grow.

The two cities enjoyed favorable geographical location for management and service operations, and both developed diversified functions within the oil industry that sustained them. Midland and Odessa were more centrally located in the areas of principal exploration and production than their regional rivals, San Angelo and Big Spring. With the opening of the Yates and Hendrick fields in 1926, activity moved farther from these cities and nearer Midland and Odessa. By 1928 Odessa was on its way to becoming the labor and supply center for the region. Subsequent activity in Ector and neighboring counties reinforced this aspect of the town's development. Midland, with its relatively abundant office and hotel space, was well situated to become the management center for operations that would stretch to more than one hundred miles in all directions, in an area that was discovered to contain nearly a quarter of the nation's oil and gas reserves, as they were identified by 1960. The same general development of regional oil-field centers occurred in other places and and at other times. Tulsa, for example, became the management center for Oklahoma oil, thus enduring as a major city long after Cushing and Sapulpa had gone through their booms. Beaumont and Port Arthur became the principal refinery sites in their region, securing an economic base more durable and secure than that of outlying oil-field towns. Tyler and Longview became management and manufacturing centers, surviving the downturn of activity in East Texas during the mid-1930s. In all of these regional centers, the business activity of the oil industry outlasted the exploration booms that had given rise to them. They thrived far after the exhilarating discoveries were made and the more regular work of establishing production was completed. Their populations, like those of other boomtowns, had swelled suddenly with the influx of boomers and mobile workers. In the Permian Basin, between 1920 and 1960, most of these newcomers were Anglo, young, and unmarried. Many were farm boys, of whom an increasing proportion were native to the Southwest after World War II; they tended to remain in the main oil towns, avoiding the long and frequent moves long required by oil-field employment. Even recent booms, like that of Snyder, nonetheless brought floods of population beyond the capacity of easy measurement and quick calculation and without precedent in the communities. In the absence of reliable data, boomtown leaders guessed wildly about population on many occasions. They tended to fall back on visual evidence and common assumptions, the most durable of which was that the boom would end as quickly as it began. It was, in fact, likely that bust would not follow boom during the postwar period because improvements in science and technology tended to sustain production employment. Decline, when it came, was gradual. Midland, Odessa, and Snyder did not go the way of McCamey and Wink.

Teamsters moving bunkhouses from Pyote to Wink, Texas, in 1928.

2.
Housing

UNLIKE RAPID URBAN GROWTH from the expansion or relocation of industry or real estate booms, oil booms cause massive short-term demands for housing. The greatest need for labor occurs during the exploration and drilling phases, while production may require less than half as many workers. In the Permian Basin, these two phases have commonly overlapped. Oil fields have been large and have produced from several structures. As a consequence, initial housing shortages have been prolonged; inadequate shelter has often served far beyond its intended term. During housing shortages, local residents of towns that existed before oil was discovered and early arrivals in the new towns cashed in by charging high rents for rude shelters.

For most workers, it was easier to find a job than it was to hire a bed. Whether in new settlements or in towns which predated oil, oil booms ordinarily taxed local housing beyond capacity. Until they could find shelter, boomers slept wherever a human body might rest with relative ease. Like California miners at the height of the gold rush, oil-field workers often camped out-of-doors until winter. In numerous towns, newcomers rented chairs in hotel lobbies and cots in front parlors of private homes by the night. They constructed every imaginable sort of temporary shelter, much of it from board and canvas. A U.S. government study of oil camps, published in 1921, described the familiar scene: "A stretch of trackless prairie sometimes becomes, almost overnight, a community numbering thousands of people who establish themselves in temporary buildings, tents, dugouts, lean-to-shelters, or even within four topless walls of burlap, or in the open. These mushroom communities have been aptly termed 'rag towns.'[1]" Some temporary structures served as dwellings; others were used as restaurants, bars, and stores.

Tradesmen in boom communities had a small advantage in housing over the transient worker; if they were able to locate suitable places to do business, those structures might often serve to house them and their families as well.[2] As late as the 1940s a dry goods merchant in Midland slept in his store for several months during the Spraberry boom, leaving his family in Oklahoma until he could locate more suitable living quarters. E. N. Beane slept on a cot in the rear of the grocery store where he worked in Crane, doing double duty as clerk and unpaid night watchman. With the twenty-four-hour pace of boomtown business, sleeping at the store was not infrequently a necessary step for an ambitious businessman, even when he had a bed elsewhere.[3]

Getting a hotel room in a booming oil town was a challenging task. Reporting on Wink in October, 1927, the *Pecos Enterprise and Gusher* noted: "The hotels and rooming houses are full, turning away people every night. It's difficult even to get a cot for the night." Newcomers to Wink who found no lodging commonly slept in their cars or, pioneer fashion, in or under canvas-covered wagons. But for those who had money and luck, temporary quarters might be quite comfortable. Midland's Scharbauer Hotel, built in 1928, had central heating, air-conditioning, and a crystal-bedecked ballroom. With an initial two hundred fifty rooms and an addition of two hundred rooms constructed during the thirties, it was both the most expensive and the most agreeable place to stay in the Permian Basin. Better-heeled oil operators frequently worked their business from rooms at the Scharbauer, and major oil companies kept sleeping quarters, on long-term leases, for prominent corporate officials. During boom times, the Scharbauer limited transient residents to a five-day stay, though it gave special consideration to newly arrived medical doctors and their families and to guests of high status who did not relish the prospect of sandy sheets and lumpy beds at a tourist court. As far as lodging was concerned, the Scharbauer Hotel was elegance in the Permian Basin. Less grand and less expensive, the Crawford Hotel in Midland and the Elliott Hotel in Odessa were still desirable places to stay. The demand for rooms at the latter was so great in 1927 that paying guests moved into the newly-constructed building before water and sewer connections were complete; cots lined the hallways. When C. C. Quinn built the Warfield Hotel in Odessa in 1930, guests moved in before the windows were installed: as long as there was a roof over their heads, lodgers did not quibble over refinements.[4]

The elegant Scharbauer aside, most of the hotels in oil-field towns were more like the flophouses in urban slums than big city hotels. Like the Miller Hotel in Wink or the Henderson and Savoy hotels in Crane, they were barracks-type structures, occasionally two-storied, built of two-by-fours and corrugated iron; rooms had rough-sawed wood or plasterboard partitions, and center hallways ran the length of the building. Rooms had minimal furnishings, amounting to iron beds and a few chairs. Beds hired for two to five dollars per night, two persons to a room; two shifts of sleepers usually rented one room. As Hood May recalled of the City Cafe and the Miller Hotel in Wink, "The chili was never hot, and the beds were never cold." Doors to rooms in such primitive hotels often lacked locks, and often there was no running water or indoor plumbing.[5] Not infrequently, these rough accommodations were moved from place to place. One proprietor, H. A. Hedberg, moved the fifty-room Rooney Hotel to Big Lake from Fort Stockton in 1925, built an addition, and renamed it the Doran House in 1926; the building was moved westward to Pyote in 1928 and renamed the Texas Hotel. It reached Hobbs in 1930. The twenty-two-room Higgins Hotel, built in Wink in 1927 and renamed the Miller Hotel in 1928, was hauled off to Mentone, sixty miles to the west, in the late 1930s. It was possible, therefore, to stay in the same hotel in several different oil towns.[6]

Even cheaper and more impermanent were the cot houses, where use of a bed for eight hours in Wink cost fifty cents in 1929. Constructed of lumber and beaver board, they generally had rough-planked floors and a window or two. Beds were arranged close together in two rows, on either side of a center aisle, down the length of the building. As in cheap hotels, cot-house beds rented in shifts; such lodgings not only lacked privacy, but they required that patrons secure or hide personal valuables. Snyder cot-house lodgers of the fifties regularly put cot legs into their steel-toed shoes before they went to sleep so that thieves would not take those most expensive parts of an oil hand's clothing; the visual effect created by a row of beds wearing workmen's boots was unusual, to say the least.[7] Though the majority of newcomers to booming oil fields had to cope with housing problems, there were, nonetheless, a happy few who could leave housing matters in the hands of their employers. In the unanimous opinion of all the interviewed participants in oil booms, the most fortunate people were those who lived in the camps and houses that were built and operated by oil companies. These facilities were, in fact, a considerable inducement for workers to remain in the oil fields, in remote locations and unpleasant natural environments. The absence of subsidized housing tempted workers to leave the oil fields, either to seek work in other locations or occupations or to return to work on farms near their original homes. If a worker and his family happened upon good housing in an oil-field town, there was strong inducement to switch employers rather than be transferred out of town. Thus, one roustabout who worked for thirteen different companies in one year recalled that he preferred to quit his job rather than lose a fine apartment he had found in Odessa: "Easier to find another job than to find another apartment." Company housing helped keep valuable employees on the payroll.[8]

Drillers, rig builders, tool dressers, and roustabouts, usually the first group to work in oil fields, stayed in nearby towns or in modest drilling camps on leases. Camps often began with a tent or two and upgraded to wood and wallboard buildings. Though many drilling camps were small and impermanent, consisting of primarily sleep shacks, some were more substantial. The Lockhart camp near Mentone, for example, included a boardinghouse and ten single-family dwellings. Companies often provided housing for transient production personnel as well. Gulf and Humble, for example, housed their mobile pipeline crews in tents when they worked between McCamey and Crane, shifting them to a boardinghouse as they neared Crane. The Pure Oil Company fed and housed its connection crew in Winkler County in a company-owned boardinghouse. In isolated areas such arrangements were necessary.[9]

When production workers and supervisors moved into an area, companies built more permanent camps. In the Permian Basin, camps were built in or near all of the oil towns, including Midland, Odessa, McCamey, Wink, and Snyder. Management and supervisory personnel had the best quarters in camp; they paid a nominal rent for houses of six or more rooms. Clerical and production workers generally lived in two-to-five-room houses, some of which included screened rear porches. Dormitories and bunkhouses accommodated single men and workers who did not have families in the area; bunkhouses sometimes lacked partitions and indoor plumbing. In the Prairie Oil and Gas Company camp in Pampa, in the Texas Panhandle, Levi Horlacher lived in a sixteen-by-thirty-foot bunkhouse with nineteen other workers. The building had one gas heater, two gas lights, and no plumbing. After he had worked for the company for several months, he moved into "the dormitory," which contained triple rooms, hot and cold water, and shower baths. Meals were taken at the company boardinghouse for forty dollars a month; the food, the best available in the oil patch, included eggs and fresh fruits and vegetables in addition to the standard items: meat, potatoes, beans, and coffee. Boardinghouses, usually under independent management and company supervision, generally packed lunches as a part of a meal contract. Prices were reasonable, and the food was safe, which could not always be said of the cafés and chili parlors of the boom town.[10]

Relatively permanent camps were usually well built and neatly finished. At times, they were very comfortable establishments. Unmarried men who worked for Shell in the Coalinga (California) oil fields in 1908 lived in spacious, clean bunkhouses, each with indoor plumbing and electricity. Recreational facilities included tennis courts, a golf course, a swimming pool, and sports fields. Company-sponsored activities included baseball, basketball, soccer, tennis, amateur theatricals, weekly motion pictures, a glee club, and a social club. Few other industries in the United States provided employees with as much.[11]

In the Permian Basin, Texon came closest to meeting the Coalinga model for company settlements. Designed to be a complete town, Texon had a library, theater, church, hospital, elementary school, golf course, swimming pool, and clubhouse. It also contained a post office, grocery stores, drugstores, restaurants, barber shops, and a company-run water softening plant. The company provided low-cost dental care to employees; it operated a volunteer fire department and an air strip. As the final touch, a landscape gardener was hired to plant and tend nine hundred rose bushes planted around the settlement. Though it did not go to quite such lengths, the Humble Oil and Refining Company made a special effort to run an appealing camp in Wink for its four hundred employees. The company carefully landscaped its camp area and planted grass, trees, and shrubs; the camp included a large community center, a baseball field, a playground, and a swimming pool.[12] Apart from the three painted wood-frame houses on "Millionaires' Row," the best housing around McCamey was part of the Marland, Texas, Humble, Dixie, Sun, Roxana, and Gulf camps. Beyond any doubt, company housing was the cheapest available; rents, running from $1.50 to $2.50 per month, included utilities, which were deducted from workers' paychecks at the end of pay periods. At a time when most McCamey residents used outdoor privies, many oil-camp residents had indoor plumbing.[13]

Not all company camps, however, were well constructed, clean, and pleasant; living conditions in those on remote leases could be quite primitive. One camp in Oklahoma, for example, operated by a relatively small oil company during the 1930s, consisted of a collection of ramshackle shotgun houses. Roofs leaked, and water oozed out of the walls in damp weather. The buildings lacked indoor plumbing; hydrants supplied residents with water. Fronting on unpaved roads, yards consisted of shifting dust and sand. Even in the best camps in the Permian Basin, sand and scorpions could be unending problems, as some former camp residents have recalled; though they have lived in town for many years, they continue to shake their shoes for scorpions before putting them on.[14]

Although oil camps often provided the best accommodations in the oil field, they were not universally popular with either labor or management. Workers objected to the elements of control and regimentation that were common to company towns. During the late 1950s, when profits were low, corporate planners realized that the camps were an avoidable expense. Companies gave most camps heavy subsidy; when better roads made it possible for workers to live in established communities and drive to the oil patch within a reasonable length of time, companies no longer needed to house employees on leases. Thus, with slackened employee demand for camp housing and increasing cost-consciousness on the part of management, many of the camps in the Permian Basin broke up during the late 1950s and the early years of the following decade.

When companies discontinued oil camps, the camp houses were either moved to new oil-fields or they were sold, generally to employees who moved them into nearby towns and cities. Clell Reed, for example, bought a house from Humble and moved it from Kermit to Odessa. The company had earlier moved the house from Wink to Kermit. The cost to Reed for the house and its transport was $275, certainly a housing bargain. When Humble closed its camp in McCamey in 1932, employees were permitted to buy the houses for $50 a room. Humble contracted with a mover, who put steel girders under the buildings, jacked them up, and moved them to Midland, all within forty-eight hours. Once new owners got company houses to town, they usually improved and added to them, the most common alteration being the addition of brick veneer on all four sides. Many transferred oil-camp houses are still sound and inhabited fifty years after they were constructed, a measure of their quality. But the boxcar and shotgun houses, once so characteristic of oil-field housing, survive in fewer numbers; they are often inhabited today by those who cannot find alternative housing. As for the camp sites in the countryside, the passerby can still find them, though their buildings have vanished, by orderly rows of struggling Siberian elms, standing starkly on a treeless landscape.[15]

Workers who brought their families to oil-field towns had knotty housing problems to solve. Frequently they found a short-term solution in tents. By any standard and with whatever improvements, tent housing was inconvenient; it was uncomfortable most of the year, even for workers who had learned to tolerate its roughness as migrant farm workers or in other oil fields. It was, however, cheap and portable. Tents hovered together on the wind-scoured Texas plains in all of the oil towns from Pampa to Borger in the Panhandle to McCamey and Wink in the Permian Basin. Beginning with Ranger, "a shack and tent town" in 1919, most of the tents were U.S. Army surplus, generally eight by twelve feet, six feet high at the peak. More affluent buyers secured twenty- by twenty-four foot tents, seven feet high at the peak, while others bought two of the smaller variety and pitched them end to end.[16]

Although most of the tent dwellers considered their quarters temporary, expecting to move on to other jobs or into permanent housing in their present locales, they made improvements to make life under canvas more comfortable. Most often, they covered dirt floors with platforms, which both raised the tent above the ground and provided a more secure anchor for the sides and the flaps. Board sides usually boxed in the perimeter of the tent and cut the chill of the constant wind, and screens kept out flies and other insects. Given location in the oil fields, it was not long before gas was available for heat and cooking in tents and shacks alike; since no one worried about wasting gas, which seemed overabundant, gas heated tents during colder months. Electricity took longer to install, and kerosene lamps or gas lights served tent dwellers in the interval. When it existed in tent cities, plumbing was found only in bath and laundry houses, and toilets were of the Chic Sale variety in most instances. Tent housewives usually tossed both wash water and garbage out of the tent; they later buried trash, or, as in Wink, incinerated it in pits fired by flared-off natural gas.[17]

There were inescapable drawbacks to tent life. Insects were a perennial nuisance, especially in unboarded tents; to keep ants and other crawling bugs off tables and beds, tent housewives sometimes placed furniture legs in cans of kerosene. During McCamey's first days, dust and flies were so bothersome that one veteran of tent homemaking recalled meals at the table being eaten under a canopy of sheets. Tent dwellers had to protect all edible items from dust and insects. Food spoilage was also a problem before the installation of electricity or the opening of local ice plants, as refrigeration was difficult. When they could buy ice, some tent dwellers constructed primitive ice boxes in holes in the ground, insulating the space between the boards and dirt with sawdust and placing cakes of ice inside the boxes. In such make-do ice boxes they could store small amounts of perishable items for a short time. Life in hot West Texas became much easier and more comfortable, however, when electricity made refrigeration readily available to boomtown residents.[18]

Storage space of any kind was at a premium in cramped tent or shack housing. A trunk or compartmented cabinet might serve to store odds and ends; in lucky instances, a shack might have a small closet or two. Those unfortunate enough to arrive in the oil fields with valuable possessions, however, soon learned that tents had little room for civilized luxuries. Ruth Godwin, who spent part of her childhood in tent housing, remembered what happened to her mother's valuables: "She just brought them along, we had no place to store them or anything, so a great number of her nice things were misused. . . . This gorgeous cut-glass punch bowl: we finally wound up using it for a fish bowl, I think."[19] The material relics of more comfortable life were at a discount. Even so, tent dwellers usually carried along some furnishings, like compartmented kitchen cabinets, radios, and musical instruments like the popular ukelele. R. V. Melton's tent in Crane, for example, was furnished with a Victrola, a sewing machine, and a Bible, in addition to standard household goods. The Victrola was especially treasured by those who lived beyond the range of any radio station because it could provide entertainment for inexpensive evening get-togethers.[20]

As an alternative to life in a tent or a shack improvised from salvaged metal, there was yet another form of boom housing, the boxcar house. Boxcar houses, portable as their name implies, were ordinarily hauled from site to site on trucks. Wood-framed and enclosed with vertically mounted wood boards, beaver board, or sheet metal, they were commonly eight to twelve feet wide and twenty to twenty-four feet long, with one window and a door in one end of the car and a single window in the center of the other end. Though they were dark and cold in the winter, dim and hot during the summer, they were still a step up from tents or cot houses. Above all, they were portable. D. E. L. Byers, for example, bought one in Jal, New Mexico, in 1935 and moved it to Carlsbad, where he lived in it on a lease. If utilities were available, boxcar houses often had running water and electricity, but sanitation facilities were still "out back." On leases, boxcar residents could usually pipe in natural gas for cooking and heating.[21]

By far the most common type of dwelling in the oil patch, however, was the shotgun house. Common enough in the South, in lumber camps and as housing for tenant farmers, shotgun houses were long, narrow boxes, somewhat larger than boxcar houses, one room wide and two or three rooms deep, with a low roof and gables at each end; they often had a porch on the front. With a living room at the front, a kitchen at the rear, and a bedroom in between (in three-room houses), they were frequently prefabricated or pre-cut, often of lumber of the size for oil-rig timbers. On the site, a carpenter could put one of them up "by ear" in a day and a half, for $20 plus the cost of materials. Pre-cut lumber for a twelve- by twenty-four- foot building, including two doors, four windows, and one partition, sold for $110 during the 1920s. Floors were built of four-inch tongue-in-groove floorboards; shotgun dwellers rarely covered them with woven rugs because rugs trapped sand and dirt that usually blew in under the doors and around window frames. More than one housewife observed that all she had to do to clean house was open the front door and let the wind howl through. Other housewives reported, even less enthusiastically, that the construction of the houses was so loose that sand could be shoveled off the floors after a windstorm. Shotgun houses broke but did not stop the relentless West Texas wind. One windy day in Crane a powerful gust blew under a local doctor's shotgun house and rolled up a newly-laid rug around his wife's legs, reducing her to tears. As her husband recalled, "She was ready to go back to Abilene or anywhere else." Whatever else can be said of them, then, shotgun houses were not luxurious. Many a woman reacted like the wife of a Monahans man: when she saw their shotgun house behind a bottling plant, she sat down on the floor and cried.[22]

After World War II, oil field newcomers in some Permian Basin communities found jerry-built housing for rent. At Midland's air field, for example, landlords converted wartime barracks into crude, drafty apartments. In neighboring Odessa, oil-field workers found rental housing in Victory Village, a development promoted during the war by the Odessa Chamber of Commerce, which wished to see housing for workers at a new carbon-black plant. Houses in Victory Village were small and box-shaped; they had been prefabricated from rejected marine plywood and shipped to Odessa on flat cars. Though it had been intended for only five years' use, oil-field workers occupied Victory Village for more than twenty years, vacating it only when oil activity slowed down in the 1960s.[23]

In recent times, the trailer, or "mobile home" as the industry would call it, displaced the cot house, the tent, and the shotgun house in oil towns. The trailer provided minimal accommodation at a price lower than conventional housing. For highly mobile oil workers and their families, it offered shelter superior to the tent cities of the past; it could be obtained and installed far more quickly than beaver board housing, and it spared its owner the need to buy a building at inflated boom prices. The Clifford Lyles, a family of two parents and five children, moved from barracks housing at Midland's air terminal into a twenty-seven-foot trailer home in the late forties, doing so in order to be able to move with Mr. Lyle's oil-field work. With only 216 square feet of living space in the trailer, daily life, as Mrs. Lyle recalls, was "pretty chaotic." Because their trailer did not have a bathroom, they had to use communal bathrooms which, varying with the trailer park, eight to fifty families might share. Fearful of the risks to health posed by such an arrangement, Mrs. Lyle made a practice of cleaning the bathrooms before her children used them. Within trailer courts, units were usually about fifteen feet apart, affording little privacy and no proper play areas for children; the baby of the Lyle family narrowly escaped injury in one court when a car of sleepy roughnecks drove over him one morning. After little more than a year, the Lyles decided to buy a larger trailer; their new home was spacious enough to allow each child a bunk and a dresser drawer of his own.[24]

For the Lyles, as for other trailer residents, living conditions were cramped and often uncomfortable. Housekeeping was particularly hectic for the mother of a large family. But trailer living did have one great recommendation, as Mrs. Lyle describes: "We lived together as a family. I could have stayed in one place and Daddy could have gone to work . . . but I wanted us to stay together. I couldn't stand to be alone. So that was the way we could be together." And, as her daughter, Karolyn, remembers, "It was terrible, but it kept us from living in places that were absolutely filthy."[25]

Trailers have been characteristic of oil-boom housing since the forties. During Snyder's boom, trailers, about twenty-five hundred of them, comprised most of the relatively new housing units in town. Some trailer owners located in parks that offered utility and sewer connections, but many found space on vacant lots and in the back and side yards of residences. In this last arrangement, a single extension cord supplied electricity from the house, and an outside tap provided water. Most of the trailer units remained in a given location for relatively brief periods ranging from two weeks to three months, and they rarely tied up to utility services during this time. Residents who remained longer, however, generally did acquire telephones and connections with electric, water, and sewer lines; they were responsible for the increase in utility connections after 1951, a time when Snyder started to lose population through net out-migration.[26]

Trailer housing was overcrowded, almost by definition: trailers rarely contained more than the usable space in one large room of a fixed dwelling, and they regularly housed more than one person. The cramped nature of trailer housing shows up in the 1950 Census of Housing, which reported that nearly half of the housing units in Snyder were overcrowded and that more than half of them lacked a private toilet, a bath, and hot and cold running water. All such rates were substantially higher for Snyder than for Midland and Odessa, which contained proportionately less trailer housing in that year.[27]

Whether in tent housing in the 1920s or in trailers during the 1950s, occupants had the same objective: to secure temporary shelter at an affordable cost. Once an oil boom crested, those remaining in town had housing that was considered substandard. Census data for Permian Basin towns reflects the cheap prices and low values of temporary accommodations that the boom left behind. In both Upton and Winkler counties, the median value of nonfarm housing in 1930 was less than $1,000. These counties reported only two houses and one house, respectively, worth more than $5,000. By contrast, Midland, which had relatively little temporary housing, reported a median house value of $3,383, with 193 homes worth more than $5,000. The 1930 census also reflected the tendency of oil-field workers to rent housing: about two-thirds of the families in McCamey, Odessa, and Wink lived in rented quarters in 1930, while nearly half of the homes in Midland were owner-occupied. By the 1940 Census of Housing, the median value of homes in McCamey, which lost population for seven of the ten intervening years, had declined by more than half since 1930, and the average value of a McCamey dwelling was one-third of that in Odessa and less than one-seventh of that in Midland. Less than 8 percent of the homes in McCamey were mortgaged, presumably because residents could afford the low-cost housing without resort to borrowing and because lenders might well have been reluctant to acquire mortgages in a declining real estate market. Some of McCamey's better homes had left with the boom, when Humble sold many of the houses in its McCamey camp to employees who moved them to Midland. Of the homes remaining in McCamey in 1940, half had outdoor privies and nearly as many had neither bathtub nor shower. The occupants of rented facilities benefited from a high vacancy rate, nearly 13 percent, as they paid average monthly rents of thirteen dollars.[28]

In Odessa, which grew rapidly from 1933 onward, the average rent in 1940 was nearly twice as high for housing comparable to rental units in McCamey. About 80 percent of Odessa dwellings were built between 1933 and 1940, and most of them were one- or two-room buildings, with indoor plumbing and baths or showers. The smaller units were built along the lines of boxcar and shotgun houses and were equipped with radios and refrigerators. The majority of them housed more than 1.01 persons per room. In short, they were modern but cramped. About one-quarter were mortgaged, a reflection of the willingness of local lenders to extend loans in the rising real estate market and of the necessity of borrowing to pay for a house that cost $1,600. In Midland, by contrast, more than 40 percent of the homes were mortgaged, for homes were generally larger and more expensive in that company headquarters town. The average value of a home in Midland was more than double that of a home in Odessa, and about one-third of Midland dwellings had five or more rooms, more than twice the proportion of Odessa and McCamey. Average monthly rents in Midland were 40 percent higher than in Odessa and nearly 300 percent above those in McCamey. The dwelling vacancy rate was barely 4 percent in Midland.[29]

Housing was relatively tight in both Midland and Odessa in 1940, a situation that worsened during the war years, when new defense installations brought in servicemen, defense industry workers, and their families. Critical housing shortages emerged in both towns during the late 1940s and the early years of the next decade. In 1950, the national vacancy rate was slightly below 4 percent, a level indicating reasonable availability of property for rental or purchase; housing was much tighter in Odessa, where only 1.6 percent of all rental housing was vacant at the time of the census. Snyder reported only seventy-six units available in 1950. Most of these facilities included one or two rooms, which were rented for more than sixty dollars per month, 10 percent higher than the rate in Odessa and Midland.[30]

In Midland the postwar upturn in oil activity and consequent population gains left the city about 1,000 homes short in 1950. During 1951 contractors built 1,323 homes. That should have left a new surplus of 339 housing units, but during the same year the population of Midland increased by about 4,000 people through in-migration. This increase alone would have required 1,276 new homes. Thus, instead of supplying the 1950 shortage and over-building for the market, construction fell behind, leaving Midland about 900 units short at the end of 1951. In 1952, about 2,334 dwelling units were constructed, which would ordinarily have left a surplus of about 1,400 units, but the population increased by about 5,300 through net in-migration. These new settlers required 1,600 units, leaving the city 200 units short by the beginning of 1953. During that year, 784 units were built, relieving the accumulated housing shortage; it also provided several hundred replacement units for the dilapidated houses that had been occupied during the shortage. By the end of 1953, Midland's severe housing shortage was over. In the following year, about 1,700 homes came on the real estate market through new construction and through net out-migration. Consequently, in spite of a slight growth in 1955 and heavy in-migration the following year, housing was still adequate in Midland by the end of 1956. For the rest of the decade, construction exceeded the minimum demand, permitting the further replacement of some sub-standard units and enabling relatively permanent residents to move into progressively better housing, on advantageous terms.[31]

In Odessa, by contrast, the pace of housing construction did not catch up with housing needs. Though Odessa had grown and built up rapidly after World War II, the city was short about five hundred housing units by 1950. Increased construction during that year cut the shortage in half, but the city was again short by about one thousand units at the end of 1951. Despite a sharp increase in construction in 1952, the shortage increased to more than twelve hundred units because substantial in-migration increased demand. Shortages of materials disrupted construction during the following year; residential construction fell off sharply, not nearly meeting demand, a situation that left a deficit of about two thousand units by the end of the year. During

TABLE 5   Postwar Residential Construction in Midland and Odessa

	1946	1947	1948	1949	1950
Midland	302	353	663	658	1,265
Odessa	470	591	869	797	982
Total	772	944	1,532	1,455	2,247

	1951	1952	1953	1954	1955
Midland	1,323	2,334	784	927	1,117
Odessa	724	1,179	1,367	969	1,238
Total	2,057	3,513	2,151	1,896	2,355

	1956	1957	1958	1959	1960
Midland	83	1,017	1,550	1,773	775
Odessa	1,225	1,385	2,206	1,572	627
Total	1,308	2,502	3,756	3,345	1,402

SOURCE: Building Permits, Midland and Odessa, 1946–60.

1954 net out-migration and new construction made about one thousand units available, relieving housing pressure somewhat, though leaving an accumulated shortage of about one thousand units. In 1955 more than twelve hundred new units were constructed; even with substantial in-migration, the housing deficit was reduced to about nine hundred units. For the remainder of the decade, however, construction never caught up with demand in Odessa, and by April, 1960, the city was still short at least one thousand dwelling units. Thus, from the end of World War II through 1960, housing was always difficult to obtain in Odessa. There was no period during which dilapidated and inferior housing could be replaced. All units were needed, and all of them were occupied.[32]

The most dramatic instance of a postwar housing shortage created by boom growth, however, occurred in Scurry County. In Snyder, the boom of 1949 through 1950 left the city more than two thousand housing units short of demand, a situation that led many Scurry County workers to commute from Abilene and other cities in the area. Nearly three-quarters of all the fixed dwellings in the town were rented, at prices about 10 percent above the going rates in Midland, and many of these quarters amounted to little more than minimally converted sheds, garages, and chicken coops. Four new subdivisions were begun during the boom years, but they provided homes for less than one-tenth of the boom population, most of whom brought their housing with them. Trailer housing was a necessity in Snyder.[33] The *Midland Reporter-Telegram* reported: "The housing problem has loomed as the main troublemaker for Snyder. The city's new citizens are finding it tough to locate a bed for the night." Many of the workers in Scurry County did not find beds: they paid fifty cents for a seat in the Palace Theater, good for an interrupted ninety-minute snooze, or they slept on the courthouse lawn, in broken-down school busses, in storm cellars, in chicken coops, or in parked cars, which lined the roads in and out of Snyder. Two men broke into the Northside Baptist Church where they were caught sleeping in the ladies' lounge. Compounding their problem, the judge levied a fifteen dollar fine on each man, but he refused to put them up for the night in the city jail. Perhaps these unlucky interlopers joined the crowds who went from door to door, hoping to rent a spare bed in a private home.[34]

The great surge in regional oil-field development, of which the Scurry County boom was a part, meant that lodging was similarly difficult to find in McCamey, Midland, and Odessa at the beginning of the fifties. Bill Briggs, a traveling representative of Dun and Bradstreet, looked for a room in Midland for five days in 1950. He finally located a minimally converted garage with a pounded dirt floor and a lavatory, furnished with army cots and divided into two areas by a blanket on a clothesline. Air-conditioning, he recalls, consisted of "breathing down my chest on a hot day." This make-do habitation, which he shared with another man, cost them a combined rental of $240 a month. In McCamey he rarely found a clean and vacant motel room; he took to sleeping in his car, using the washroom of a filling station, at $2 per day, to wash up. The same sort of experience may have motivated enterprising thieves to steal a twelve- by eighteen-foot shack from behind the Rambling Rose Dance Hall in Odessa in 1955: they not only gained a roof over their heads but also enjoyed the distinction of having committed what the *Odessa American* described as "the largest theft ever reported here."[35]

Though they ordinarily did not force people to steal buildings, the housing shortages so noticeable in Permian Basin towns in the 1950s were the inevitable result of oil booms, and by the 1950s they had been part of the oil field population's experience for decades. Earlier generations who followed oil lived as they could, in tents, shacks, or temporary lodgings; responding to so obviously an unpleasant feature of oil-field life, companies tried providing housing in camps. But whether he found shelter in a cot house or a camp, no one who worked in the oil field expected housing to be luxurious. Makeshift, crowded, and substandard shelter was something to be endured; like constant mobility, it was part of the price paid to get ahead. No one expected to live in a tent or shack for long, and as they waited for the next move, oil-field workers and their families could hope that they would live in something better at the next stop. If they saved enough money to buy a trailer, they could at least know what their shelter would be like in the next town. The substitution of the trailer for the tent and the shotgun house, a change which began in the thirties, marked the greatest change in boomtown housing between 1920 and 1960. Trailers, better roads, and workers' desire for town life all helped spell an end to the company camp. Like the cable-tool rig, the company camp remained in use from time to time and from place to place after 1960; but it was more often only a memory. The housing problems that the company camp aimed to solve, however, remain an enduring part of oil booms.

Roughnecks, roustabouts, and teamsters in Wink, 1928.

3.
Public
Services and
Education

THE MOST CHARACTERISTIC FEATURE of a boom, the initial flood of newcomers, creates immediate and inevitable public problems. While newcomers can find their own food, shelter, and employment, collective action is necessary if they are to have drinkable water and a safe means to dispose of garbage and human waste. In a booming community these two needs require action by public agencies; should they go unmet, the community will risk epidemic disease. Depending upon the composition of the newly arrived population, one more immediate need may arise: if the booming community receives many families with young children, public law requires it to provide schools. Where schools exist, the community must enlarge them; where they do not exist, the community must create both schools and the machinery to run them. These basic problems of water and waste disposal, and of the provision of schools, are likely to loom large in any boom community, and communities booming from petroleum development are not exceptions.

Oil booms have had historically distinctive characteristics that often complicated the public problems accompanying growth. Like hard-rock mineral booms, the majority of oil booms have taken place in remote, rural areas. In such areas, the public problems created by an oil boom were without precedent, and the villages and small towns confronting them had to make strenuous efforts to modify existing government machinery or to bring new institutions into being to handle them. The booms which took place during the development of the oil fields of the arid Southwest gave rise to particularly difficult problems of water supply; in places like McCamey and Crane, for example, oil was discovered where there was no drinkable water. Pressing need to solve the problem of water supply was, as we shall see, a prime motivation in the establishment of municipal government in such places. With some notable exceptions like Oklahoma City and Long Beach, California, then, oil booms have not taken place in areas ready or well able to support the sudden arrival of many newcomers.

As already indicated, oil booms did not bring a representative cross section of national population to the oil fields, and booming oil communities had a younger population than the nation as a whole. The relative youth of oil boom population had a number of implications for community development. With respect to public health, for example, the population of booming oil communities was far less susceptible to chronic degenerative disease than to infectious illness, venereal disease, and automobile accidents. Because oil-field work was physically demanding, oil-field workers had to be reasonably strong and healthy. Their stamina was, in a sense, an asset to community health. The youth of oil boom population also meant that families moving with oil activity tended to have young children. In oil boomtowns, therefore, the lower grades of schools were always the most crowded. Uneven distribution of school population is well illustrated by an example drawn from Midland's school enrollment of 1930–31. During that year, as oil activity shifted from the Permian Basin to East Texas, enrollment in the two elementary schools dropped by 73 percent; at the same time, enrollment in the junior high school increased slightly, while high school enrollment changed little.[1] School enrollments in oil boomtowns did not grow at a uniform rate over all levels of instruction, a phenomenon which complicated school planning.

The distinctive pattern of population growth in oil booms, a pattern in which the greatest influx of population took place with exploration and development rather than with production, explains why problems with water and waste became critical during the early months of a boom. Public authorities had no lead time to improve water or waste systems; nor could they plan for growth from the development of a major oil field. Only the use of extensive manpower in drilling proved, beyond question, that a large amount of oil was present in producible quantities; growth took place in the course of defining the potential of the field. The headlong pace of an oil boom, moreover, far outstripped the pace of procedures usual in public business. Before one newcomer could draw a glass of water from a new city water tap, plans had to be drawn, funds voted, bonds sold, bids taken, materials purchased, and supply assured. While the pace of progress on large-scale public projects was best measured in years, that of oil activity was best measured in months. Even if public authorities acted decisively, they were not usually able to catch up with oil-boom development.

When population began to move away from an oil boomtown, it often did so at a rapid rate. There was thus the possibility that boom-time projects would be complete only after the persons who were to use and pay for them had moved away. The rapidity of population loss depended on the richness of area oil fields and the level of regional activity. With the refinement of scientific oil-field technology and the development of secondary recovery methods, public planners had a greater chance to make rational decisions about the probable level of future oil activity. But during the first sixty or seventy years of American oil-field development, the only indication of an oil field's potential was the size of wells brought in; the rest was guesswork. When large wells were brought in in the Ranger area in 1918 and 1919, for example, most people assumed that a giant field had been discovered, rather than the shallow pools which soon played out. Civic leaders in Ranger and experts at Humble Oil alike were mistaken about the oil resources of the area.[2] With the difficulty of predicting an oil field's future, a planner had to ponder bleak examples from past petroleum development: production declined, fields seemed exhausted, and bustling settlements turned into quiet hamlets. The initial hesitation of civic leaders in a booming oil town to plunge into expensive public works was understandable. Who would need public projects if the oil ran out? And would the oil really run out? Community leaders were not in a position to answer these questions.

Notwithstanding the peculiar difficulties petroleum development posed for those who tried to provide public services, most oil boom-towns coped successfully with public problems. In only one of the examples which follow (Wink) did unusual local conditions result in irresponsible management of community needs; only Wink had any resemblance to the wide-open oil boomtowns so often described in oil-field folklore. The problems communities took on were similar; styles of coping with them varied.

The early history of McCamey illustrates not only how need for drinkable water brought a government into being, but also how well an oil town could fare if its residents included a large number of civic-minded company employees. Like most other oil boom settlements, McCamey lacked an adequate supply of drinkable water for its population. From the days of the Pennsylvania oil booms onward, the quality of water used by oil-town residents commonly was poor, for the oil and waste accompanying petroleum development polluted the streams and rivers that furnished early boom towns with their water supply. Smart oil field dwellers with money bought their drinking water at Pithole, Beaumont, Red Fork, Ranger, and Burkburnett; the less wise and fortunate drank from local taps and came down with dysentery.[3] But in all these places, there was at least a local water supply. Like the many towns which sprang up with oil development in arid West Texas and New Mexico, McCamey had no streams, rivers, or lakes which could supply water. Oil, not water, dictated the town's location. As in Crane, which developed twenty miles to the north, and Borger, in the Texas Panhandle, in new-born McCamey water wells brought up fluid so heavily laced with mineral salts and, on occasion, oil, that it could not be used for washing, much less drinking. In consequence, the first residents of these southwestern boomtowns had to import their water. McCamey dwellers bought water that came in on railroad tank cars from Alpine, a hundred miles away, and that sold from Model T trucks at one dollar a barrel. The price of water prompted many McCamey residents to improvise elaborate domestic water recycling schemes, which might begin with dishwashing, procede to family bathing, and culminate in laundry. Thrifty hotel guests, given one pitcher of water in their rooms, could follow suit, as one oil field veteran recalls: "We first washed our faces—there were two of you in the room—next you shaved, next you took a spit bath, next you washed your socks, and finally you threw the water out."[4]

The saving grace of this arid situation was the near impossibility of water-borne disease. Waste water, thrown out of the tent or shack door, quickly evaporated into the hot West Texas wind; similarly, garbage and other human waste dried rather than rotted.[5]

Less than three months after the filing of McCamey's town plat, a group of residents, motivated by their need for a more regular supply of water, forwarded a petition for municipal incorporation to the Upton County commissioners. McCamey voters approved incorporation on December 27, 1926, and on February 18, 1927, the new Board of City Aldermen assembled for the first time. The board's first business was water. Councilmen immediately authorized the mayor, Dr. F. E. Gibbons, to begin negotiation with landowners under whose property there might be a supply of usable water. Three days later, councilmen divided up responsibility for finance, civic improvement, sanitation, and fire and police protection, and at their third meeting passed twelve ordinances, including regulations for sanitation and taxation. A mere ten days after its initial sitting, the McCamey Board of Aldermen authorized drilling the first city water well.[6] There could be no doubt that city government was in earnest about meeting community needs. By August, 1927, the city had taken bids on water mains and sewers; contracted for street lights; purchased fire-fighting equipment; built an incinerator; and selected a chief of police, a sanitary inspector, and a waterworks superintendent. McCamey found the answer to its water problem in an underground source seventeen miles south of town, but that did not leave city leaders idle. By the end of 1929, they had addressed themselves to problems of public health by having the city haul away trash and by passing ordinances relating to sanitary food handling.[7] Among Permian Basin towns, McCamey's city government was a model of decisive action.

If McCamey's need for water brought about municipal government, the legal requirement to provide schools led to the establishment of the McCamey Independent School District. Like most West Texas counties where ranching, rather than farming, prevailed, the only school in sparsely populated Upton County was located in Rankin, the county seat. In 1925, six teachers taught 150 students in twelve grades in the Rankin school. But the following year, the number of school-age children who lived in McCamey surpassed Upton County's entire pre-oil population.[8] McCamey was too far from Rankin, or any other town with schools, for its children to go to school elsewhere, so Rankin's school superintendent hired eighteen teachers for McCamey's 550 students and arranged for the construction of a four-room tin building. His efforts fell far short of local need. Accordingly, in December, 1927, McCamey succeeded in establishing its own school district. In the following year, work on permanent brick school buildings got underway; in the interim, classes met in space borrowed as it could be had, primarily from fledgling churches. Classes were crowded; one schoolteacher recalls that her first-grade classes enrolled 40 to 45 students; the desks were squeezed in so closely that "you'd walk down between them . . . [and] your hips would hit on each side."[9]

The new McCamey school board faced many more problems than makeshift and overcrowded facilities. It had to find money to meet operating expenses and to pay bills due, long before it could approve a budget or levy taxes. The board turned to the State National Bank of Alpine, from which it received a series of short-term loans for the next year; in McCamey, as in other oil boomtowns, future taxes guaranteed such loans, ordinarily an uncomplicated matter. But the new school board soon faced an extraordinary situation: school officials in Rankin, suddenly aware that the bonanza oil discoveries were located in the new school district, promptly brought suit to reclaim part of the oil-rich land taken from their tax rolls. Once the suit was filed, a number of owners of oil properties in the area under dispute declined to pay their school taxes until the two districts settled their differences.[10] Worse yet, legal difficulties with Rankin made it difficult to sell bonds for school building. One bond purchaser told the board that it would advance the school district $100,000 of a projected $150,000 bond issue, pending the outcome of the suit. Were Rankin to win, McCamey would have to return the advance and look elsewhere for a buyer.[11]

While the challenge to its jurisdiction raised unusual financial problems, the McCamey school board found that the process of collecting taxes was not as simple in a boomtown as elsewhere. Like public officials in many another oil town, the McCamey school trustees had to levy taxes on a type of property whose value was difficult to estimate. No doubt a parcel of land with producing oil wells was valuable, but how valuable it was depended upon the value of the oil that could be produced from it. Arriving at a valuation of oil property was no simple matter, and the average rural tax assessor was not equipped to do so. After a year McCamey school trustees decided to employ a professional valuations firm, Thomas Y. Pickett Company, to handle oil property. By the time they took this step, the school tax rolls were in an awesome muddle, and not only as a result of the inexpertise of the school tax assessor. Even as early as 1928, when the McCamey school board began to handle business, the peak of McCamey's oil boom was past. The town still bustled with regional activity, but the boomers were moving on: to Wink, Crane, and Ector counties, where activity was high-pitched. In July, 1929, several months after the school district's first tax assessor-collector resigned, the new tax assessor told the board that, of properties on the tax roll, 194 lots were unrendered, the owners of 240 lots were unknown, and 917 tax items were delinquent; a total of 63,720 acres were listed under unknown ownership and unrendered.[12] As was common in oil boomtowns, the winding down of drilling activity left tax rolls in chaos. There was no way to collect taxes on property whose probable owners left town without a forwarding address.

Knotty financial problems notwithstanding, McCamey's school officials resolutely managed business at hand. By 1930, when it settled boundary differences with Rankin, the school district had completed permanent high school and elementary school buildings. Along the

way there were incidental problems: the contractor for the high school
went broke, leaving the school board to manage its completion, and the
enlargement of Humble Oil's McCamey refinery in 1929 crowded
grade schools beyond capacity. But the school district coped well, in
part because it benefited from civic interest among the oil company
management personnel residing in large numbers in McCamey. Such
personnel served on the school board, and they brought their companies to make tangible contributions to school programs: pipe for
fencing, trucks to move furniture into new buildings, governors for
school busses, and materials for home economics programs.[13] Though
oil company employees were liable to sudden transfer from town, they
were an educated and capable asset to government bodies.

   While McCamey showed how well an oil boomtown could tackle
problems, booming Wink showed what could go wrong with a new
community's government. Wink had the dubious distinction of being
"wide open." Apart from the context of law enforcement, that meant
that city officials pursued their own gain and neglected community
needs. School officials were not in the corrupt league of their city
colleagues in government, but they were inexperienced in administration and unready for pressing problems. During its first and greatest
growth, Wink lacked a corps of capable, disinterested civic leaders who
were able to control public business. The result was both colorful and
costly for the community.

   Like McCamey, Wink depended upon oil for its existence. Before
the discovery of the Hendrick field, there had been no settlement on
Wink's remote sand-dune site. To this isolated locality oil brought both
oil-field workers and numbers of persons who sought their money;
gamblers, bootleggers, and prostitutes arranged the new town's government to suit their enterprises. On June 4, 1928, Wink's city government, consisting of a mayor, J. R. Ostrom, and two commissioners,
began doing business. The new city officials' first concern was for jobs;
they appointed a city secretary, city marshall, special police, and a city
health inspector. It would appear that the last appointment was but a
token gesture toward public health, since the city commissioners
passed no ordinances relating to health until 1929. On October 16,
1928, the district judge for Winkler County declared Wink's incorporation election void, so it was necessary to begin municipal government
afresh. Ostrom was once again elected mayor, and Roy Leake and J. J.
Gleese filled the commissioners' places.[14]

   Once city government was underway, much of Wink's municipal

budget was allotted to what passed for law enforcement. The city payroll included a chief of police, two policemen, a jailer, a jailer-fireman, and one person whose job was "police services." The distinctive character of the Wink police force was indicated by one police chief whose past career included bank robbery and escape from prison. In December, 1928, the city built its first municipal building, a jail. Paying for that improvement was of no greater concern to Wink city officials than handling city finance in general. The city did not bother to appoint a tax assessor until March, 1929, and it issued 6 percent scrip to pay bills until the following year.[15] This casual approach to administration carried over to legislation, for Wink's new government did not rush to pass laws. In January, 1929, for example, with a rare burst of energy, the city commissioners passed four ordinances, regulating peddling and sales, automobiles and trucks, payment of taxes, and interference with fire fighting. In February they regulated transport of explosive materials, in March they regulated pipelines within city limits, and in May they set up fire zones. But, while city officials continued to appoint a sanitary inspector, they did not get around to legislation on sanitation until June, 1929, when they passed Ordinance 14, for the "Disposal of Garbage, Trash, and other Filth"; a year earlier, Roy Leake had helped award himself the city contract to haul garbage. The city gave Leake a twenty-five-year water franchise in March, 1929, its first action on water supply.[16] Wink residents, however, did not depend on the city for their water, as they could obtain drinkable water from wells sixty to ninety feet deep. Unlike McCamey, what Wink did about water aroused little public concern.

To judge from their ordinances, then, Wink city officials were interested in legislation only when it had potential for jobs and profit. On these terms, protecting public health had low priority. Wink city officials even managed to exploit a health crisis when they established quarantine tents for smallpox victims in 1928 and gave the tent concession to one of the mayor's friends.[17] But they did little to promote sanitation, made no attempt to ensure the purity of water supply, left food handling unregulated, and passed no building or zoning codes. Ostrom and his friends acted for themselves rather than for the public.

The effect of Wink's *laissez-passer* in city government was reflected in its mortality rates during its first boom.[18] In 1929, the town's death rate from typhoid fever was nearly ten times that of the nation; deaths from gastritis, enterocolitis, and infectious dysentery occurred at more than four times the national rate. Gastrointestinal infections were clearly a threat to public health in booming Wink, though, in this respect, Wink was not unusual. In both Odessa and Midland, for example, boom growth from the thirties onward shows up in death records as sudden surges of mortality from gastrointestinal infection.[19] Yet Wink, whose city officials did nothing to regulate food handling, ensure pure water, or control insects, had health problems of apparently greater magnitude than other comparable oil boomtowns. Wink death rates from contagious diseases were usually higher, often by several times, than those of McCamey. In 1929, Wink residents died of gastrointestinal infections at a rate twice that of McCamey inhabitants. While there were no deaths from typhoid in McCamey in the three years following 1927, Wink continued to have a high mortality rate from the disease through 1930, long after the machinery of city government was in place. Even the crude death rates of Winkler and Upton counties present a contrast. In 1929, that of Winkler County was 15.1, as compared with Upton County's 8.3 and the national rate of 11.9; in 1927, the year of McCamey's maximal initial growth, Upton County's death rate had been only 10.3. That Wink was more notable for violent mishaps than McCamey does not explain its higher death rates; the percentage of deaths by violence or accident was very slightly higher in Upton County in 1927 than in Winkler county in 1929.[20] Bacteria, not bullets, were the real peril of Wink life.

While Wink's corrupt and irresponsible city government made more public problems than it resolved, Wink's school administration at least succeeded in building and running schools. School officials tried to do their jobs. Their inexperience and the magnitude of the problems they faced meant that the school system's first years were not easy ones. As in McCamey, there was no school system within negotiable distance capable of taking in the numbers of children who came to Wink between 1927 and 1928. A handful of children went to school in tiny Kermit, but that was nearly ten miles away, across the dunes; when the wind blew hard, the track across the shifting sand was impassable. During the first part of 1928, the Wink Chamber of Commerce made a strenuous effort to run half-day school sessions in a sheet-iron building. Wink residents meanwhile petitioned the Winkler County commissioners for a local school district, and in May, 1928, after twenty-three voters turned out to elect a school board, the Wink Independent School District began business.[21]

The first task the new school board took up was the construction of permanent school buildings; the board hired an architect at its first sitting, and two days later it called for a $225,000 bond issue to meet construction costs. All forty-six persons who bothered to vote on June 9 approved the project. But brick buildings take time to construct, and on August 9, school officials suddenly realized that facilities would be necessary for the coming school year. The board hurriedly purchased lots and called for bids on four three-room school buildings, twenty-four by ninety feet in size. Four local lumber companies offered bids. Rather than accept the low bid, school officials decided with egalitarian unorthodoxy to let each company build one building. The temporary buildings had water, gas heat, toilets, and ventilation; the board later decided to add the relative frills of paint and weatherboarding to them.[22]

Having done this much toward accommodations, the board left provision for instruction to the superintendent, A. E. Lang, whom it hired in June. Lang spent the summer recruiting teachers from teachers' bureaus in Denton and Canyon, and he ordered books and supplies from Dallas. Neither he nor anyone else had any idea precisely how many school-age children there were in or around Wink, but Lang estimated that the school system would handle roughly 400 pupils. On the first day of school everyone's calculations were confounded: 724 pupils enrolled. Within the first week, school enrollment swamped existing facilities, and three more school rooms had to be built over the weekend. It was necessary to build additional temporary classrooms during the remainder of the school year; by May, 1929, over 1,300 students attended school in twenty-seven classrooms, more than three times the number of pupils the school board originally expected.[23]

That Wink school officials should have been mistaken in their estimates of community growth is understandable. Even veterans in school administration in other booming oil towns made similar errors. Experience, however, could have headed off other mistakes and would certainly have quickened the pace of school business. On April 6, 1929, the board attempted to hold a trustees' election. Unable to assemble a quorum of members for the rest of April, board members did not try to canvass election returns until May 2, at which time they had to admit that they had conducted the election improperly and it was void: "The condition of the returns are such as to show that it is impossible to determine what would have been the result of the election if it had been properly held; . . . there are no certified poll lists; the returns show no oath taken by the election officers; . . . all affidavits filed are lacking in essential requirements to be of a valid basis for voting." The school trustees decided, somewhat belatedly, that they needed to retain an attorney for the school district.[24] When they tried to take bids on a permanent school building, school officials showed similar want of expertise; having accepted a bid from a Lubbock contractor in August, 1928, they found they had used incorrect procedures and had to call for bids a second time in February, 1929.[25] School-board members might have avoided much unnecessary difficulty, embarrassment, and delay if they had been familiar with the rules of public business.

Problems with inexperienced public officials were, in part, the result of the community's newness in places like Wink. New oil boomtowns did not have a ready supply of long-time residents willing and able to fill public places. The mobility of boomtown population meant that even if civic-minded officeholders could be recruited, they might move on after only a few month's service. During its first two years of business, thirteen persons served on the seven-member Wink school board. None of the original board members of May, 1928, remained on the board by May, 1930, and only two served out their terms. To fill the vacant places of those who moved on, school boards in both Wink and McCamey commonly appointed persons whose bids for election to school trusteeships had been unsuccessful; perhaps school officials reasoned that these persons were at least interested in the job. But such appointments did not always have happy results. One appointed member of the Wink school board, for example, missed an entire year of board meetings, after which she resigned.[26] Constant turnover of board membership was a handicap to smooth transaction of public business.

In September, 1929, Wink school officials proudly opened the handsome brick building which they began planning at their first meeting. As oil had made the building necessary, so oil would pay for it: the school district's tax rolls listed a total of $23,690,775 in valuations. The future seemed so bright that when the new Baptist church offered to buy one of the temporary wooden buildings, the board decided against sale, keeping it "for probable future use."[27] As in many other oil towns, however, the passage of some months brought radical changes to the community. Hit successively by national depression, collapse in oil prices, and shift of oil activity to East Texas, Wink rapidly lost population. Property valuations on the school tax rolls plummeted from $16,165,124 in 1930 to $8,915,179 in 1931 and $5,297,754 in 1932. School officials retrenched. They sold temporary buildings, reduced teachers' salaries, cut back on staff, and ended summer programs. The end of the boom, however, was not the end of the Wink school system. After two years of hard times, between six hundred and seven hundred students continued to go to school in Wink, and the tax base of more than $5 million generated enough income to pay for their education. Despite Winkler County cowboys' joking predictions, the new Wink school building was never used to store hay.[28] Even some five decades later, when Wink's total population amounted to less than school enrollment in 1928, consolidation and bussing from remoter areas kept Wink's well-funded schools in use.

The early histories of McCamey and Wink not only identify problems faced by towns brought into being by oil, but they also illustrate how greatly the styles of dealing with public problems could differ, even between two oil towns of similar age, situation, and size. Composition of population may have made the telling difference between governments in the two towns. By 1926, seven major oil companies had leased most of the land around McCamey; a large number of persons who came to McCamey were major company employees and management personnel. Most important among the majors in McCamey was Humble, for it not only built large camps but transferred its regional headquarters from San Angelo to McCamey and built a refinery there. By 1926, many major oil companies, Humble among them, had adopted personnel policies which emphasized hiring steady, reliable workers—solid citizens who would stay with the company for long periods. These were the sort of oil workers present in McCamey. Humble, moreover, encouraged community activity and service. Any community would have benefited from large numbers of such newcomers.[29]

In the Winkler County oil fields, by contrast, independent and smaller operators were especially active, and the presence of the major companies was not as overwhelming as in Upton County. Major companies did extensive work in developing Winkler County, but few of their higher-echelon management personnel came to live in Wink. Isolated in the sand hills and far from major transport routes, Wink was not suited to be a management center. The tough reputation the town acquired early in its career made it even less attractive as a base of business operations. Those civic-minded persons who, nonetheless, did reside in Wink received no encouragement to look into public business from those who controlled town government. As low turnouts in school elections would indicate, many Wink residents may have thought it best to show no interest in public affairs. Public life in Wink was thus emphatically different from public life in McCamey.

Most other oil towns were neither as decisive as McCamey nor as negligent as Wink in handling the problems of explosive growth. Odessa, Midland, and Snyder predated oil development, and when rapid growth took place, they had the advantage of some existing governmental machinery to deal with new needs. Midland and Snyder were incorporated before the coming of oil, and Odessa was incorporated in 1927, as it began to grow from oil activity to the south of Ector County. All three communities had local schools, and all three were county seats. Fast-paced growth meant that existing machinery of government needed some additions, improvements, and modifications; by the mid-fifties, for example, all three towns had adopted the city manager form of government. In most general terms, government bodies in the three towns faced similar problems in public policy. They had to identify priorities for action in the midst of hectic, unfamiliar development; they had to try to keep up with growth while managing their finances responsibly; and they had to make the most of present prosperity in planing for the future. None of these towns ever experienced the anarchy of oil boomtowns as presented in folklore. Oil booms brought about an increase, rather than a decrease, in government, and they did so of necessity.

With rapid growth underway, which problems city governments tackled first depended on local perception of conditions. As construction suddenly went forward at a headlong pace in what had been a sleepy small village, the new Odessa city council passed its first ordinance in 1927; it defined the city fire district and established building standards to which all construction had to conform. By way of contrast to the notion that boomtown governments made no attempt to control development, it is worth noting that the measure was a tightly drawn piece of legislation, requiring building within the fire district to be of brick, stone, portland cement, or "other incombustible materials approved by the City Council." The city, moreover, was strict in its enforcement of the ordinance, refusing to grant building permits for wood frame, composition board, and Sheetrock buildings.[30] There was nothing "wide open" about this part of Odessa government, and there were sound economic reasons for regulation. Conservative investors were shy of placing their money in oil-town growth, not only because of the historical rise and decline of towns like Batson, Ranger, and Desdemona, but also because the typical oil boomtown, with its shacks and wooden buildings, was notoriously vulnerable to fire. If property were to be insured and mortages granted, municipal governments had to act on problems of fire protection and building practices. In 1928, Midland responded similarly to growth from regional oil development by passing its first comprehensive building code, which included fire regulations.[31]

While Odessa's first ordinance regulated construction within the city fire district, town development outran district limits during the boom years of the late thirties. That development made it necessary to reexamine building codes and devise zoning plans; in 1937 the Odessa City Council decided to revise regulations with a view to helping entrepreneurs get "better and larger building loans."[32] What the city needed was a model on which to base its building and zoning measures. For cities like Midland, whose development resulted in an identifiable "downtown," the Southern Building Code provided a usable model for growth. But Odessa's rapidly growing business community, dominated by oil-field supply and service, did not form a tight downtown concentration. The Ector County commissioners energetically promoted the city's growth as a regional oil supply center by constructing main highway arteries to the oil fields, and Odessa sprawled along the roadways as it grew. Businesses of all sorts settled along the oil field roads: lumberyards, oil-field equipment dealers, tank builders, oil-well service contractors, garages, cafés, motels, retail outlets, and residences lined main roads at random outside the city fire district. A rigid zoning ordinance would have been unrealistic and unworkable. Odessans, therefore, found what was needed in another oil town, Pampa, whose zoning code the city council decided was "a good and appropriate ordinance." With only four zoning categories, the Pampa code was more permissive than most: it allowed a mixture of one and two-family dwellings and of retailing and light manufacturing, both of which were common in Odessa.[33] When it adopted the Pampa Code, Odessa legitimized a pattern of development already well established.

The same growth that prompted municipal incorporation and a city building code brought about Odessa's water and sewer service, both of which were unnecessary before growth from oil. In 1927 the city won voter approval for $157,000 in water and sewer bonds, and it began purchasing lots on which it drilled city water wells. By 1949 Odessa's water supply came from sixty-four area water wells and several small city water fields. But by this time it was also obvious that these purely local efforts would not meet the needs of either boom growth or long-range development. Summertime water shortages occurred regularly in the late forties, and city water wells declined in rate of gallonage by 10 to 12 percent a year: with good reason, since water consumption more than trebled between 1938 and 1948. During the decade which followed, water consumption showed a sevenfold increase. Rather than let town prospects dry up with waning water supply, the Odessa city council successfully promoted joining the Colorado River Municipal Water District Project in 1950; they told the public: "The industrialization of Odessa is solely dependent on an adequate, assured water supply."[34] The city received its first water from the regional association in 1952.

Even when public officials reacted promptly, they could not install water mains and sewers quickly enough. In Odessa, as in Midland and Snyder, early fifties boom-growth outran city services. In one year, between 1951 and 1952, the city water system added eleven hundred new purchasers; many homes nonetheless remained without domestic water.[35] Numerous houses and trailers were without adequate sewage disposal as well. Not coincidentally, a series of epidemics struck the community: measles in 1949, poliomyelitis in 1950 and 1951, gastroenteritis in 1951 and 1952, and influenza in 1953. The city responded as best it could with sanitary measures. It carried out insecticide spraying programs, made trash collection mandatory, tightened regulations applying to sewer hookups, and promoted community cleanup campaigns. As well intentioned as such stopgaps were, they did not put an end to epidemic infection.[36]

In handling formidable problems in public health, Odessa's city government was especially lucky to have the cooperation of Ector County officials. Unlike McCamey, Wink, and Midland, Odessa was not gerrymandered into one county commissioner's precinct; Ector County commissioners shared its representation. County government was attentive to urban problems and promoted urban growth. During the epidemics of the early fifties, county commissioners cooperated with city sanitary efforts by hiring sanitarians, carrying out county spraying programs against flies and mosquitoes, and creating a county-wide sanitary district. These efforts did not take the place of functioning sewers, but they may well have lessened the toll taken by infectious disease. Nor was this the only instance of city-county cooperation. During the boom years of the late thirties, county officials worked with city and school officials to fight an epidemic of venereal disease; cooperation on that problem eventually brought about the establishment of a county health unit.[37]

Just as the drawing of county precinct lines seems to have made Ector County commissioners singularly responsive to city needs, the consolidation of Ector County schools into a district coterminous with the county appears to have promoted cooperation between county and school officials. Ector County school trustees looked for help from the county in 1926 when their school, a small wooden building without indoor plumbing or running water, was crowded beyond management; the county let the school district borrow space in the courthouse. During the next two years, while a permanent, large school building was under construction, school enrollment tripled.[38] In the decades that followed, as oil fields came in throughout Ector County, the school district had to scramble to keep up with growth, not only in the city of Odessa, but also in the outlying communities of Penwell, Goldsmith, and Notrees. The school district had to decide both when and where to build its schools.

Like school trustees in most places, Ector County school-board members tried to locate schools on the common sense plan of serving populous neighborhoods. In boom times, however, it was not easy to predict where neighborhoods would grow most and where enough permanent residents would settle so that school buildings would be needed after boom days. Odessa's constant growth after 1935 ensured that schools built within city limits would always serve an ample number of students. During the late forties and early fifties, Odessa schools were usually overcrowded. In 1948, for example, the district was especially hard-pressed for elementary and junior high classrooms; it borrowed a store building and rooms in churches for interim use, but it was still necessary to resort to half-day schedules in some grades.[39] Within city limits, wherever the school district could build schools in the early fifties, they quickly filled to capacity.

Odessa, however, was not the only place within the school district to grow. In 1929 the bustling little communities of Penwell and Badger sprang up in the new oilfields of western Ector County; in 1935 a small town began to grow at Goldsmith in oil fields north of Odessa, and in the late forties the aptly named settlement of Notrees appeared in the northwest corner of the county. The school district tried to serve the Penwell area by bussing students to Odessa, but when Penwell and Badger residents requested local schools in 1930, the district built a two-room schoolhouse at Penwell. Students at the little Penwell school were almost without exception members of oil field families, and when oil activity fell off, the school district found itself with a near-empty building. In 1937 school trustees took some of the pressure off Odessa classes by holding first and second grades at Penwell, but by 1940 it was clear that there was no longer need for a school out in that oil field.[40]

Though Penwell demonstrated the short-run use of school building out in the oil field, the Ector County school system also built schools in the oil fields at Goldsmith and Notrees. In each instance, relief of extreme crowding in Odessa classrooms may have been as important in the decision to provide local schools as educating students close to home. At the time that schools seemed to be needed in these settlements, however, both places seemed to have a promising future. When school officials decided to put a school in Goldsmith in 1937, the little town had a full complement of stores, cafés, filling stations, and oil-field lodgings. In later years, discovery of deeper pay zones and the establishment of gas plants and large company camps spurred Goldsmith's growth. The Ector County school district enlarged the Goldsmith school and built a school at Notrees in 1948, putting up housing for teachers and administrators in both locations. But, as sensible as this seemed at the time, by the end of the next decade the school at Notrees had to be closed, and that at Goldsmith was underenrolled.[41] Not only had oil activity dropped off in the area, but companies began to shift workers from houses on leases and in camps into town, a trend the school district could not have foreseen. In the long run, then, bringing schools right into the oil fields was not a success.

Since one school system served the entire county, the great oil fields discovered in Ector County between the thirties and the fifties all enriched school district tax rolls. Oil crowded schools, but it also paid school bills. That was fortunate. The school district had to build eight schools during the forties and ten schools in the five years between 1950 and 1955. Hurried construction, characteristic of boom growth, brought about a spectacular increase in the school district's bonded debt. During the fifties alone, the Ector County Independent School District sold $17,527,000 in bonds, nearly two and one-half times the total bonded debt of the thirties and forties. Since Ector County, like other school districts, was at the mercy of prevailing rates in the bond market when it had to build schools, the school district refinanced its debt a number of times, in 1935, 1939, 1942, and 1955, whittling its interest rates down from a high of 4.25 percent to 1.75 to 2.25 percent.

Debt service ate up a high of 32 percent of the district's total tax revenue in 1945, but that burden dropped to an average of 21 to 24 percent in the fifties.[42] As the school district's debt demonstrates, boom growth meant heavy obligations.

For Odessa's schools and city government alike, the expense of meeting public needs in the late forties and early fifties was not as great a difficulty as simply trying to keep up with continual development. That Odessa had regional economic importance, ensured that oil development anywhere in the Permian Basin would make the town grow. Whether oil came in Scurry, Andrews, Yoakum, or Lea counties, pipe, supplies, and services were as likely to come from Odessa as were the oil-field workers who brought in the oil. In the fifteen years following World War II, Odessa had little respite from pressure on public services, no slack time in which schools could end classroom crowding or in which the city could catch up with water and sewer-line construction. To some extent, Midland's position as a regional management center placed that town in a similar situation. The level of oil activity throughout the Permian Basin during the late forties and fifties brought great numbers of company personnel to Midland. At the same time, development of the Spraberry trend fields in the county gave Midland its own local oil boom. As in Odessa, despite the efforts of city and school officials, public services always lagged far behind public needs.

Compared to Odessa, Midland was disadvantaged in two respects. Unlike Odessa, the various bodies of local government in Midland did not ordinarily cooperate in solving problems of growth. As one urban observer lamented in 1967, "Each has—to a distressing extent—gone its own way in the development of its own facilities and in solving its own problems."[43] With the representation of all Midland placed in one county precinct, three of the four county commissioners maintained a determined disregard for city problems; the city and the school district wrestled with their problems alone. Moreover, while Midland grew from regional development, Midland County's oil development did not create a taxable El Dorado for the city or school district. City and school district boundaries did not encompass Midland County's oil fields, and those fields were not as spectacularly rich as finds in Ector County. Much of the cost of rapid growth, thus, fell on residential and commercial property rather than upon a bonanza on the oil tax-rolls.

By the Spraberry boom of the early fifties, Midland had long had municipal police and fire protection, a municipal water and sewage system, and building and zoning codes. Since the new oil fields were some miles from town, many oil-field workers did not live within city limits, where reasonably strict ordinances covered locating trailers and trailer courts, but out in the oil fields and along oil-field highways. The city nonetheless faced sharp strain upon water and sewer services, a strain aggravated by past sins of omission. Hard-pressed to keep up with growth during World War II, Midland had postponed some long-needed improvements in the forties, most notably the extension of water and sewer lines through the city's black and Mexican-American neighborhoods. The practice of waiting for residents to pay for installations before constructing lines further delayed delivery of public water and sewer systems to poorer residents.[44] Nor had the city resolved questions about future water supply. Though water shortages in the late forties brought the city to investigate the option of joining other Permian Basin communities in a regional water authority, in 1949 a city council whose majority was new to office decided not to participate in the Colorado River Municipal Water District Project. Rather than assign Midland's water reserves to the District and ante up a $5 million payment to join, the city decided to seek self-sufficiency in water supply. It negotiated water rights and plunged into water field development in neighboring Andrews and Martin counties. But the result of its independent enterprise was disappointing: by December, 1951, only two of sixty-five test holes produced prospective water wells.[45] At that time, boom growth was underway.

As grave as Midland's water problems were, sewage disposal caused a real crisis in public services in the summer of 1952. It was not without warning: neighboring Odessa had had problems with water and sewage, and with epidemics as well. After months of overload, the Midland sewer system finally gave way in July, 1952. Sewer lines in south Midland overflowed from drainage of developments farther north, and raw sewage bubbled up from manholes which, in some instances, had to be surrounded with earthen dikes. A new sewage treatment plant was under construction but not near completion; the existing plant reeked from burdens beyond its capacity, and swarms of flies and mosquitoes thrived in untreated effluent. Fearing a polio epidemic, the city undertook an insecticide spraying campaign and urged citizens to put trash in covered cans. Whether these efforts had much result is uncertain, for an epidemic of diarrhea hit the community. In four weeks, between the end of July and mid-August, health authorities recorded 833 cases of that infection. City construction crews worked seven-day weeks to relieve sewer problems, and city spraying crews fogged streets and alleys. The city also launched a drive to promote sewer hookups in poorer neighborhoods and decided to waive sewer installation charges for indigent persons. Only completion of new sewer lines and the new sewage treatment plant ended the crisis. Easing of pressure on the city disposal system, however, was only temporary; the following year, though there was no epidemic, the city sewer system was again overloaded, this time by more than 25 percent of capacity.[46] For the rest of the decade, the city sewer system remained far behind the pace of demand.

While the crisis in public services that Midland experienced in 1952 was striking, it was not peculiar as a phenomenon in a booming community. Oil booms ordinarily place an immediate heavy demand on water supply and waste disposal systems. Midland's city officials struggled to cope, meeting at weekly, and sometimes daily, intervals to handle public business. The city, however, confronted unusual demands at an inopportune time, just after it had had to pay for wartime growth, and it faced expenses which could neither be passed on nor postponed. Between 1950 and 1957 the city took on $7.2 million in bonded debt for water and sewer improvements; when it took on construction, it was pinched for cash. As the Midland City Manager complained in 1952, when Midland Memorial Hospital asked for free water, with water and sewer improvements, "Expense is always ahead of revenue."[47] Nor was cash the only thing in short supply. That the city was in the midst of a drilling boom had a peculiar impact upon efforts to put in water and sewer lines, because drilling created a tremendous demand for all varieties of metal pipe. Given strong demand from the oil-field contractors, the pipe needed for public services was not always available. In 1953, construction on water and sewer mains stopped when Midland ran out of pipe and could not restock its supply.[48] When pipe could be found during an oil boom, its price was likely to be high.

While the city toiled in the wake of growth and public need, on the first floor of the courthouse the Midland County Commissioners maintained an Olympian aloofness from the development taking place around them. A decade before oil development, the county had found money to put up mailbox stands for county residents on rural mail routes, but throughout the oil-rich fifties, Midland's county commissioners did their best to shed fiscal responsibilities onto the overburdened city. In 1952 the county commissioners contributed ample funds to build a road to the regional Boy Scout camp. The same year, despite the city's plea that growth made immediate expansion of health services imperative, they refused to increase their contribution to the city-county health unit. Similarly, six years later the county commissioners told the city that they wished to end joint projects like the health unit, the child welfare program, and maintenance of Ulmer Park; they offered to trade off, taking on the cost of the relatively inexpensive child welfare program, for example, if the city would take on rural fire protection. With narrowly drawn rural interests at heart, county officials shrugged off city problems as none of their affair.[49]

In planning, as in other matters, Midland city leaders were left to their own devices. Turning to professional advice, in 1950 the city hired the Dallas municipal planning firm of Koch and Fowler to develop a comprehensive plan to serve Midland for the following ten or fifteen years. The consultant's recommendations ranged from lengthy schemes for roads and parking to such matters as "civic attractiveness." As well conceived as the plan was, boom growth soon made it obsolete. Eight years later the city rehired the firm to draw up a new city plan; the firm's representative commented that city growth had so outmoded the 1950 plan that "it was almost like not having one."[50] When city officials tried to plan and control growth, they ran afoul of various real estate developers and speculators. Because they could decide which land to annex and where to extend city services, city officials had potential control over development: they could, in effect, make some parcels of land more desirable to build on than others. It was in the city's interest to see building take place within city limits, within the framework of water and sewer lines already complete or underway. But the greatest possibility for profit to developers lay in cheaper land outside city limits; ideally, the developer would persuade the city to annex his low-priced land and bring city services to it; he would thus enjoy the resulting rise in its value. Development did not take place in a tidy fashion, according to city plans and systems, but leapfrogged outside city limits, pushing up the cost of public services once annexation took place. In 1960 the city finally tried to get developers to take on the cost of drainage, one of the most expensive burdens of annexation, but the developers refused; four years before, they had similarly headed off a city scheme to assess developers for municipal improvements in advance of development.[51]

That Midland's rapid growth proceeded on an uneven geographical pattern created problems for the school system as well as the city. The Spraberry discovery and the postwar baby boom made school enrollment shoot upward, from 3,686 pupils in January, 1949, to 9,162 by fall, 1955, and 14,647 by fall, 1959. To accommodate a fourfold increase in the scholastic population in a decade, the school district built twelve additional elementary schools, three more junior high schools, a modern junior-senior high school for the black community, and fourteen additions to existing buildings.[52] Most construction took place on sites which were windswept fields in 1949. While growth was at first most rapid in the northeast part of town, it shifted to the west and southwest in the course of the fifties; minority neighborhoods in south and east Midland grew rapidly as well. School officials did what they could to meet the needs of developing neighborhoods. They acquired old barracks buildings from Midland's air field and shifted them around town, musical chairs fashion, according to the most pressing need; they rented space in neighborhood churches. Even with these expedients, however, classes were crowded: by February, 1956, some classes had more than forty pupils in a room.[53] In 1958, having run out of old barracks buildings, the school trustees decided to put temporary frame buildings near the most crowded schools. At that point, they crossed purposes with the City Planning and Zoning Commission, which required them to make their temporary buildings of steel.[54] Permanent construction forced the school district to try to second-guess developers, and in the mid-fifties they were continually short of space in western Midland. By September, 1957, the district's superintendent resorted to canvassing developers for construction data in areas near existing schools, in an effort to predict locations of greatest growth. The school district also hired professional consultants from Austin in 1956 to project expansion over the next five years. The experts predicted a doubling of school enrollment, from roughly 10,000 to approximately 21,700. At that rate, the school district would have had to build at least four new schools a year![55]

Fortunately for the Midland school system, the experts were wrong: they overestimated actual growth by more than half.[56] The apparent reason for their error was the assumption that school enrollment would grow at a constant rate, across the board. In booming oil towns, however, growth was rarely that easy to predict. Indeed, as the experience of Permian Basin oil towns often showed, peak school enrollment usually took place after the fast initial period of overall population growth. Historically, mobile workers whose jobs were in some phase of work related to production were the most likely to have sizable families, and they came to town once fields were established. In a management town like Midland, central office operations grew once regional fields were proven. But, once such personnel were in town, barring the discovery of new fields, immigration subsided. When low oil prices dampened oil activity, as they did in the early sixties, the cities experienced a net loss of population. As Midland illustrates, when planners in oil communities overlooked the peculiarities of growth based on oil, projections went awry.

Compared to the experiences of Odessa and Midland, Snyder's boom was tidily compressed in time, between 1949 and 1952. Like other oil boomtowns, Snyder had predictable problems with water supply, sewage, and crowded schools. But because rapid growth was briefer in duration, resolving public problems was neither as stressful nor as expensive as in the larger cities. Snyder was the only sizable settlement in a county of new oil fields, and the outward signs of boom struck anyone who came to town. Throngs of persons and quantities of automobiles jammed the courthouse square, where Snyder's shops and cafés were concentrated. Not surprisingly, the first response to boom growth taken by the Snyder City Council was to congested traffic; much to public disgust, the city installed parking meters downtown in the spring of 1949.[57] City officials were somewhat more hesitant to tackle other, potentially more expensive problems, but once the baking heat of summer arrived, it was plain that the city did not have enough water to go around, and deficient sanitation became more noticeable, to the nose as well as to the eye. The hallmark of Snyder's boom, the trailer house, appeared in backyards throughout the city. Unrestricted by city ordinance, property owners rented space to transient trailer residents, whom they supplied with water by running garden hoses from the nearest taps. Arrangements for waste water and sewage disposal were at best improvised, for many parts of town had neither city water nor sewers; one Snyder resident, Joel Hamlett, who was a mailman during boom days, recalls seeing waste water from trailers allowed to run out on the ground. In June, 1949, Snyder's mayor, Forrest Sears, warned the city council that something would have to be done about "deplorable sanitary conditions."[58]

Thus prodded to action, the Snyder City Council began discussing water and sewer improvements with engineers, and in November it called for a vote on $350,000 in waterworks bonds and $400,000 in sewer bonds. Not until spring, 1950, however, did the council act on the most glaring hazard to sanitation, the ubiquitous trailer; in May it required that trailer parks be licensed and that trailers be connected to a sewer line. To back up the ordinance, the city took on inspection of trailer parks, and owners of parks had to get a permit to operate from the Health Department. Regulating trailers was probably the most effective step the city took to safeguard public health, for water and sewer improvements were, as usual, tied to the slow progress of finance and construction. Snyder's new city water plant was not completed until 1954.[59] By that time, the boom was over.

Like the city, Snyder's school system did not complete the projects growth made necessary until boom days were past. When school enrollment began to grow at the rate of thirty pupils a week, late in 1949, school officials thought of a stopgap; they bought a large old school building in Crane, 130 miles away, and moved it to Snyder. The school district, however, counted on permanent growth, and between 1949 and 1954 it took on an ambitious building program, which included three elementary schools, new junior and senior high schools, a school for the growing black community, and an administration building. So large a five-year building program might have strained the resources of another system, but the consolidation of all schools in Scurry County into the Snyder district in 1947 meant that oil wealth throughout the county paid for expansion.[60] By the time oil activity diminished, the Snyder school system had a thoroughly modern plant.

In Snyder, as in other oil towns, oil companies took more than a passing interest in school budgets and programs. Companies and school districts not uncommonly reached cooperative understandings on business; often, as in McCamey and Wink, company personnel on school boards eased cooperation.[61] In 1953, 68.6 percent of all income the Snyder Independent School District received came from taxes paid by oil companies. Not surprisingly, the school district took to regular consultation with oil company representatives on financial matters. When, in September, 1950, the school district faced a shortage of money to meet immediate needs, Standard Oil of Texas guaranteed a loan of $50,000 against future revenue; in May, 1951, the same company loaned the school district $75,000.[62] School officials met with company representatives in 1950 to confer about a bond issue to fund expansion, and they met again with the oil men in January, 1951, to settle on the amount of valuation on oil property. During boom years, the school district seems to have had little difficulty in reaching understandings with oil interests. In 1953, however, as local oil activity was winding down, oil company representatives made their first determined objection to the size of the proposed budget for the school year to come. To the school district plan for a tax roll of $138.5 million, the oil companies argued for a maximum roll of $130 million. On this occasion the school district dug in its heels to resist stringent budget reductions and was willing to cut its original proposal by only $2.5 million, despite company protests. That falling out was atypical of relations between school officials and their most substantial tax-payers.[63] With respect to school finance, oil interests in Snyder were watchful, but generally cooperative.

As the experience of the various Permian Basin oil communities illustrates, oil booms did not produce anarchy. They did create specific problems in the delivery of public services. In the unforeseen heavy burdens on water and sewage systems, and the crowding of school facilities, oil booms resembled other types of booms; like other booms, they placed short-term strains on local budgets and forced communities to take on long-term obligations. But the pattern of peak pressure on public services, early in development for water and sewers, somewhat later for schools, was a pattern shaped by the way oil-field development took place. The rapid pace of petroleum development made it likely that some public needs would not be satisfied as they occurred. With the opening up of oil fields in the arid Southwest, for example, boomtowns with acute water shortages came into being. Water problems took time to solve, even when, as in McCamey, citizens created government to deal with them. Though petroleum development posed problems, in the long run, oil paid the incidental costs. Once communities overcame the logistical difficulties of calculating the value of oil properties by hiring professional valuating services, oil-based tax revenue was adequate to meet the costs of expanded public services. The same growth that presented problems frequently brought educated and energetic oil company employees to booming towns. When, as in McCamey, these newcomers took part in civic affairs, and even held elective office, they supplied the management experience needed to meet current needs and to chart a course for the future. Though oil development brought pressing community problems, it also contributed both material and human resources for their solution.

Relic of boom days, a three-room shotgun house in Odessa.

4.
Women and the Family

WOMEN AND CHILDREN have always been among the newcomers that booms bring to communities. Like men, women have looked for better paying jobs in boomtowns; with their children, women have also followed husbands in search of well-paid work. Because oil exploration and production have been an emphatically male activity, few descriptions of oil-boom life have given women much attention. When authors have acknowledged their presence, they cast women either as messengers of civilization, with a mission "to stabilize and dignify society" through churches and clubs, or as paradigms of vice: "gamblers, women, liquor peddlers, vultures, harpies, and the riffraff of the country."[1] Sensational journalism, popular literature, and scholarly writing alike identified boomtown women as an element in the vague but alarming notion of "social chaos": the "working women" who came to oil communities were identified as prostitutes or dance hall girls.[2] Consideration of women in oil-boom communities has thus begun and ended with reflections on the virtues of church socials and the horrors of vice.

To pass beyond sensationalism, it is worth asking a few questions which might lead to some concrete knowledge about the part women took in oil booms and development of boom communities. How many women came to boom communities? What brought them? What were their reactions to the milieu in which they found themselves? What problems did they encounter in earning livings, maintaining homes, and raising families? Few women were directly employed in the exploration and production of oil, but many found employment in boom times. Many more settled into new communities and learned to cope with challenging living conditions. Though men outnumbered women in the mobile labor force, just as they outnumbered them in new oil communities, women were more numerous in both areas than might at first be supposed.

Women did not take part in the initial phases of oil exploration, but they arrived in numbers with the growth of oil field communities, as the experience of the Permian Basin communities makes clear. In 1920, for example, Upton County had only 119 female inhabitants, Winkler County only 36. By 1930, after the establishment of McCamey and Wink, Upton County had 2,741 and Winkler County 2,928 female inhabitants. Ector County had a total female population of 331 in 1920. In 1930, with activity still high in the Penwell field, the female population of the county had increased more than fivefold. In the city of Midland, which took its initial steps in evolution to a center for oil management operations in the twenties, the number of women over fifteen doubled in the decade of the twenties. During the first two years of the Scurry County oil boom, the female population of Snyder tripled; nearly three-quarters of the female population were women fourteen years of age or older. Boom activity, then, brought women as well as men to the oil fields.[3]

Considering the above figures entirely by themselves, one must regard the notion that most boomtown women were honky-tonk floozies as merely one more part of folklore. Even the most dissolute of communities could scarcely support a female criminal population of the proportions indicated in these population increases. What, then, brought women to oil boom communities? Though family obligations were of greatest importance in making oil-field women mobile, opportunity for employment in the new communities was also a powerful drawing card. In that context, it must be noted that there were many women in the early twentieth-century mobile labor force. Wives of sharecroppers and casual field laborers accompanied their husbands from tenancy to tenancy, from job to job, sometimes working in the fields and sometimes serving as temporary domestic help to the farmers' wives. Boardinghouse operators, waitresses, and domestic help were also among those who followed job opportunities from area to area. Teachers at the beginning of their careers often moved along until they found a place and a community that pleased them.[4] In the course of the twentieth century, as employment opportunities for women increased, more women entered the mobile labor force. The business and clerical skills a small-town girl could acquire in high school created possibilities for secretarial and retailing employment in other communities. Many of the women who came to booming oil communities, then, came either with jobs or with the expectation of finding them.

For working men and women alike, oil boomtowns were attractive not only for the number of jobs available but also for the higher wages jobs offered. Boardinghouse keepers could expect a ready supply of boarders able to pay premium prices for food of better quality than that offered by cheap cafés; rooming-house operators could cash in on the scarcity of lodgings. Women followed the booms, setting up boarding and rooming houses from place to place. Thus Slim Jones described a boardinghouse keeper at Cross Roads, Arkansas, in 1925: "A lady who has made all the booms, and knows almost every oil-field worker who walks in her door."[5] Waitresses who found work in oil towns found their jobs hectic, but their tips ample. Teachers, too, were attracted by higher salaries offered in new oil towns. One might not make a fortune, but, male or female, one could expect to make a good living in a booming oil town.

Few women who found work in oil boom communities worked directly for the oil industry. Of those who did find direct employment in petroleum, very few found work outside the office. In 1920, for example, there were only thirty-five female wage earners, excluding clerical and technical employees, in the petroleum and natural gas industry in the whole state of Texas. In 1930 there were two female roustabouts working in Texas: that there were as many as two is remarkable, given the general exclusion of women from such jobs! To say that women were a minority of wage earners in the oil industry between 1920 and 1960, then, is rather an understatement.[6] Oil-field work was heavy work. Living arrangements for unmarried employees in new oil fields accommodated men, not women, for work in the field was assumed to be man's work. In the absence of women workers from the oil fields, then, West Texas was no different from other Mid-Continental petroleum regions.

Though oil companies seldom employed women in the field, they did employ them in company offices. The most numerous group among women to be directly employed in oil were the clerical workers: stenographers, typists, file clerks, and others. Their employment shows up in the census data for towns like Midland and Odessa; in Upton and Winkler counties, where there were no management operations, only a handful of women were employed in oil by 1940. Not surprisingly, more women found work in oil in Midland between 1940 and 1960 than in any of the other West Texas communities described in this study, for by 1940 Midland was the leading management center for oil company activity in the Permian Basin. Midland had the offices, and women did the office work. During World War II, wives of military men in training at Sloan Field, Midland's air base, found jobs in oil company offices; in later years, Midland attracted many young women from smaller area towns to work in its clerical labor force.[7] Midland's development as a center of regional management operations, however, also made it the residence of another small group of women who worked in company offices: the geoscientific professionals.

Career openings for women in petroleum-related geosciences only appeared with the increased application of a scientific technology to oil in the twentieth century. In the 1920s, the larger oil companies recognized the importance of subsurface geology in exploration, and they hired women who had geological training to process and analyze samples collected in the field. One geologist who did some subsurface work recalled that this development opened real career opportunities for women because "a lot of men don't like to sit at a desk and do tedious work."[8] The novelty of using science in the oil business sometimes worked in favor of women geologists who were beginning their careers. One company, based in California, found that deeper drilling in the Big Lake area brought them to formations common in Oklahoma but not in California, and went to the University of Oklahoma to try to recruit a geologist for their staff. When they explained what they needed, they found themselves hiring a woman. "Dr. Monnett, who was head of the department there, said, 'Well, before we go any farther, I have one question to ask, . . . do you have any objections to employing a woman?' Well, these two men . . . looked at one another, and one of them said, 'Well, do we?' and the other said, 'No, I guess not.' It just never had occurred to them to hire a woman, so they didn't have any built-in prejudices."[9]

Since it was not necessary in subsurface work to sit on wells or rub shoulders with roughnecks, women in that specialty could make careers in petroleum. In the early days of the development of the Permian Basin, there were a half dozen or more women at this work in San Angelo; one woman worked in subsurface analysis in the Humble field offices in McCamey. But there was a drawback to the cloistered nature of subsurface work: there was just so far a woman could pursue a career in subsurface geology done in the office. Beyond that point, advancement as a geologist required work in the field, and some companies, especially among the majors, were not willing to give women field assignments. Oil companies, moreover, were not enthusiastic about hiring or keeping on women married to men working for other oil companies, for they feared that in such circumstances confidential information would be leaked from employee to employee. For a married woman, finding professional employment was more difficult than for her single female colleague.[10]

For the most part, then, the women employed directly by the oil industry worked in management offices and not in the oil fields. There was, however, one exception to this general rule. When new oil fields opened up in isolated areas like Upton, Crane, and Winkler counties, the oil company camps which were built in these places usually contained company boardinghouses. Women often ran these boardinghouses, hiring other women as waitresses, kitchen workers, and cleaning help. Often the women hired for the boardinghouse work would be wives of company employees. Thus, a professional boardinghouse keeper and the wife of a Humble employee ran the Humble boardinghouse in McCamey; they in turn employed two black women to help in the kitchen and set up tables. The company provided the boardinghouse operator with housing in the house itself.[11]

Because every new oil field contained so many people who needed to buy their meals, boardinghouse operators, café owners, and waitresses found a good income in boomtowns. Not all boardinghouses were oil company-owned; Texas Electric Service Company maintained company boardinghouses which employed women, and independent boardinghouse operators also fed oil company employees on a regular basis. Indeed, one woman in Wink made a good living by running a boardinghouse near a company camp. She was a better cook than the company cook.[12] Oil-field workers were so hungry for good food and a family setting that Alice Keene recalls being pressed into running an impromptu boardinghouse in her tent residence: before she knew it, she was cooking breakfast and dinner for nine boarders on a small oil stove. She did not find this a satisfying arrangement: "It took all my husband's wages and part of [son] Don's wages and what they paid me to keep the table a-going. . . . I had the awfulest time getting rid of them; Fred [her husband] just had to insult them."[13] Demand for food and lodging also shows up in boomtown census data on the employment of women in hotels and restaurants. In Wink, for example, the 1930 census revealed that hotels and restaurants employed 156 women; 13.2 percent of all Wink women worked in this area! Similarly, in 1950 nearly 19 percent of the total female work force in Snyder worked in eating and drinking places.[14] The provision of food, drink, and lodging in oil boomtowns, then, always provided employment for women.

When married oil-field workers succeeded in finding both work and housing, their families usually joined them. As a result, after a few months of boom activity, growing schools needed teachers, and this opened another opportunity for employment to qualified women. School superintendents in boomtowns found that keeping schools staffed was challenging work, as additional teachers often had to be found at short notice to cope with surges in scholastic population. They preferred to hire single women, but single women were not always willing to come to towns like Wink, which had a reputation for being tough.[15] As a result, boom activity gave married women teachers the chance for work, at least until their husbands transferred to new locations. Many married women taught in McCamey, Wink, and Odessa in the late twenties. With the Great Depression, however, employment for married teachers dried up, and teachers in Midland or Odessa who married automatically lost their jobs; not until the pressure of wartime growth renewed demand for teachers did school districts drop restrictions.[16]

For teachers, higher pay was the principal attraction of booming oil towns. In 1929, for example, a grade-school teacher in Midland, where oil had not as yet been discovered, made an average of roughly $90 a month: in Wink, during the same year, a grade-school teacher could expect to receive a minimum of $150 a month.[17] Higher pay, however, did not mean a life of luxury, as teachers who took boom jobs soon discovered. Because of high cost of living and the shortage of available housing, single teachers often shared quarters in rooming houses; finding an inexpensive place to eat was no easy matter, for café food was expensive on a teacher's salary. There were other limitations on a teacher's style of life, for whatever might be asserted about the free-and-easy atmosphere of boomtowns, Permian Basin school officials expected teachers to exercise a tight control over their personal lives and feelings. The airing of personal opinions could have serious consequences. In May, 1930, Mrs. Murtle Dancer was said to have told a café companion that the Wink school board was "a bunch of old maids with pants on"; she was fired without a hearing.[18] Miss Allie V. Scott, who taught in McCamey, recalls tight discipline: "You did as you were told. You never voiced an opinion of any kind when you were in the school. . . you didn't open your mouth."[19] Even personal freedom of movement could be subject to limitation: in 1934, teachers who wanted to spend more than one weekend a month outside Odessa had to receive permission to do so from the superintendent of schools. That boomtown teachers tended to come and go was understandable. As one former Wink student remembers, "The teachers couldn't stand it. They came and went faster than the worst people."[20]

The demand for various types of services in oil boomtowns provided women with a wide range of job opportunities. Even new oil towns soon had some provision for medical and health care services, and women who had trained as nurses thus found employment. Beauty shop operators and hairdressers in the dusty boomtowns had an ample supply of customers with money for regular appointments. Oil money also created jobs for women, especially women from minority groups, in domestic service. Business which grew with oil activity—oil-field supply, building, lumber, transport, for example—employed women as clerical help. In towns where telephone service was available, telephone operators found steady work. Boomtown growth multiplied openings for women as sales clerks in supermarkets and other retail outlets. In short, as population and business activity increased, so did jobs available to women. As Allie V. Scott recalls, "If you wanted a job you could get it."[21]

While many women found jobs, most women who came to oil boomtowns were not themselves looking for work. By World War II, more than 80 percent of all petroleum workers were married and had families; the majority of women who came to new oil towns came because husbands or relatives had found steady employment.[22] A wife's initial reaction to a West Texas boomtown was not likely to be favorable. It took fortitude to accept the first sight of any boomtown, but first encounters with the new oil towns of barren West Texas could try even seasoned veterans of oil-field life. Not a few women, used to lush greenery of regions to the east, burst into tears as their husbands helped them off the train in towns like Midland and Odessa: and those towns were oases of civilization compared to new towns like McCamey and Wink.[23] Upton and Winkler counties were remote and forbidding, so much so that some newcomers vowed to move on when they found themselves in an environment whose harshness and isolation surpassed anything they had known. Alice Keene remembers, "We was going to stay two weeks 'til we made a payday; we was going to get out of this.

Where I lived, you know, we had trees and vegetation and everything. Well, where he [her husband] lived in Henrietta . . . it was nothing compared to this. This was outside of the world."[24] L. V. Gill, an oil-field veteran who made the Wink boom, arrived in Pyote by train one cold winter morning at two A. M. and could see nothing of town except the shack which was the depot: "I looked around and I told that conductor, 'I'm going with you to somewhere. . . . I'm not going to stay here," and he laughed, and I said, 'I'll go with you somewhere if I have to go to California!' "[25]

So common was a newcomer's initial dislike of the remote new oil fields that the *Odessa News-Times* of September 25, 1936, reported a domestic spat at the Sunshine Tourist Court as a story with a moral. After a woman told her male companion, "You can't make me stay here all winter," motel guests saw him knock her out with the car crank, throw her in his car, and drive away at top speed. The paper concluded that "back of it all is a very worthwhile lesson for Odessa wives who are given to weeping about living in 'this terrible country' and wailing for a return to the old homestead for good": persuasion had to be physical and drastic to settle some newcomers into the oil fields.[26]

With the uncomfortable sense of isolation, newcomers to West Texas boomtowns were immediately aware of omnipresent wind and dust. Dust kicked up by heavy oil-field traffic over dirt roads supplemented the sand and dust normally wind-borne in arid country. Dust seeped in everywhere, into tents, shotgun houses, and more substantial houses alike. Tent dwellers wakened to find everything but the spot on which they had slept covered with sand. Town residents who shook their curtains showered themselves with dust. Merle Montgomery, who ill-advisedly made a jellied salad for her first Thanksgiving dinner in McCamey, found it permeated with sand by the time it was solid.[27] Cafés set crockery upside down on their tables; one café used a bicycle pump to blow grit out of its coffee cups. Women used to keeping tidy homes ruined hands and tempers in the futile job of coping with dust: as Alice Keene recalls, "My hands was so sore, not being used to it. . . . Every time it'd sand, I'd think, 'Well, I have to clean it up.' I couldn't stand it you know."[28] It was not unusual for a sandstorm to deposit as much as three or four gallon buckets of sand in a small house. One Crane housewife remembers that she could never get rid of the dust: "You just rearranged it."[29] To be caught out in a sandstorm was not an experience a person would choose to repeat. One woman who was caught in an Odessa sandstorm of the thirties discovered when she got home that the sand had shredded her stockings and cut her legs. It is no exaggeration, then, to say that it took moral grit to adjust to the physical grit always in the West Texas air.

Apart from coming to terms with dust, the greatest adjustment that women who followed husbands to the oil fields had to make was that of turning the housing their husbands had found into decent comfortable homes for their families. Oil boom housing was substandard and in short supply; whether in older communities, new towns, or on leases, space was usually cramped and decor would vary from plain to primitive. Wives lucky enough to find themselves living in a small house or duplex in towns like Midland or Odessa were able to keep house much as they might have in other towns; they could have groceries delivered, send laundry out to commercial launderers, enjoy the use of electricity and gas, and even hire occasional domestic help. Wives whose husbands were among the first to arrive in the oil fields of Upton and Winkler counties, however, carried on under much more challenging conditions; arriving before towns were established, they had to wait for boom growth to bring in shops, services, and utilities.[30]

For women who kept house in tents and shotgun houses in the oil fields, daily life had a liberal lacing of hard work. Women who went through the rigors of tent and oil lease life have vivid recollections of doing laundry. Where domestic help was available, as in the East Texas oil fields, housekeepers could sometimes find black women who went from home to home doing laundry. But in remote West Texas settlements there was no such help. Housewives used gasoline or kerosene to remove the sticky black accumulation of oil on work clothes; then they washed the clothes on a rub board and soaked them in boiling water in a tub or a sawed-off oil drum. If a housewife had too free a hand with gasoline or kerosene, she might see her boiling wash-water burst into flame. Some men helped their wives by sponging work clothes down with gasoline; others used steam boilers at their work to give dirty clothes a preliminary cleaning.[31] But nothing could turn laundering into easy work. Even when wives were lucky enough to have running water, electricity, and washing machines, laundering was drudgery. As Martha Lyle recalls of oil-lease life near Seminole, Oklahoma: "We had an old Maytag washer. It was in the kitchen, and that's how we did laundry. I used to despise washday. I just despised it. I'd wake up and hear that washer going, and here would be piles of laundry, here and everywhere, you know. It was horrible. It took Mother all day. She'd wash all day on that Maytag washer."[32] Once a housewife had her clean clothes hung out to dry, it was not unusual for a dust storm to coat them with muddy grit, making it necessary to wash all over again.[33]

Notwithstanding the rigorous character of cooking, cleaning, and laundering in a tent or a shack, women often had time to spare. Some used the time in sewing, making clothes for their families, or doing fancy work. Some spent spare time with their children.[34] But card playing offered the most ready amusement, and in growing towns of the twenties and thirties, women who liked cards turned in droves to bridge. Bridge offered a way to meet other newcomers, socialize pleasantly, and pass the time. Accordingly, one of the first groups to be formed during the initial months of McCamey's development was a ladies' bridge club. Bridge could become a large part of a woman's life: "I liked to play. . . . And I found myself under great pressure to finish things that I needed to do at home in order to get away early in the afternoon to go play bridge. And then, before that was over, I had made arrangements to go out that evening and play bridge."[35] In the forties and fifties study clubs assumed the importance that bridge clubs had had earlier. If a woman liked reading, she could send away for books and magazines. Merle Montgomery unearthed a list of "100 Books Every Person Should Read" and proceeded to work her way through the list; when she found she still had time to spare, she decided to adopt and raise a child. She also wrote music in idle moments: as she recalls, "There was nothing you could do other than something that was inside you."[36] A woman who could draw on such personal resources for occupation was indeed fortunate and unusual. It was more often true that a homemaker who completed her chores found time heavy on her hands, and there was little that a husband who worked a twelve-hour day could do about that.

Though women on remote leases endured a physical isolation that women in boomtowns did not share, most women in McCamey and Wink in the twenties found themselves isolated by convention from the boomtown bustle which offered amusement to men. Some husbands and fathers flatly forbade their wives and children to walk in town without their escort. Women did not do shopping, run errands, or find entertainment without their chaperonage.[37] There was some practical sense behind this rule: drunkenness and occasional street fights in boomtown main streets did not add up to the best of environments for anyone unescorted, male or female. Boomtowns had a fearful reputation for toughness and violence. Yet it was convention more than actual physical danger from assault that seems to have influenced behavior;

women who did not venture to town on their own nonetheless recall no sense of physical danger when they were in town. Going about alone looking for amusement was simply something a respectable woman did not do, especially at night. As Allie V. Scott remembers, "At night you didn't go out by yourself. No woman did. Except maybe those who walked the street."[38] In a boomtown like McCamey or Wink during the late twenties, where young men greatly outnumbered women, an unescorted woman could readily find diversion. Bessie Leonard, who walked home from her work as a nurse, recalls, "Oh, I'd have guys drive up and say, 'You like a ride home? Like me to take you home?' I'd say, "I live two doors up here and we'll go up and ask my husband.' And they'd take off. Well, you know, guys is guys."[39] How seriously one took such a casual encounter depended upon one's view of boomtown life. Getting picked up by strange men, however, was not something a respectable woman did.

Despite the rough environment of new oil towns, despite their removal from comfortable, visibly respectable surroundings, many women made a valiant effort to raise their families in accordance with their notions of respectability. These notions were essentially the same as the canons of small-town propriety which predated oil, when society was, as one native of rural Texas recalls, divided into two classes, those who were respectable and those who were not: "To a large extent, people associated with their own class. Standards of morality were strict—especially for women, and we—were conscious of the fact that there were people with whom we did not associate."[40] The inhabitants of boomtowns made such a distinction among the people in their communities. The difference between the two classes, which one lady separated into "those that tried to live decent and those that didn't," was clearly recognized.[41] Some couples chose friends with care, as they did not wish to associate with "the low sort"; some parents would not let their children play with children whose families were not respectable. The high mobility of oil town population was no barrier to such selectiveness. As one Crane resident explained in the choice of her children's playmates, "The town was small enough that you had a pretty good idea of who people were."[42] As in rural communities in the days before oil, family standing in the oil community was not so much determined by wealth or possessions as by behavior. Since oil people, moreover, followed oil activity from place to place, many acquaintances from one community reappeared in the next community a family visited; one could not shed a bad reputation by a move from McCamey to Wink. Because many oil-field workers, especially in the twenties and thirties, were part of what amounted to a mobile community, the type of control over individual behavior that sociologists have observed in rural and small-town life was transplanted to the oil fields.[43]

Even in brand new communities, then, inhabitants made class distinctions between those who lived on the right and wrong sides of the track, and moral distinctions between those who lived right and those who did not. In existing communities that experienced oil-boom development, residents made similar distinctions, as oil people sometimes found to their discomfort: pre-oil residents and outside observers alike distinguished between settled residents and oil-field people. Don Dittman, whose father was a cable-tool contractor from Pennsylvania, recalls how some long-time Fort Stockton residents reacted to oil-field newcomers in the late twenties: "We were White Trash. I have been refused a meal in the cafés in Fort Stockton in '26 and '27. You'd go in and set down to eat and some of them would tell you, 'We don't serve White Trash.' Oil Field White Trash. And others would just let you sit there 'til you got tired and got up and walked out."[44] To a Dun and Bradstreet representative who visited the Permian Basin boomtowns of the fifties, townspeople and oil people formed "two levels of society."[45] This distinction was most perceptible in towns experiencing their first oil boom activity. Confronted with a crowd of newcomers, older residents were cautious. As one Snyder resident remembers, "We were a little reserved and didn't know how to accept the oil people here for a few years."[46] The picture of boomtown crime and violence presented in the popular press worked against newcomers, for journalists regularly linked oil workers with crime and social disorder.

Against these instances of reserve on the part of settled residents, however, must be set numerous efforts to welcome oil families to the community. During Midland's rapid growth of the late twenties, local ladies welcomed newcomers with large-scale bridge parties at the Scharbauer Hotel. Even women who were not devoted to cards found these parties pleasant.[47] During Snyder's boom, members of the local Woman's Club happily expanded the number of their study groups to include new members, though their first effort to do so by founding a garden club misfired: none of the newcomers had gardens![48] Though some newcomers may have felt snubbed, then, local residents received others cordially.

While men often entered oil-field work at the prompting of a relative or friend, following oil-field activity usually meant giving up frequent contact with relatives and old local friends. For wives and mothers this meant that in time of family crisis there was no mother or grandmother at hand to offer advice and support, no kindly aunt or cousin available to help keep the family going, and no family connections to ease adjustment to a new community. In place of help from kin, however, there was the neighborly support of other oil-field workers. Many people who worked in the oil fields and followed oil activity came to know one another and to feel as though they were part of "a large family," "kind of a cadre," a moving community. Sharing the rootlessness of mobility, they were eager to make friends: as a former McCamey resident remembers, "Everybody was from somewhere else and everybody was anxious to get acquainted."[49] They shared experiences and living conditions; they lived in such close proximity that it was impossible to ignore other people's problems. And in time of crisis they filled the place of family by helping one another out. Bessie Leonard thus recalls that when their tent in McCamey burned down, fellow workers and neighbors made up a purse to help them get started again. In time of sickness, neighbors would help keep a household going; if doctors and nurses were not present, people with medical skills would be hunted up by word of mouth to help deliver a baby or treat illness.[50] This sort of neighborly assistance during boom days met practical and immediate needs. It operated in place of relatives, social agencies, and institutions.

The most striking example of neighborly aid was the help given to a family in the event of a death. Such help, traditional in rural communities, carried over to oil towns where families, generally of rural origins, were miles from the loved ones who might have offered them support. For the residents of new oil towns like McCamey or Crane, the nearest funeral parlor was many miles away over difficult roads. At first, those who died were most likely to be buried elsewhere, in whatever place they had originated, but when a local burial was necessary, neighbors carried it out. One Crane resident describes the burial of an oil-field worker: "They were poor people and they just built a wooden box and the women put cotton padding in it and a thin cloth of some kind like lawn and lined the casket. The men just put him in the casket and nailed it up."[51] The men then carried the casket to a small cemetery, where they had dug a grave, and friends and neighbors held their own burial service at the gravesite.

The people who moved with oil, then, could find social and psychological support from those who moved as they did and lived around them. In hard times they shared problems of intermittent work and low income; Ruth Godwin remembers: "During the depression . . . you got closer than ever [to those around you] because everybody depended on everybody else." An oil-camp veteran recalls: "It was like being relatives, like being kinfolks, so to speak, because we all depended on each other, and we all helped each other, and that was what made it a highly attached group of people." To sum up in the words of a former Humble camp resident, "It was kind of a family deal."[52]

The sense of supportive community filled individual longing for family ties left behind. For some young people, oil field associates—bosses, colleagues, acquaintances—filled family roles. Alice Keene recalls her son's acquaintances calling her "Mom"; one oil-field worker recalls even stronger ties to his supervisor: "Newt's situation there with his boys, we all felt like that he was the father and we were the sons, and we looked upon him for guidance both financially . . . and a lot of times from the moral aspect."[53] It is not surprising that many older oil-field residents reminisce with fond nostalgia about the close-knit oil community.

Notwithstanding the positive support families could find from the oil-field community, it is undeniable that oil-field life commonly placed considerable stress upon family unity. Oil-field work often separated fathers from families, a circumstance that may well have been harder on children than anyone else. One oil operator found that during the early part of his career he was away so much his daughter "wondered if she really had a Daddy."[54] Oil-field workers in the twenties worked twelve-hour days, seven days a week, which left them with little time and energy for their families. The development of better roads in the forties and fifties meant that oil workers could live at some distance from the field, but commuting time ate up the spare time shorter hours of labor created. The dangers of oil-field work meant worry for some wives; others found isolation, hard living conditions and boredom hard to accept. One oil-field worker of the twenties felt that oil-field wives were almost "invariably dissatisfied" with their lives: "During the idle hours a woman thinks of the inconveniences and loneliness of the life—like an idle person thinking about the state of her health until she actually becomes sick." Yet, to the same observer, the amusements of parties, dances, and drinking were an even worse influence on marriages.[55]

With these sources of stress in family life, there was economic

uncertainty of intermittent oil-field employment. Periodic unemployment was usual in the oil fields; for casual laborers and "boomers,"
being in and out of work was a way of life. For this reason, one oil-field
worker noted that few of his acquaintances were able to save their
earnings: "The wages paid compare favorably with, and are possibly
better than, the average paid by other industries for similar labor. Yet
few accumulate or save any money and are in debt from one payday to
another. More to be desired than high wages would be steady employment for then it would be possible to . . . balance expenditures with
income."[56] The popularity of gambling in oil-field amusement also
interfered with workers' savings for a rainy day. While taking oil-field
work gave a man a better income than farm work, it was thus no
panacea for money worries.

Stresses commonly encountered in oil-field marriages had their
reflection in skyrocketing divorce rates in oil boom areas. As in the
California goldfields of the 1850s, young men so greatly outnumbered
women in boomtowns that a married woman looking for another
companion had no trouble locating one.[57] Divorce proceedings took
time, and for that reason divorce decrees always lagged somewhat
behind boom activity; divorce rates often continued high for a year or
two after boom activity petered out. The rise in divorce rates in counties where oil fields opened up was striking, and rates themselves could
be spectacularly above national and regional divorce rates. The divorce
rate in Winkler County during the second year of the Wink boom was a
stunning 35.7, at a time when the U.S. rate was 1.7. With the coming of
oil in Ector County, there was a tenfold surge in the divorce rate in two
years. No wonder the Ector County clerk observed, "Newtimers don't
seem to stay hitched like the old-timers."[58] Even during the bleak first
years of the Great Depression, the divorce rates in Winkler, Ector, and
Midland counties remained many times higher than the national rate,
though by 1932 it was obvious that in West Texas, as in the nation,
fewer people could afford divorce.

Divorce rates were far higher in the booms of the twenties and
thirties than in later booms, perhaps because by the late forties and
fifties living conditions in the oil fields were not as rugged as they had
been. Better roads made it possible for men to live with families in town
and commute to work. When house trailers became increasingly available in the forties, they became an alternative to either separated
families or commuting; with all their uncomfortable crowding, trailers
kept families together.[59] The comparatively low divorce rates for

TABLE 6   Divorce Rates in Some Oil Producing
Counties during Selected Periods of Oil Activity

Year	Winkler	Ector	Midland	Scurry	Rate, Total U.S.
1926	--	4.6	3.6		1.6
1927	--	19.4	6.4		1.6
1928	22.9	47.7	8.3		1.7
1929	35.7	34.6	8.4		1.7
1930	22.6	37.4	19.9		1.6
1931	25.5	27.0	22.5		1.5
1932	11.0	25.5	12.3		1.3
1934	17.5	11.9	15.9		1.6
1935		26.3	11.2		1.7
1936		28.2	12.9		1.8
1949		19.4	10.1	7.4	2.7
1950		17.6	10.2	9.0	2.6
1951		17.2	13.7	4.2	2.5
1952		18.2	11.9	6.1	2.5

SOURCE: District Court Civil Fee Books and Clerks' File Dockets for Winkler, Ector, Midland, Scurry Counties; Population estimates, Appendix 1; *Statistical History of the United States*, p. 30. There is a discrepancy between figures reported in the Annual Reports of the Texas Judicial Council and the records in local courts, especially for the period before 1937. Local figures have been used in preparing this table.

Scurry County during its boom, then, may reflect changing conditions of oil-field life. Many oil-field workers who took part in the Scurry County boom, however, resided in adjoining counties, so their marital problems were not reflected in data for that county. Allowing for all these matters, it was still true that rising divorce rates went along with Scurry County's oil boom.

Though divorce rates rose and fell with oil activity, divorce was not the necessary outcome of boom activity or oil-field life. Many oil-field marriages successfully weathered the stresses and problems of boom-town environments. To couples sharing common goals and aspirations, even temporary separation, hard living conditions, and unemployment were surmountable problems.[60] Some oil-field marriages evolved in a very companionable way, as wives took an active part in their husbands' businesses. The wife of a busy well shooter, for example, not only handled all his bookkeeping but also learned how to figure how much nitroglycerin would be needed for a well described in a customer's telephone conversation. The wife of a fledgling oil operator helped transport equipment to a well site. And, in a shadier enterprise, more than one man and wife were partners in bootlegging operations. In these examples, the pace of boom activity brought wives into business and reinforced marriage partnerships.[61]

More to the point in considering boomtown divorce rates was the nature of boomtown population. The majority of newcomers to Permian Basin oil towns came from Texas or contiguous states, a geographical area in which such religions as Roman Catholicism and Orthodox Judaism, which are strongly opposed to divorce, are not relatively strong. This west and south-central geographical region, moreover, had, as a whole, a higher divorce rate than a region like New England or the Middle Atlantic states; divorce was much more easily obtained in Texas than in New York. Even before the coming of oil, Ector and Midland county divorce rates were higher than the national rate. Divorce rates have always been high among the young and the mobile: and these were precisely the people most numerous during peaks of boom activity when divorce rates took rapid climbs. Many people who followed oil activity were of rural origins; the process of their adaptation from rural to industrial and urban life meant an uprooting of existing ties and controls over behavior. It is likely, then, that boomtown divorce rates reflected not only the domestic problems which could result from a rugged life-style, but also the presence in boomtown population of a large number of persons whose ages and backgrounds made them more likely to resort to divorce than the inhabitants of other places.[62]

In considering family life in the new oil-fields, what is more impressive than the number of families that broke up, is the number of families that endured the hardships of a rugged life without domestic upset. People put up with living conditions that would dismay a modern observer: yet persons who can recall moving from boom to boom in a Model T and living in tents are by no means uniformly negative about having done so. Far from trying to escape the oil fields, many sons went on to follow in the footsteps of oil worker fathers; many daughters married men from the oil patch. It was not uncommon for virtual dynasties to emerge from oil-field families, in which men and women of several generations took part in oil-field employment.

Thus, in one Texon family of the twenties, the grandfather was a tool pusher, the grandmother ran a boardinghouse, a father and uncle worked as drillers, a son became a roustabout, and a granddaughter later married an oil-field worker.[63] By the fifties, in towns like Odessa, many children were of the third or even fourth generation in the oil community.

There is no denying that it took stamina to make the best of boomtown living conditions. On the other hand, there was always the hope that the dirt and discomfort were only temporary, that this boom or the next would mean a lucky break: most people came to boomtowns knowing they would eventually be moving on. Perhaps it was hard for wives to keep a household without the consolation of solid furniture and nice things; but among families who were obliged to travel light, there was little reason to envy neighbors' possessions. Bessie Leonard remembers that "it didn't seem like anyone had anything more than the other guy."[64] If intermittent employment could pose financial problems, costs of living could nonetheless be quite low. For a family living in a company house, for example, groceries, clothes, and gasoline might be the only expenses to be met from a paycheck; rent was automatically deducted. As Bessie Leonard recalls, "They don't have a light bill to pay and they maybe had only $1.50–$2.00 to pay [for rent]; we didn't have the worry we have today."[65]

Being young helped in tolerating boomtown life. Merle Montgomery, who was a "bright-eyed young bride" of twenty-two when she came to McCamey within a week of its founding, reflects that she was not aware of rough conditions as an older person might have been: "It was very primitive, but I didn't mind it. Oddly enough, I didn't mind it. I was happy, really was very happy."[66] Bessie Leonard echoes this perspective: "I was young. You didn't mind it too bad, you know. And although I'd come from Tulsa, Oklahoma—that was a big city even at that time, you know—we just didn't really pay that much attention to it, I guess. It was kind of a lark in a way."[67]

It cannot be assumed, moreover, that the living conditions families encountered in boomtowns were drastically worse than what other people without much money were familiar with. To oil workers who grew up in rural environments, for example, long hours and hard work were usual. Modern comforts were not common in early twentieth-century farm life; as late as 1940, fewer than one-fifth of all American farm homes had running water, flush toilets, or central heating.[68] To a person who had grown up in the average farm home, the gas heat, piped water, and communal bathrooms of Wink tent life might not have seemed primitive. Women worked no harder at raising families in boomtown shacks than did their counterparts on farms: indeed, they were spared much hard outdoor work that farm wives routinely performed. For those who came from the farm, then, oil-field life might not have seemed quite as rough and uncomfortable as it sounds today.

What did take endurance, especially for wives, was the uncertainty of oil-field life, particularly a life following booms, and frequent tedium. One wife of an oil operator saw little choice for an oil-field wife but stoic acceptance of her life: "She could whine if she liked, and that meant an unbearable life of misery. Or she could comfort herself that it wasn't as bad as the boom before."[69] Women who did not live in town, but in isolated tents or shacks on leases, had the hardest lot to endure, for they were without the neighborly support which made town and camp life bearable. One oil company executive who believed that "when you hire a man, you hire his wife," admitted in 1922 that "if it were not for the downright courage of some of these women, more than one man would fail and more than one lease would be handled inefficiently."[70] But husbands as well as wives were courageous enough to hold families together in times of crisis. One mother's only child died of polio when the family was living on a remote lease. She had no one but her husband to help her bear her grief:

I went into shock and was in shock two or three years. I did my work and everything, but I couldn't remember anything, and they'd tell me the things I did. Oh, my. The doctor said we had to move from out there because I'd stand in the door and look out to the cemetery from the time . . . my husband would leave for work . . . he'd come in and there I'd be, you know. The doctor wanted to take me to some of my folks, thought of getting me away. [Her husband said] "No, I'll just keep her here."

He moved his wife to town, away from the prospect of the cemetery and the barren horizon. And, she reflected, "I guess I dealt him a life, too."[71]

The courage to accept a hard life, to make the best of unpromising circumstances with the hope of betterment, stands out time and again among those who came to the new oil towns of West Texas to make a living and raise their families. Cramped, substandard housing in remote places and constant mobility with oil activity presented major challenges to women who had to move with their families from one oil boom to the next. Domestic life was not ideal, certainly not romantic, yet it had its compensations. If it was not glamorous, it was not terrible. Those who recall boomtown life do so less with appreciation or dislike than with bittersweet nostalgia. Alice Keene, a fifty-year resident of Wink, often reminisces about old times with a former neighbor: "And she'll say, 'Alice, those were the happiest days we had.' And I'll say, 'Yes, but weren't they hard ones.' "[72]

Busy times on Hendrick Boulevard, Wink,
in 1928; right foreground, the bus to Pyote.

5.
Black and
Mexican
Americans

ON NOVEMBER 1, 1927, the *Odessa News* reported that the Ector County Clerk had just issued a marriage license to a black couple, the first black couple ever to be married in Ector County. Commenting on this novelty to the *News* reporter, the clerk reflected, "There just hasn't been any [blacks] living here in past years, however, the colored population of the city is increasing with the growth of Odessa."[1]

Like other types of booms, oil booms attracted members of racial and ethnic minority groups by their promise of more jobs and better wages. But, until recent years, oil booms have had a historical peculiarity with respect to minorities. Though oil booms always created a great demand for labor, few blacks, Mexican Americans, or members of other minority groups found jobs in the exploration and production phases of petroleum development. Oil companies hired blacks to work in refineries and to clean office buildings, but they kept most work in the oil field as the preserve of the Anglo majority. That minority group members who came to booming oil towns found themselves barred from direct participation in opening up oil fields contrasted with the opportunities open to them in hard-metal booms. During California's great gold rush, for example, blacks and Latinos prospected, mined, and made fortunes in the goldfields.[2] In order to take part in that mineral boom, it was usually sufficient to have a pick, a pan, and plenty of muscle. To drill for oil was quite another matter, a business which increasingly took amounts of capital beyond the reach of a poor but ambitious individual. Few blacks or Mexican Americans in the early twentieth-century Southwest had the capital resources necessary to look for oil. Nor was there much reason for blacks or Mexican Americans to take an interest in oil. The working of traditional patterns of racial and ethnic discrimination, patterns of both regional and national practice, defined employment opportunities for minority group members: and oilfield jobs were among the types of work seldom, if ever, available to blacks and Mexican Americans.

The effect of oil booms on Permian Basin population was thus paradoxical: the very development of the oil fields from which minority group members were generally barred resulted in the growth of minority communities in oil-field towns. Here, traditional patterns of discrimination in employment were at work. While oil booms created an abundance of oil-field work which blacks and Mexican Americans could not get, they also multiplied jobs in types of work customarily done by members of minority groups. Heavy, hot, dirty, and unskilled types of work, such as clearing land, doing laundry, cooking and washing up in cafés, cleaning houses and buildings, and carrying baggage, had always been open to blacks and Mexican Americans, and oil booms resulted in an abundance of these jobs, spun off from oil prosperity. Blacks and Mexican Americans thus came to oil communities in search of work in these areas.

There were few blacks or Mexican Americans in the thinly-settled counties of West Texas before the coming of oil. Ranchers and farmers hired an occasional black or Mexican-American hand, and the annual cotton harvest always brought in migratory black labor from East Texas. But the gradual agricultural development of the Permian Basin counties in the early twentieth century did not bring in any great number of minority residents. As many a small farmer discovered to his grief, the arid West Texas plains were no place for those without much land or money; without considerable capital, one could not weather hard dry times like those during and after World War I. Apart from agriculture, which suffered memorably hard times just before the discovery of oil, there were few economic opportunities open to minority group members. Those that were there generally entailed hard work and low pay, jobs unattractive to the local Anglo labor force. The handful of blacks living in Midland worked, for the most part, as domestics and lived in servants' quarters. Occasionally employed at clearing land, road construction, and agricultural labor, Mexican Americans most often found work on the railroads as section hands, forming small communities in the town of Midland and at Metz in Ector County. The construction of the Roscoe, Snyder, and Pacific Railroad to Snyder in 1908 brought the first Mexican American residents to that town; Snyder's first black residents came with the establishment of a cotton oil mill whose operation meant work in heat the local Anglo labor force was not willing to endure.[3] Compared to West Texas, many other areas offered more attractive economic opportunities to minority group members, for the hard times that preceded oil development meant economic contraction, which affected all elements in area population.

That growth of minority population accompanied the discovery of Permian Basin oil, stands out most clearly in census data. In 1920, of the five counties considered, three—Ector, Upton, and Winkler—had no black residents whatever.[4] The census reported 16 blacks living in Midland County; Scurry County, with its greater number of cotton farms, had a total black population of 128. The largest Mexican-American community of the five counties was that of Midland; there the 1920 Census recorded that 132 residents had been born in Mexico, and total population was roughly 200. In 1920, 58 Mexican-born persons lived in Snyder. By 1930, after its first years as a petroleum management center, Midland's black population had grown to 259. During the same decade of oil discovery in Ector, Upton, and Winkler counties, all three counties had black residents by 1930. The black population of Ector County was 123, but the boomtowns of McCamey and Wink each had roughly twice that number of black residents, a reflection of greater local oil discoveries. By contrast, the black population of Scurry County, where no one had found oil in quantity, reflected only a natural increase of 19 persons. Similarly spectacular increases took place in the Mexican-American population of the five counties during the twenties. The most striking growth took place in Midland County, where the Mexican-born population increased to 1,123, nearly 14 percent of total county population. Upton and Winkler counties had, respectively, 144 and 65 Mexican-born residents by 1930. Oil prosperity alone, however, does not explain the increase in Mexican-American population in the Permian Basin, for Scurry County's Mexican-American population also increased more than 1,000 percent during the decade. Escape from abject poverty and political turmoil in Mexico may have been as important in drawing immigrants to the five counties as immediate economic opportunity.[5]

Oil activity was slow during the depths of the Great Depression, but by the mid-thirties new finds in Ector, Ward, and Winkler counties, as well as renewed development in Upton County, meant that the Permian Basin offered job opportunities when times were hard elsewhere. To judge by the information gathered from death records, the late thirties were a time of substantial black migration to Midland;

the 1940 Census revealed that Midland County's black population exceeded 1,000, most persons residing in the city of Midland. Similarly, Ector County's black population quadrupled during the thirties. The rate of growth of the black population slowed during the forties, but shot up again in the fifties; by 1960 Midland's black population was 6,313 and Odessa's 4,875. Similar rapid growth of black population took place in Snyder during the fifties, as the number of black residents increased from 51 in 1950 to 414 in 1960, an increase of more than 800 percent.[6] Judging from local records, the amount of black in-migration to Midland reflected the pattern of community growth. Thus, in-migration was substantial in the late twenties, dropped off markedly with the worst years of the Great Depression, picked up slowly in the late thirties, and became heavy in the forties, particularly after World War II. Much the same pattern was true in Odessa.[7]

When oil activity subsided, black population in the twenties boomtowns of McCamey and Wink declined, but small black communities remained in both towns. The black and Mexican-American communities in West Texas oil towns never expanded or contracted at the headlong rate of Anglo population, for, unlike Anglos, few blacks or Mexican Americans held jobs in the petroleum industry and had to move with development. It is difficult, however, to arrive at a precise picture of the growth patterns of West Texas Mexican-American communities, for census records contain far less information bearing on the matter than on the growth of black population. The number of Mexican-born residents of communities offers one indication of growth: in 1960, for example, there were 1,828 Mexican-born residents of Midland and 2,318 of Odessa. Local records, however, indicate that by 1960 the majority of Mexican-American residents of both towns were native Texans. In communities having separate schools for Mexican-American children, school enrollments also reflect community growth; in Midland, for example, there was pronounced overcrowding at the Mexican-American school in the late twenties, and in the late forties and early fifties, indicating that growth of the Mexican-American community was quite substantial at those times.[8]

The growth of minority population in oil towns reflects substantial in-migration of blacks and Mexican Americans. Birth and death records show the overwhelming majority of black newcomers were native Texans. Of 60 parents recorded for black births in Ector County in 1949, for example, only 9 came from outside Texas: 3 from Alabama, 2 from Arkansas, 2 from Louisiana, and 1 each from Oklahoma and Mississippi. The movement of blacks within Texas may explain why

Texas was one of the few southern states to lose only a small part of its black population through out-migration between 1940 and 1950.[9] Of 152 parents recorded for Mexican-American births during 1949, 125 were born in Texas, 20 in Mexico, 2 in New Mexico, and 1 each in Colorado, California, Iowa, and Kansas. By 1949 many Mexican-American parents had come from areas south and west of Ector County, from towns in Presidio, Brewster, and Pecos counties. Such numerical superiority of Mexican-American Texans, however, is characteristic of births only after the thirties; for 21 Mexican-American births in Ector County between 1928 and 1931, only 3 parents were born in Texas.[10]

The majority of black newcomers to West Texas came from the river valley land of rural East Texas and Central Texas, an area whose limits extended from Waxahachie to Tyler, south from Tyler to Houston, west from Houston to San Marcos, and north to complete a rough rectangle; the counties within these boundaries are those from which blacks moved westward. Anderson, Bastrop, Burleson, Cherokee, Ellis, Falls, Fayette, Grimes, Henderson, Houston, Limestone, Madison, Milan, Robertson, Walker, Waller, and Washington counties all fall within this area; all are among the places of birth cited in West Texas records, and all lost population between 1920 and 1960. There were no large cities within this river-bottom area; it was and is a rural area. Much of the farm land in these counties was cotton land, but livestock gradually outstripped cotton in agricultural importance. Some blacks came from the Longview-Marshall area, and some came from such south-central and southeast counties as Gonzales and Wharton: they, like the handful of blacks from San Antonio, Austin, and Dallas, were in the minority.

That so much of the area from which blacks came to West Texas was cotton land is important in explaining how they chose to come to West Texas, for it was cotton rather than oil which first brought many blacks to the Permian Basin. Since there was no large supply of resident labor to pick West Texas cotton, there was a need for seasonal migrant labor, and that labor came from East Texas cotton land. Mrs. Willsie Lee McKinney, a retired school teacher who grew up in Jacksonville, Texas, recalls that as a youngster she heard adults talk of going to West Texas to pick cotton for the Scharbauers and Faskens. She describes the movement of labor:

Many negroes migrated out of East Texas after they would get through with their sharecropper crops. Many of them didn't have anything left [after they paid what was due the landlord]. And they would get through with their cotton picking perhaps about the middle of October in East Texas, whereas the cotton was just opening up good in West Texas. And while cotton picking was at the lowest ebb of wages per hundred there, a man that could pick 500 pounds of cotton could make $5 a day in West Texas. Whereas if he picked 500 in East Texas he might have only $3.75. So they migrated to West Texas.[11]

One could make better money in West Texas than back east. As West Texas gradually became a major dry-land cotton-growing area, more and more blacks found attractive seasonal employment. Not surprisingly, many decided that permanent residence in West Texas would mean a chance to get ahead. Barbara Bass Lane describes her father's decision to move his family to Midland from Calvert, Texas:

My Daddy had heard about out here. Somebody had come back very disillusioned, you know, about the living out here. He came out here, but he liked it. He liked it so well that even though work wasn't out here like what they had led him to believe it was, he still didn't want to go back to East Texas. They had to work hard, do FIELD work and something similar to plantation life in Calvert. Being out here *was* a whole lot better than what they were accustomed to. They sure made more money . . . even then out here than back there.[12]

With the great expansion of dry-land cotton farming in West Texas, the minority population of the Permian Basin might have increased even without petroleum development. But oil prosperity added a dimension of economic opportunity for both black and Mexican-American newcomers. In older communities and new towns alike, oil booms meant jobs for cooks, hotel porters, general laborers, domestics, and laundry workers. Midland's development as a management center with multi-story office buildings created jobs for elevator operators and janitors; its large Scharbauer Hotel hired many black men and women as porters and maids. The work of keeping house in dusty West Texas meant that domestic workers found constant demand for their services, and because there was, in effect, a sellers' market in domestic service, wages compared favorably with those in other places. Willsie Lee McKinney, who first worked in Midland on the Pliska farm, explained her decision to go to work in booming Midland as a matter of high wages:

The thing that caused me to stop here in 1949, . . . I could make one dollar per hour for domestic work: cleaning house, washing, and ironing. So if I worked ten hours that day, I had ten dollars. Ten dollars per week was a good wage back in East Texas. So I thought, "Well, this is it. I'll stay here and make me a little money and go back to school." So that one dollar per hour for domestic work really interested me; and I know that there were many others who had come earlier who were like me.[13]

Because there were many jobs to be had in a booming oil town, individuals of all racial and ethnic groups often held more than one job. Depending on his stamina, an individual might hold two or three jobs, considerably enhancing family income. A head of a family might hold daytime and nighttime custodial work; one Mexican-American mother of a large family combined daily laundry work with evening kitchen work at a restaurant.[14] If other family members found work, family finances improved still further. Thus, two of the early black residents of Midland, Fred and Mary Bass, worked as a custodian-night watchman and a maid at the Scharbauer Hotel, respectively; they also led the Mount Rose Baptist Church, which they founded. Their children all found work when they were old enough to do so: Barbara Bass Lane remembers, "That was the standard in our family: when you got old enough, you worked."[15] Boomtown demand for labor meant that employers sometimes resorted to hiring children of minority families to fill adult jobs. Oralia Corrales, who grew up in Midland during the fifties boom, recalls her first job, at age nine, washing dishes in the café where her mother and sisters waited on tables; several years later she and her sisters took turns working in a twenty-four-hour restaurant. One or another member of the family was always on shift, giving the family round-the-clock income. Local farmers also hired children in Midland's black and Mexican-American communities to pick cotton in area fields, for adults could find better paid work in town.[16] In this respect, while oil activity resulted in directly improved incomes for minority families, it clearly did so at a human cost.

Traditional hiring practices, language barriers, and educational differences meant that blacks found different types of work than Mexican Americans, and blacks held a somewhat greater variety of jobs than Mexican Americans. Nevertheless, there was one thing that jobs open to members of minority groups generally had in common: they paid less than other jobs. Members of minority groups bettered themselves relative to earnings prior to coming to oil towns rather than relative to Anglo wage earners in the area. For blacks, domestic and personal service jobs were those most often available, especially to black women. In 1950, for example, 89 percent of Odessa's employed black labor force worked at jobs that fell into this category; somewhat more than two-thirds of Midland's labor force held such jobs. Domestics were 27 percent of the total employed Odessa blacks; most domestics were women. Within the personal service category there were jobs as cooks, porters, and waiters. Laborers were the third most numerous category of job holders among blacks. In 1950, one of every six employed blacks in Midland worked as a laborer; in Odessa, roughly one of every eight.[17]

This pattern of employment for blacks contrasted with the pattern of job holding for Mexicanos indicated by information contained in local birth records at roughly the same period. In Odessa in 1949, for example, of seventy-four Mexican-American fathers identified by occupation, 69 percent identified themselves as laborers. Forty-eight percent of the Mexican-American fathers in Midland in 1951 identified themselves as laborers. A somewhat greater percentage of Mexican Americans than blacks worked as truck drivers or in the building trades; far fewer Mexican Americans than blacks worked in domestic or personal service jobs. The contrast in patterns of minority employment was especially noticeable in hotel-restaurant and local government employment. A far greater proportion of the black labor force worked in hotels and restaurants than Mexican Americans; there were some Mexican-American cooks but no Mexican-American porters. More Mexican Americans than blacks, however, were on municipal and county payrolls, working at road construction, street cleaning, and garbage collection. An occasional black custodian showed up on municipal and county payrolls, but only in places like Wink, where there was no Mexican-American community in boom days, were blacks employed at municipal road work. Both blacks and Mexican-American railroad employees appeared in public records; blacks worked as porters, while Mexican Americans worked as section hands. Both black and Mexican-American women worked as domestics, but, from evidence in local records, a greater percentage of black women were thus employed than Mexican Americans.[18]

In explaining these patterns of employment, it must be noted that the heavy concentration of black employment in domestic and personal service jobs was characteristic not only of West Texas but of Texas and the nation as a whole between 1920 and 1960. The number of blacks employed as cooks, for example, reflected the customary hiring of blacks in that area of employment. In the Southwest, blacks had long worked as cooks, not only in eating places but on chuckwagon gangs; even during the California goldrush, cooks were the most numerous group of skilled workers among blacks.[19] Land clearing, railroad work, farm labor, and road construction were similarly usual jobs for Mexican Americans in the Southwest. So common was Mexican-American employment on road work, that Luis Saenz Ramos found work paving Midland's Main Street simply by walking to the work site: the foreman told him, "Go get a shovel and a pick and get to work," and he did so. After the work on Main Street was finished, he returned to work for the Texas and Pacific Railroad.[20]

Language and educational barriers were as important as custom in the employment patterns of oil towns. As minority communities developed, so did the need for professional services of doctors, dentists, lawyers, and teachers in those communities. Among professionals, teachers usually appeared first in the black community. But the access to higher education which blacks had, albeit with some handicaps, did not have a counterpart in the Mexican-American community. To receive an education, Mexican Americans had to master English, as it was spoken by Anglo teachers. Mexican Americans attended Anglo schools in Snyder and Odessa; in Midland, and later in McCamey, there were separate Mexican-American grammar schools. But Mexican-American students seldom received encouragement to continue their education beyond the sixth-grade level. Not surprisingly, there were fewer Mexican-American than black professionals. Mexican Americans were more tightly locked into laboring jobs than blacks, by virtue of educational barriers common in the region.[21] In jobs which involved personal services to the Anglo majority, whether as porters, waiters, or domestic servants, language also acted as a barrier to Mexican-American employment. The combination of language and educational barriers worked against Mexican-American access to office or retailing jobs.

As minority communities grew in the larger oil towns, both blacks and Mexican Americans established small businesses. In Midland and Odessa there were eventually black and Mexican-American grocery stores. Places of entertainment—bars, dance halls, and pool halls— found a community clientele. Midland had a notable black nightclub, The Swanky Night Club, which brought in name entertainers; the size of the Midland black community supported a hotel and a number of cafés by the forties. One Mexican-American Midland resident, Alvino Rodriguez, owned two dance halls, the Cinco de Mayo and Benito Juarez; the latter also served as a movie house.[22] Both blacks and Mexican Americans entered the taxi business, though in Midland such municipal regulations as the requirement that taxi drivers "be able to speak, read, and write the English language," were no aid to their doing so.[23] Barbers, beauticians, tailors, mechanics, auto repairmen, and service station operators also found work in growing minority communities.

Though few members of minority groups found oil-field work between 1920 and 1960, the exclusion of blacks and Mexican Americans from the oil field was not absolute. Where customary employment patterns overlapped with oil-field needs, minority workers found oil-field jobs. Opportunities in such areas meant that there were a few blacks who were mobile workers and boomers. They were the founders of the black communities in McCamey and Wink.

When minority group members found jobs out in the oil field, those jobs were usually in janitorial work, cooking and boardinghouse maintenance, dirt work, teaming and hauling, or pipelining. Most minority employees of major oil companies had jobs which fell into the first two categories. Mr. and Mrs. Allan Patterson, for example, both worked for the Humble Oil Company in McCamey; while Humble hired Patterson as a janitor for company offices, Mrs. Patterson worked in one of the Humble boardinghouses and did part-time independent cleaning, washing, and practical nursing. After several years' work in McCamey, Humble moved the Pattersons to Penwell, Sandhills, Wink, and Hobbs; in all, Patterson worked for Humble for forty-two years.[24] Major companies and small operators alike employed black cooks. Both black men and women cooked for drilling crews that were at work on remote leases; there were black cooks on the crews that drilled two of the greatest Permian Basin discovery wells of the twenties, the No. 1-A Yates in Pecos County and the Hendrick well in Winkler County.[25]

Yet another occupation traditionally open to blacks was mule skinning. Before the thirties, dirt work and hauling in the oil field was done with teams of horses or mules. Teams hauled derricks and other heavy equipment and dug slush pits and storage tanks. Blacks thus found employment as oil-field teamsters in the early twentieth-century Gulf Coast fields, in Eastland County in 1918–20, in Burkburnett, and in the Panhandle oil fields of the twenties. In the late twenties they also came to Crane and Winkler counties, for shifting sands made the routes to new oil fields impassable to trucks with heavy loads and required the use of wagons for transport. Among blacks, mule skinners were the group most likely to move with oil-field development; as retired West Texas oil-field workers recall, many blacks who worked in the Permian Basin oil fields had begun their work in Louisiana or on the Texas gulf coast.[26]

Throughout the West Texas oil-field development of the twenties and thirties, blacks outnumbered Mexican Americans in the oil fields; Mexican Americans do not appear to have shared access with blacks to employment as drilling-rig cooks or teamsters. By contrast, in South Texas, where there were a greater number of Mexicanos, independent dirt and construction contractors hired many Mexican Americans; Mexicanos there worked in connection work and pipelining.[27] With the labor shortages created by World War II, however, Mexican Americans began to hold a variety of West Texas oil-field jobs. By 1949, for example, the second most numerous occupational category for Mexican-American fathers listed in the Ector County birth records was that of "oil field laborer." Mexican Americans worked as pipeliners and oil-field truckers, as well as in oil-field supply. By contrast, none of the Ector County black fathers listed in 1949 had oil-field jobs. There was no great breakthrough for minority labor in the oil fields of the late forties and fifties, but as Mexican-American employment shows, the pattern of employment shifted. It was no longer usual to have oil-rig cooks, and heavy machinery had taken over the work previously done by teams: that cut oil-field opportunities for blacks. But for Mexican Americans, access to oil-field work increased in the postwar period as, with mechanization, they took over part of the work black teamsters had once done.[28]

As minority population increased in booming oil towns, customary residential segregation led minority communities to emerge as distinct entities within the community as a whole. Thus Midland had its "Mexican town" in the area to the northeast of the center of town, around what is now De Zavala School, while its black community grew up around Lee Street, east of the center of town and south of the railroad tracks. Odessa's black and Mexican-American communities developed on the south side of town, initially in the area between Jackson and Texas streets. Even in new towns like McCamey and Wink, blacks lived in a separate part of town.[29] In many instances, minority communities had separate schools; they developed their own businesses, churches, clubs, and civic organizations. Despite separation, however, residents of minority communities shared such common boomtown problems as shortages of housing, slow growth of public services, and pressure on school facilities. Indeed, boomtown problems were usually more acute and of longer duration in minority communities than in oil communities as a whole.

In new oil-towns, where the absence of any existing housing forced most residents into tents and shacks, blacks and Anglos alike shared the discomfort of inadequate housing. There was little difference in either Wink or McCamey in the rudimentary shelter used by black and white residents. Similarly, during Odessa's late-thirties oil boom, Anglos as well as minority group members lived in tents and flimsy shacks built from salvaged tin. But because housing development and construction catered to the more affluent Anglo consumer, during the later booms of the forties and fifties, housing was especially short in minority communities in both Midland and Odessa. Paid less than Anglo workers, minority group members could not have competed with other consumers for high-priced housing even had residential segregation patterns not kept them in clearly identified neighborhoods.[30] Minority group members thus had to find housing within a limited geographical area in oil towns in which housing was already in short supply. As a result, they paid high prices for what housing there was, and when that was occupied, newcomers often had to move on. The combination of oil activity and wartime growth of Sloan Field, then an Army Air Corps base, brought black workers and servicemen to Midland in large numbers, but housing was so hard to find that most of the married servicemen had to reside at the airfield. Some G.I. housing was eventually constructed; tenants coveted it, not only for its sound construction, but also for its indoor plumbing. Before the fifties, the latter convenience was rare indeed in minority housing in Midland and Odessa. Willsie Lee McKinney remembers that rooms for rent in houses with indoor baths and hot and cold water were hard to find in the late forties: "You paid a premium just to share one with somebody, where you could have hot and cold water for a bath and indoor bathrooms." A shared room without such facilities might cost as much as sixty to seventy-five dollars a month, and the luxury of modern plumbing commanded a higher rent.[31] There were hotels and rooming houses in both the Midland and Odessa black communities, but lodging was still in short supply. The remaining option in minority housing was residence in servants' quarters. Few newcomers found this alternative acceptable, and those with families found such accommodations especially difficult.[32] The shortage of housing in both Midland and Odessa's black communities during the rapid growth of the forties and fifties took its toll in community development, as many newcomers decided to move on. Scarce housing meant that Midland and Odessa saw transient black population in the late forties and fifties, but this was a population on the move for a different reason than that motivating the Anglo oil-town boomers: living conditions, rather than better employment opportunities, led blacks to move on from booming oil towns.[33]

Such public services as street paving, effective drainage, water mains, and sewers were slower to arrive in boomtown minority neighborhoods than elsewhere. In Midland, neither Lee Street nor the adjoining streets were paved in the forties; Odessa's black neighborhood had but two paved streets until the city carried out additional paving in the late forties.[34] In both towns water and sewer lines were not generally available to residences until the fifties, though the black business district in Midland received city water service in the forties. During the early forties both black and Mexican-American civic leaders urged the Midland City Council to extend water and sewer lines to their communities, but not until the health problems of the early fifties did the city make real progress in serving minority neighborhoods.[35]

Primarily because of traditional regional segregation in public places, public recreational facilities, never overabundant in booming oil towns, were almost nonexistent in minority neighborhoods. Blacks and Mexican Americans could not use the parks and libraries in Midland and Odessa. On receiving special permission from the city council, Midland black groups were, on occasion, able to hold special functions in Cloverdale Park, but no other facilities were open to them, nor were there any parks in minority communities until the late forties. By 1945, after much effort on the part of black civic leaders like E. L. Jordan and the Reverend H. F. Doyle, the city established a park site in the Midland black community; two years later the city council approved building a recreation hall and library on park grounds.[36] Ector County created a park for blacks and Mexican Americans in the late forties; in 1948 the Ector County commissioners established a library for blacks, and three years later they provided a building for a library and kitchen at the minority park.[37] By the fifties, then, some provision had been made by local government for separate recreational facilities, but like segregated arrangements in other parts of the nation, they were not of the same quality as such facilities used by the majority.

Minority communities fared somewhat better in the provision of schools, for in that area even small towns usually made an effort to meet educational needs as mandated by law. When oil activity brought a sizable black population to new towns like McCamey and Wink, local school boards provided schools for black children. In McCamey, black children went to school at the black Baptist church during 1928, and the following year the school system furnished a two-room school for them. It was necessary to enlarge the school when Humble expanded its refinery and office operations; by September, 1931, there were over 100 black children of school age in McCamey.[38] There were fewer black children of school age in Wink, but they had their own school until August, 1930; at that time, as boom activity in the Winkler County oil fields was over, the superintendent of schools reported that there were but six black children of school age in the district.[39]

In communities that predated petroleum development, considerable improvement in the educational facilities available to minority group members followed oil prosperity. In Snyder, for example, black children could obtain only a rudimentary primary education until 1952, when a brick building housing eight grades opened; four years later, the addition of rooms to this school permitted black students to pursue a high school education without leaving town. By 1956 there was a total of ninety-two students attending Snyder's black school.[40] Both Midland and Odessa provided primary schooling for black children in 1929, hiring one teacher to teach eight grades. As in Wink, however, the end of the oil boom meant considerable out-migration of Odessa's black population, and in the fall of 1931, the Ector County Independent School District's board of trustees decided that there were too few black pupils to warrant employing a teacher. A year later, a teacher was again hired, but only eight pupils enrolled. Not until 1938 did enrollment increase enough to warrant adding another room to the two-room school building on Muskingum Street. During the next decade, however, the growth of Odessa's black community proceeded at so rapid a rate that by 1948 black students attended school on a half-day schedule. In December, 1948, Blackshear, a new junior-senior high school, and Douglas Elementary School opened, but by 1952 it was necessary to construct another school building. Later growth during the fifties required additions to these buildings.[41]

Because Mexican Americans were of the same race as the majority but unwelcome in Anglo institutions, the provision of education for Mexican Americans in West Texas oil towns did not follow as consistent a pattern as the traditional segregated education provided for blacks. In small towns it was not usually feasible to construct a separate school for Mexican Americans; local authorities had a choice of permitting

Mexican-American children to attend Anglo schools or discouraging their attendance at school altogether. In Odessa, for example, the school district considered setting up a separate school for Mexican-American children in May, 1923; a month later it abandoned the idea and decided that these students would continue to attend the Anglo schools. After this triumph of pragmatism over prejudice, there was no hard and fast separation of ethnic groups for many years. Similarly, in Snyder the few Mexican-American children in town went to the Anglo school.[42]

In Midland, by contrast, the school system organized a school for Mexican-American pupils in 1920 and enrolled 38 students; until 1929, when the Mexicano student population was over 200, it hired only one teacher for that school. In 1931 there were 53 students in the first grade alone at the school, and the first of numerous additions was made to the building. For the next three decades, the "Mexican School," which came to be named De Zavala School, was consistently overcrowded; after many years of additions and temporary buildings, a modern school building was constructed in the fifties. The Mexican-American school did not provide for students beyond the first six grades. Until the mid-forties, interviewees recall that, while an occasional Mexican American attended school beyond that level, most Mexican Americans could not continue their education beyond the sixth grade. Oralia Corrales, a former student at De Zavala School, recalls of higher education: "There was no written law, but it was just known you could not attend."[43]

Despite all too common disadvantages faced by minority group residents of oil boom communities, prosperity generated by oil extended to both blacks and Mexican Americans. Though generally barred from oil work, blacks and Mexican Americans took advantage of other job opportunities created by growth and prosperity. These opportunities were, for the most part, in unskilled labor, but they could yield an income better than that which the same work might bring in other areas. The median income of black families in Midland in 1950, for example, was $1,558; in only four other Texas cities were black median incomes higher than in Midland. Even in notably low-paying occupations like domestic labor, wages were better in Midland than they were in other parts of Texas, and domestic workers had reason to be optimistic about the possibilities for getting ahead.[44] Because more boomtown jobs were open to them, blacks may have been somewhat greater beneficiaries of oil prosperity than Mexican Americans. On the other hand, more Mexican Americans than blacks found oil-field employment in the fifties, and when oil-field work opened to minority group members after the civil rights legislation of the sixties, more Mexican Americans than blacks entered oil-field work.

Though minority group residents of oil boomtowns did hard work for wages below those of Anglo workers, at least some of the heady optimism characteristic of a booming oil town found its way into black and Mexican-American neighborhoods. Barbara Bass Lane, who grew up during Midland's renewed oil prosperity of the late thirties and forties, recalls,

When Midland finally did break loose, you could almost walk down the street and pick up money. Money was flowing just that much. Even the poor had it made. I remember seeing my mother get her first expensive dresses . . . well, it was expensive to us: a ten dollar dress was a lot of money. And we had plenty of clothing, plenty of shoes, plenty of food, plenty of everything. This was when everybody else [in other parts of the country] was having it hard. And remember now, this was a family of ten, so you know that it really must have been *good* for us. Mom and Dad had built their first home, you know. And they paid practically spot cash for it and bought their first furniture. We had our first indoor bathroom. And, like I said, we were living good. This was in 1937.[45]

Allowing that what is described here is the situation of a more than ordinarily enterprising family in which more than one family member worked, the boom prosperity reflected in this recollection reached other families in minority communities. And if even boom times were not without personal hardship, they did offer individuals a chance to better themselves and their families. Over a period of more than six decades, Luis Saenz Ramos of Midland worked at clearing land, road construction, railroad work, trucking, retailing, cotton picking, and cotton growing, and his perspective perhaps best sums up what oil development meant in minority communities: "I didn't lack for a job. There was work to be done. There was always something you could do."[46]

Midland, Texas, July 1929. Midland County courthouse (left) and jail (right) frame the new Petroleum Building.

6.
Crime and Vice

IN THE SPIRIT OF Tombstone and Dodge City and of their fabulists, journalists have generally described oil boomtowns as perilous places, where murder and other violent crimes were commonplace. Earl Gray, for example, recently wrote that the boomtowns in the United States were "as well known for saloons, dance halls, gambling halls, vice, robbery and murder as the most desperate towns in the cowboy stories of the old west."[1] Images of violent men and bloody deeds have long been transferred from yellowed dime novels to fresh newsprint, without critical reflection. Now that historians have proved that cattle towns and mining camps were much less violent than previous writers led the public to believe, however, one might well wonder if the oil towns were singularly violent.

A sizable group of historians and journalists have claimed that they were. Sam Mallison, for example, asserted that in Best, near McCamey, a dead body would turn up "every few days."[2] The truth of it was that only one murder occurred in Best in 1925, its boom year. In many instances, writers have picked up hyperbole and some colorful prose from participants in the booms. Carl B. Glasscock, recollecting Ranger in 1919, asserted: "The body of a dead man lying in the street created no great excitement."[3] Readers could hardly say the same of Glasscock's statement, or of those of a number of other authors, who peppered their pages with colorful and fervent denunciations of "highly concentrated evil" and of "the wickedest place that ever existed on earth." A godsend for any sensationalist was the discovery that an oil town contained a saloon named The Bucket of Blood. And it was not difficult to find one with that name: Borger, Big Spring, McCamey, and Wink are among the cattle and oil towns that had one. Having dug up a mention of a Bucket of Blood Dance Hall in Bradley's Corner, near

Burkburnett, Boyce House made the most of it: he warned his readers that "the title was no empty boast." An industrious splasher of purple ink, House enjoyed passing along a common oil-field town anecdote, that a dead body was found in the gutter every morning when shop-keepers opened up their stores. He applied it to Desdemona in one instance, though, in fact, that town recorded no murders during more than half a year, at the height of its boom.[4] The image of the corpse on the doorstep was irresistible.

The same sort of wide-eyed exaggeration has been characteristic of descriptions of most oil towns, including those of the Permian Basin. One old-timer, speaking of Wink in 1928, claimed: "It was pretty rough, with somebody getting killed here about every day." A good story no doubt, but only that. In fact, there was a homicide every four months or so in Wink during 1928 when drilling activity hit its peak. Old-timers not uncommonly impressed newcomers with the rip-roaring days of old. When a schoolteacher arrived in Odessa in 1945, she was given a local version of the mud and blood legend by a new friend: "When she was a child there used to be a killing in Odessa . . . every Saturday night . . ."—*before* the town's first oil boom.[5]

In fact, there is no reason to suppose that lawlessness was common in oil boomtowns or that they were more perilous places than other towns, when due allowance is made for the composition of boomtown population. Problems in law enforcement were generally limited to the first few months of settlement, when boomers and drifters were a sizable proportion of the population. William Franklin ("Hot Shot") Ash, once a well-known member of the underworld in both Borger and Wink, Texas, explained the initially high incidence of crime as the response of boomers to the immediate problem of finding eating money: "Ace Borger advertised in every major paper in the world and everybody came down there from New York, Chicago, and Detroit. They didn't come down there to rob nobody. They come down only to see what was goin' on. They'd all get busted, they had to rob some-body."[6] The boomers and drifters furnished the clientele for the gamblers, bootleggers, and prostitutes; relatively high wages paid in the oil fields could support a flourishing underworld, even in small towns. The existence of victimless crime, however, was not peculiar to oil boomtowns. Gambling was a common rural pastime, no more so in the oil towns than in farm-market settlements; tough bars and prosti-tutes abounded where large numbers of single young men found work, no less so in mining, cattle, and military-post towns than in the oil centers.[7]

After national prohibition was established, gambling shifted to the backrooms of the most wide-open places, and local bootleggers, café owners, and druggists often provided alcoholic beverages, ranging in quality from locally made Choc beer to imported Scotch whiskey, smuggled from Mexico. It was provided for a price, and it was consumed at a cost. But most drillers were willing to tolerate hung over or even slightly drunk workers on the job, as long as the well was drilled without delay.[8]

Bars that catered particularly to the oil-field trade were often on the peripheries of boomtowns, commonly along the roads and highways that connected oil fields and settlements. Named, variously, the Cattleguard, the Dew Drop Inn, and the Permain [sic] Club, they ran long hours; they had a table or two for cards, and left dice on the bar. Workers between jobs and roughnecks who had completed tours settled in for serious drinking, with consumption of one case of beer by one man a reasonably common occurrence. The drinking was just as hard at the in-town joints, which differed from the rural hangouts in that the premises were more carefully appointed. Heavy Brackeen's City Cafe, in Wink, for example, boasted an ornately carved mahogany bar, shipped out from El Paso. Like many of the country spots, the city bars often carried the names of their owners: in Hobbs, New Mexico, one of the hot spots was Ramona's. Occasionally, however, local wits were more inspired, as in Hobbs, where one of the seedier dives was the Petroleum Club, in outlandish mockery of the more pretentious establishments of the same name in Tulsa, Dallas, Midland, and other oil centers. Whether in or out of town, the oil-field worker's bar provided diversions in various forms, "booze, broads, and brawls," as the common phrase put it.[9]

Fights usually broke out as the evening wore on. The regular scrappers had at each other, over and under the pool tables, until they dusted themselves off, settled back in hardwood chairs, and cooled down with bottles of beer. Many of these frays were more or less friendly affairs, repeated on a regular basis, by older hands who had worked together for years. After watching two rig builders, George Anderson and Bill Wooster, tangle nightly, Slim Gabrel, the stoic proprietor of a pool hall in Odessa, reflected: "Them sons of bitches plays worse than anybody I ever saw fight."[10] Many of the oil-field workers' bars were fairly tough places where a roustabout could pick a fight to let off steam, to settle a grudge, or to celebrate payday. Occasionally the fights were in deadly earnest, as convictions for maiming indicate. In other instances, it amounted to rough sport. As one former roustabout put it, it was a "matter of pastime and good exercise."[11]

Prostitutes in the oil towns were often alcoholics, some of them tragically young, like the high-school girls in Ranger who took to whoring to pay for bootleg whiskey. "They didn't know much what they were doing," one retired oil-field worker recalled, "but they wanted the whiskey."[12] It is fair to say, however, that most of the fancy ladies in the oil-field towns knew full well what they were doing, and that many of them carried on their profession in several different oil towns. In Wink, for example, many of the two dozen or so prostitutes had worked in towns in Oklahoma and in Borger before they went into business "on the line" behind Hendrick Boulevard, Wink's main street. Like gamblers and many bootleggers, they moved with the tide of workers, from field to field and town to town. When the masses of young men who did the heavy work in the field moved into an area, prostitutes and pimps were not far behind. In a few instances, prostitutes settled down and stayed in a town. One boasted to the deputy sheriff of Winkler County: "I rode into Wink on the first load of casing and I'll ride out on the last load of sucker rods!"[13]

Though one could buy liquor legally in most of the oil fields, except in Oklahoma, in some counties and precincts in Texas, and during national prohibition, gambling and prostitution were outside the letter of the law. Illegal status, however, was no particular brake on these activities because most boomtowns were broadly tolerant of "victimless crime," as it is called today. There was precedent in rural as well as urban experience for such toleration. In mining camps in the nineteenth century and in the rural areas of most of the country, gambling was the only readily available recreation for farmers and workers. As such, it was accepted by most of the community and it was tolerated by local lawmen. Cattle towns were perhaps more tolerant of gambling, drinking, and prostitution than most other settlements. Big Spring, a cattle town, the West Texas railroad center for the Texas and Pacific Railroad, and the principal city in the Permian Basin before oil, offers a suitable example. Arrests for moral offenses were infrequent in Big Spring. In 1893, for example, only thirty-seven of seventy-three indictments in district court were for moral charges, and these were primarily for gaming, with a few indictments for prostitution. Local authorities customarily overlooked both offenses, except when card players became violent or when disorderly houses were actually disorderly. As one perceptive student of the town's history put it, "The important function of the law in these cases was to maintain control rather than to punish all offenders."[14]

In more recent times other Permian Basin towns similarly tolerated victimless offenses. In Midland serious card playing was generally confined to hotels, and law officers rarely intervened. Before 1926, the county sheriff staged a full-fledged gambling raid once a year, stepping up the rate to two per year in 1929, during the boom, then tapering these raids off to a few during the following decade. Permian Basin residents showed a like degree of toleration for bootlegging, as a bootlegging case or two was heard each year in Midland courtrooms before, during, and after the boom of the late twenties. Thirty years later, law officers in legally "dry" Scurry County similarly tolerated illegal liquor. The sheriff routinely arrested rumrunners once a month, a practice that continued during the Scurry County boom. Fine and fees paid, liquor offenders resumed their trade without interference for another month or so. Thirsty workers were thus able to find beer and liquor at drive-in restaurants and other places.[15]

Like bootlegging, the established towns tolerated prostitution as long as prostitutes did not openly solicit on city streets and carried on their profession without scandal. Soiled doves were good for business in cattle towns and oil boomtowns alike, and law officers were unlikely to be more severe in prosecuting the women than public opinion required. Midlanders referred to one motel as the "riding club," while Odessans called the top floor of an Odessa hotel the "athletic club," all in a jocular way. As long as vice was restricted to well-known locales, it did not offend the sensibilities of citizens of oil-field towns. Operating from hotels and boarding houses in McCamey, from four-room shacks in Wink, and from a converted army barracks in Snyder, prostitutes generally escaped legal hassles.[16]

In the newer oil towns of Borger, McCamey, and Wink, prostitutes went about their daily lives with little direct censure from other women in the community. Borger residents knew of and tolerated the fancy women down on Dixon Street, just as McCamey and Wink inhabitants knew their local soiled doves. In Wink, prostitutes patronized the same stores and shops as more respectable women; the beauty shops always placed a folded newspaper on the seat of a chair that a prostitute had occupied before a respectable client sat on it. In both McCamey and

Wink, prostitutes ate on meal contracts at the same boardinghouses that fed the employees of the major oil companies. On occasion, they served as bankers, holding and lending money in Wink, which had no regular bank during its principal boom. Though relegated to the demimonde by "the church people" and many oil-camp dwellers, the prostitutes were important to the social and economic life of the oil towns, and they received appropriate consideration from local law officers.[17]

In established communities like Corsicana, Wichita Falls, and Midland, lawmen kept the tolerated lawbreakers—gamblers, bootleggers, and prostitutes—under control by occasional raids and by vigorous prosecution when they took part in robbery or violent crimes. In most of the new oil towns, such as Borger, Best, McCamey, and Wink, lawmen found it difficult to manage this element, for it had arrived on the site even before the towns were incorporated. In the new boomtowns, the pre-boom county sheriff coped as best he could with rough characters, beyond his ken. He often did so alone. In Upton County, for example, the county commissioners did not authorize hiring a deputy for McCamey until 1927, when the boom was in full swing. Such deputies, selected from the small group of pre-boom residents, rarely had experience in law enforcement. They were thus of limited value on the job. The new deputy in McCamey might well have been discouraged at the outset; he was the only officer for McCamey, with nearly five thousand people, and for Crossett, a smaller neighboring settlement that was a haven for gamblers and whores. For several months, the lawman in McCamey lacked so much as a rudimentary jail. Like his counterparts in Wink, Carlsbad, and Borger, he chained prisoners to trees, buildings, pipes, and hitching posts until they could be brought to trial.[18]

The greatest single difficulty confronting the lawman in a new oil boomtown was that social and political life had already settled into a channel of a sort before he arrived on the scene. Considerable toleration for victimless crime and of drunkenness and fighting developed during the hiatus between settlement and regular attempts to enforce the law. An overly zealous deputy thus would find himself increasingly cut off from the general community, with scant support and short tenure in his post. Even the raw recruits to the job were aware of these possibilities, and when it was inescapably necessary to impose order, sheriffs and deputies generally turned to the state for help.

In response, the Texas Rangers visited most of the new oil boom-towns on several occasions. The Rangers usually moved into town quickly, raided gambling dens, roughed up a few of the local toughs, and intimidated the more intractable operators before they moved out, leaving the sheriff's deputy to keep a lid on things as best he could. Thereafter, one or two Rangers passed through town to demonstrate the presence of the law. As one Crane resident recalls, "Sometimes they would arrest a few. Sometimes they wouldn't."[19] The Rangers also bore down on Borger, though they were less successful in intimidating the well-entrenched lawbreakers there than they had generally been in the other oil towns. After the local officials and the Rangers failed to maintain reasonable order, the governor of Texas placed the Borger area under martial law in 1926 and sent in the National Guard to restore it.[20]

So drastic a recourse was never necessary in McCamey, where following municipal incorporation in 1927, city officers succeeded in curbing the most flagrant and dangerous violations of the law. More a townsite than a community in 1927, Wink lacked a sizable group of residents who had any great interest in controlling bootlegging, pros-titution, and gambling. A loose-knit clique of rumrunners, gamblers, and allied politicians dominated Wink during its boom. Wink had no law officers of its own for a full year after settlement began because it was not an incorporated place. Thus, until mid-1928, Sheriff Will Priest represented the law from Kermit, an hour's drive away. The justice of the peace and the county and district judges all conducted trials in the county seat. The sheriff, who had taken office when Winkler County contained a handful of land-poor ranchers, made an effort to enforce the law in the beginning: in April and July of 1927, he cooperated with federal officials in raids on local beer joints, arresting ten suspects, all from Borger, on the first incursion and eight during the second raid. The saloons, which had run wide open according to the editor of the *Pecos Enterprise and Gusher,* thereafter closed down when the revenuers neared town, resuming business at full tilt after federal agents returned to San Antonio.[21]

Victimless crime was big business in Wink. That few residents were willing to make local efforts to curtail it became obvious when Nan Hillary Harrison, the first editor of the *Wink Broadcaster,* attempted to rouse officials and citizens on the issue: she found no support. The Wink "syndicate" brought pressure to bear on advertisers, who withdrew their patronage from the paper; they forced a hotel manager to eject the editor from her room, and they paid a local thug to go push her around on the main street in midday. It is not surprising that Ms. Harrison hurried out of town and that crusading journalism disappeared from the pages of the *Broadcaster*. By mid-1928, there was some cause for optimism among those who wished to see law and order in Wink without placing local trade or local necks in jeopardy: Sheriff Priest hired a special deputy for Wink, and the bewildered Winkler County commissioners built a twelve-by-eighteen-foot wood-frame jail in the town. Unfortunately, these measures produced few changes. One lone deputy did little more than follow up on violent crimes already committed, and the new jail was so primitive that prisoners had to be chained to the floor beams to keep them from kicking escape holes in the walls. On one occasion, when the deputy arrested a dozen gamblers, local bosses dispatched their musclemen to the jail, where they freed the prisoners, roughed up the deputy, and bound him with chains. One green lawman and a crackerbox jail posed no more than minor annoyances for the gamblers and hoods who ran local operations.[22]

On occasions, in 1927, 1928, and 1929, the Texas Rangers moved into town, collared a few gamblers, and headed on. During their first raid, in 1927, they arrested two of the reputed kingpins of Wink crime, Henry Fields and Charles ("Heavy") Brackeen, for keeping gambling houses. Fields was also charged with possession of liquor, a minor offense. Thereafter, local officials tipped off the big operators well in advance of Ranger visits, and they discreetly shut down their gambling tables and whiskey stills for a few days, making up for lost time after the Rangers moved out. One of the big wheels among the bootleggers, William ("Blackie") Laughlin, escaped arrest altogether during the boom years; not until 1931 did he appear before a court, for possession of large quantities of Jamaica Ginger ("Ginger Jake") and beer for sale.[23]

Visits by the Rangers were not of long duration, and when the Rangers left town, law and order were once again in local hands. Even conscientious local lawmen were no match for their opposition, and residents of Wink knew it. In October, 1928, for example, the ranchers and the few male residents of Kermit who made up the Winkler County Grand Jury reported that the jail in Wink was inadequate; that the disappearance and intimidation of witnesses commonly made the law a dead letter; and that some law officers had been "slack and derelect in duty, if not guilty of official misconduct." The grand jury wanted the Rangers back and, presumably, wished for more vigorous action from Sheriff Priest. It also wanted privacy and security for its meetings, because several members had been threatened by the well-informed Wink syndicate. Little came of the courageous work of the grand jury, though Sheriff Priest, the object of some of its criticism, decided not to stand for reelection. His successor, Ray Clapp, hired a new chief deputy, Calvin A. Stewart, who was primarily responsible for the control of minor crimes, such as bootlegging, in Wink. Stewart had no more zeal for this task than Sheriff Priest had before him. When lawmen located a cache of booze, for example, they often sent the found treasure to friends and relatives, who drank up the evidence. Even had the deputies and sheriffs been bearish on prohibition, they might well have found their efforts frustrated by judges and juries. One-time District Judge Charles L. Klapproth, for example, told one interviewer that he was not "too sympathetic" with the liquor laws, that he was not overly strict in enforcing them, and, with regard to prohibition, that "the thing should be repealed."[24]

Facing a well-entrenched opposition and judges who disapproved of prohibition, Winkler County lawmen opted for highly selective enforcement of the law. Police, sheriffs, and deputies made strenuous efforts to arrest, and district attorneys to prosecute, all robbers and murderers. When two men, who had recently arrived from the Oklahoma oil fields, held up a Wink feedstore, they were tracked down by the deputies of Winkler and Ector counties in full force; but hijackers, the lone holdup men who specialized in robbing workers on payday, generally escaped arrest and trial. Brawls that resulted in maiming or other serious bodily injury led to arrests and indictments. These efforts to enforce the law, however, often ran aground when district attorneys sought convictions. Witnesses in hijacking cases often found it healthier to leave the county than to testify. Even murder cases, such as that brought against A. W. Morris for an alleged homicide in 1929, were dismissed after all of the witnesses had left town. As a result of such disappearances, cases were dismissed after long delays.[25]

The inadequate numbers of lawmen, reluctant witnesses, and broadly tolerant community standards made the enforcement of the law in Wink a sometime thing. In 1929, for example, apart from indictments for murder and armed robbery, judges in Winkler County tried only twenty-four defendants on other charges, which included sixteen motor-vehicle violations, four arrests for vagrancy, and four miscellaneous offenses, including tipping over a frame toilet.[26] The infrequency of indictments for victimless crimes in Winkler County indicates shortcomings in law enforcement, which gave Wink the atmosphere of lawlessness that was remembered by some town residents. Thus, when F. E. Summers came to Winkler County in 1931 to serve as a deputy in Wink, he observed that "a lawless element controlled some of the police officers, mainly in the city. I also found that the majority of the people either condoned what they were doing or [they] kept their mouths shut or pretended they did in order to stay alive."[27] Summers arrived in Wink after Sheriff Priest had made a political comeback by taking the census in 1930, thereby meeting all of the voters in the county. Safely back in the office he occupied until his death in 1937, Sheriff Priest continued to show considerable toleration of gamblers, bootleggers, and prostitutes in Wink. As Deputy Summers saw it: "I don't think anybody tried to clean up the town. All they did was try to keep the fights down and keep somebody from killing somebody, and pick up the drunks. That was about all the law enforcement they had."[28] According to Wink residents, the police were not even particularly zealous about arresting drunks, especially if there were two or more of them in one place.[29]

That law enforcement during boom days in Winkler County was difficult and not especially thoroughgoing is undeniable, but that does not explain Wink's unique lawlessness in the Permian Basin, where other communities were successful at maintaining a more conventional level of law and order. The explanation lies in the existence of an exceptional situation in the Winkler County boomtown: in addition to the prevailing tolerant view of victimless crime and ill-prepared law enforcement agencies, Wink had both a well-organized underworld and a corrupt city government. The combination was unbeatable, and it lasted as long as easy money flowed in Wink.

The kingfish of the Wink underworld, by all recollections, was Heavy Brackeen. He ran one of three large poker, black jack, and dice parlors in town and shared control of the flow of alcohol from Juárez and New Mexico with Henry Fields and Blackie Laughlin, both of whom also ran gambling houses. Heavy, a sullen and bulky man, had made half a dozen or more boomtowns in Oklahoma and Texas, most recently Borger. Ruthless with competitors, he was a soft touch for even bare acquaintances who looked for small handouts. Lewis Gray, once his bartender, remembers him: "Old Heavy Brackeen was one of those thugs. He was a good man, but he was a thug. Do anything you want for you; shoot you next morning. But he was a nice guy."[30] Heavy was not a man to be trifled with: nor could one take Hot Shot Ash, his right hand man, lightly. Ten years younger than Brackeen, Ash drifted from Burkburnett to Ranger to Three Sands and Cromwell, Oklahoma, then to Borger and Wink. At various times, he was a professional baseball player in the minor leagues and a carnival worker. The talents refined as a bouncer were applied freely at Heavy's prompting and Hot Shot, small, wiry, and armed, kept rowdy workers and would-be competitors in line. Under his eye, small local operators sold beer and ran small games, on license from Brackeen and his associates. For a small fee, local drugstores were allowed to do a lively trade in Jamaica Ginger, which they obtained from a St. Louis supplier and sold for two dollars per two-ounce bottle. As long as the small fry observed limits of scope and territory, they were safe from private violence and public prosecution. Wink lawmen were no challenge to Brackeen and Ash; as the latter put it plainly, "Heavy owned them." Sheriff Priest, familiar with many of the more colorful establishments, observed the "live and let live" conventions, stepping out of line on only one occasion, when he hired an overly zealous young deputy. When the deputy shut down several of the rougher gambling parlors, Heavy Brackeen responded by kidnapping Sheriff Priest at gun point. For several hours, Heavy, Hot Shot, and other Wink toughs, explained the salient facts of Wink life to the bewildered sheriff. Had there ever been any question as to who ran Wink, there was none after this widely talked about episode: Wink was an open city and Heavy Brackeen kept it that way.[31]

City officials were not likely to interfere in Heavy Brackeen's enterprises, for the two commissioners and Mayor J. R. Ostrom had their own lucrative ventures. The two commissioners, for example, took personal interest in public utility franchises, while the mayor turned the municipal court into a proverbial gold mine in the form of fines on oil workers arrested for misdemeanors. The legal proceeds from Ostrom's office, Mayor and Recorder of Corporation Court, came to more than six thousand dollars per year. The mayor was also said to have released prisoners, including prostitutes, without charge and trial, for twenty dollars paid under the table. The mayor's group extracted protection money from bootleggers and gamblers, as well as a percentage of gross revenues from prostitutes who worked the line. In this environment and with official protection, even the narcotics traffic proceeded openly in Wink. Some druggists and many bartenders sold codeine and morphine on demand, and one dentist routinely administered powerful opiates in his waiting room. When Ross De-Lacy, Wink's first police chief and, by all accounts, no dissenter to the mayor's various schemes, hired a drug informer in 1928, the city council fired the chief, paying off the informer several months later. The Wink syndicate also had its allies in county government; a county commissioner was closely identified with Brackeen.[32]

The extent of Wink lawlessness and corruption came to light in a series of underworld slayings in 1929. In November, 1928, Big George Hilmer, proprietor of a cothouse and erstwhile rig builder, balked at the wholesale liquor prices charged by Brackeen, Fields, and Laughlin. He entered competition with the trio, apparently without making a realistic calculation of his risk, and took to carrying a pistol. His precaution proved inadequate: an unidentified assailant shot him to death three days before Christmas.

Hilmer's murder was the beginning of a murder spree that lasted through most of 1929. Shortly after his death, a waiter who did not make good on gambling debts was dragged to death behind a car that sped up Hendrick Boulevard. During the months that followed, local thugs murdered another waiter and a cook after they peddled bootleg whiskey "without a license." By midyear the easy alliance between the city government and the Wink underworld showed signs of strain, as state and county officials reacted to the rising level of violence. Rufus N. Gilbreath, Wink's second police chief, began to cooperate on occasion with the sheriff and the Rangers in planning raids on major gambling and bootlegging operations. Word of Gilbreath's disloyalty apparently reached the syndicate: he was gunned down by an unidentified assailant on Wink's main street in broad daylight.

Yet another murder followed. John Harrison Northcutt, a former Texas Ranger, decided to break with Brackeen and set up as an independent bootlegger. He might well have made good on his effort, for Northcutt was known as a violent and ruthless man whose favorite barroom boast was that he had shot a waiter in Oklahoma City, "because he was a Chinaman." In Wink, he had been a particularly effective enforcer for underworld bosses, so much so that his threats were taken seriously, when he extended them to the sheriff, a local attorney, and Heavy Brackeen. Brackeen took matters into his own hands without delay and cut down Northcutt from ambush with a shotgun. A Winkler County jury, hearing the case two years later, decided that the killing was committed in self defense.[33]

Following the death of Northcutt, an abortive attempt was made to oust the Ostrom-Brackeen faction. In 1929 a loosely knit group of local businessmen and oil company employees decided to beat Ostrom at the polls. Realizing the potential danger to their lives, they organized and moved without a public campaign, and they seem to have caught Ostrom napping: the would-be reformers succeeded in obtaining appointments as election judges from Ostrom before their plans were known. On election day, however, the mayor learned that the reformers intended to keep his coalition of drunks, bootleggers, and gamblers from voting on the grounds that they had not established residence in Wink. In swift response, he turned to Heavy Brackeen, who sent a gang of professional toughs to the polling place, where they ejected the election officials. Intending to see their cleanup campaign through, the reformers turned to the county judge for relief. He obligingly threw out the results of the contest, which Ostrom had rigged after ejecting the reformers, and he ordered a new election. When the day came, Ostrom, now wary of the reform group, staffed the polls with his own men and kept Brackeen's supporters at the door to bar entrance to voters who were thought to sympathize with his opposition. In reaction, the reformers made another appeal to the county judge, who referred the matter to the county attorney, who brought it to the grand jury, which found inadequate evidence for indictments: thus leaving the Brackeen-Ostrom syndicate in control of Wink and frustrating Wink's single organized attempt at reform.[34]

The combination of broad toleration of bootlegging, prostitution, and gambling; sporadic and ineffective enforcement of laws; and municipal corruption made Wink almost as violent and lawless as the oil towns are usually said to have been. Even so, a number of observations on Wink's experience must be made in the context of boomtown crime. Wink was unique in the Permian Basin. No other community experienced the degree of lawlessness that prevailed in Wink. Its year of violent crime, moreover, involved no oil workers; it occurred while drilling and population were both declining. In any event, dead bodies did not appear inexplicably in the streets. Men were murdered, but far less often than the "blood and mud" writers have claimed: and for reasons well understood in the underworld.

Among the Permian Basin oil towns, Wink held the record homicide rate in 1929, about 85 per 100,000 inhabitants, when the national rate was 8.6. Quick computation reveals other startling homicide rates: 125 in Odessa, 85 in McCamey, and 38 in Midland, all in 1927. These figures might well suggest that homicide was relatively common in oil-field towns and that high rates of major crimes commonly accompanied oil booms in the region. In fact, such figures are highly misleading. The homicide rates are based on a small number of incidents, on a narrow chronological base, and on populations that were not representative of that of the whole nation. With a small number of homicides and relatively small populations, the oil towns, like other similar settlements, could generate astounding crime rates for short periods of time. That statistical freaks produce misleading conclusions is illustrated by another Permian Basin example. In 1921, before the discovery of oil in the area, Upton County had a homicide rate of 148: it was the result of only one homicide, and there was not another killing for six years. With one killing in 1926, Ector County's rate was above 150, but there had been no homicides in the preceding ten years.[35]

Though life was not cheap in them, oil boomtowns could still be relatively rowdy, and court records reflect a high level of illegal activity. In two months, June and July, 1927, there were a murder, an assault, a robbery, two embezzlements, and six thefts in McCamey. Misdemeanors included seventy-six convictions for vagrancy; local authorities often used this charge in lieu of prostitution, gambling, and bootlegging because it was less reliant on tangible evidence and rested only on the lack of a visible means of support. Additional offenses included blocking the alley, gambling (22), disturbing the peace (26), and drunkenness (10). One year later, the pattern was much the same, with a murder, an assault, a forgery, 2 embezzlements, 2 liquor violations, and a statutory rape case. Vagrancy (84 arrests) was still the most common misdemeanor charge, but arrests for fighting and disturbing the peace were only half of the 1927 level, possibly indicating a decline in street and saloon violence, as the boomers moved on and married production workers replaced them in the population.[36]

Snyder, to take an example from the later period, was even less violent during 1949–51, the high point for oil development in Scurry County. Its homicide rate was actually lower during this period than it had been during World War II. Local judicial records indicate that its principal law enforcement problems, like those of Midland and Odessa during the late 1940s and early 1950s, were oil field thefts and bad checks. In 1949, in addition to a single murder, there were 3 assaults, 4 thefts, and 1 burglary. During the following year, more than one-half of the indictments in district court were for passing bad checks; other indictments consisted of 6 assaults, 2 thefts, and single indictments for bigamy, possession of narcotics, swindling, and sodomy. The greatest number of county court defendants—96 in 1949 and 308 in 1950—were charged with drunkenness. The next most common offenses during both years were the illegal sale of liquor and the presentation of bad checks. Assault cases averaged 3 per month at the highest point, during 1950.[37]

Passing bad checks was one of the commonest oil-town crimes. The rapid turnover of the oil boom population made the bad check problem particularly difficult to deal with; a boomer might work through several areas of the Permian Basin, moving frequently and leaving a string of bogus checks behind. Lawmen, moreover, were concerned with violent crime; compared to assaults or holdups, bad checks were small change.[38] Once oil-field equipment became both sophisticated and expensive, oil theft grew to be a perplexing problem for law enforcers; by the fifties, theft of oil-field material was frequent in Permian Basin towns. In Midland County, Sheriff Ed Darnell and his deputies staged elaborate all-night stakeouts to trap thieves, detering but not stopping traffic in stolen materials. Drilling pipe, casing, tubing, engines, drill bits, and other items often disappeared from rigs and supply yards. A loose syndicate fenced stolen goods, moving them to Louisiana, Wichita Falls, and other oil producing areas. At times, these middlemen sold scarce equipment back to the original owners who needed pipe and tubing more than the doubtful satisfaction of seeing thieves and fences behind bars. Misappropriation of natural gasoline or "drip gas" was so common that it was thought to be more like borrowing than theft, and local lawmen did not try to prevent small-scale pilfering.[39]

For most oil-town residents, what mattered was getting on with the job and living with a sense of personal security: crime played no part in their lives. Even boomtown residents who still enjoy telling a few tall tales about the "rootin' tootin' days" recall no sense of personal danger:

Those days your husband went to work in the evening, all night . . . and you'd go to bed in that open tent: you never thought a thing in the world about it. We was never molested in any way whatsoever. Well, a whole lot of that [talk about violence] was press stuff. I think most any of them was a lot safer to be in in those days than some of these little towns are now.[40]

Midland, Odessa, Snyder, Tulsa, and the other towns that predated the discovery of oil in their regions, all had at least rudimentary police and legal systems before oil activity began. Just as important as their police

and judges, these towns also had standards of lawful and moral con-
duct, which they generally maintained, even under boom conditions.
In the newer towns, by contrast, there were seldom enough lawmen on
the job, and victimless crime was often subject to little day-to-day
regulation. The relatively large number of young, single, mobile men
in the oil-field work force attracted gamblers and prostitutes to all of
the boomtowns of the Permian Basin, and the failure of Permian Basin
law officers, like their counterparts in most other parts of the country,
to enforce prohibition laws strictly made it possible for bootleggers to
flourish. But a general toleration of victimless crime, prevalent in the
area's cattle towns before the discovery of oil, posed special problems
only when public officials were corrupt or inept, or both, especially in
new and remote boomtowns. No doubt, the Permian Basin oil boomtowns were often rough. The person who did not drink or gamble
heavily, however, was unlikely to be threatened by crime: he might well
have felt more secure then than now. The Bucket of Blood, whether a
scruffy saloon or a piece of purple prose, has long provided entertainment, but it belongs in the world of folklore, local wit, and imagination.
It is no more suitable a symbol of actual oil-field life than Pinkie's Mecca
Cafe in Hobbs is of oil-field religion.

Fifth Street in McCamey, 1928.

7.
Spare Time and Legal Amusements

ON BEING ASKED what he and others did for entertainment during the years he worked in the West Texas oil fields, one oil field veteran replied without hesitation, "You didn't have time for entertainment."[1] The pace of action in booming oil fields did not leave those who worked, whether in oil fields or the towns in them, with much spare time. Until the Great Depression years, when major companies shortened the length of tours, an oil-field worker would commonly work a twelve-hour day, seven days a week. He could, in other words, expect to work eighty-four hours a week, as compared to today's forty hours, excluding overtime. A pumper was on duty twenty-four hours a day; though he would not be working all the time, he was, as it were, always on call. Similarly, boomtown lumber yards, oil-field service companies, and auto and appliance outlets experienced twenty-four-hour demand. At the peak of boom activity, work was more important than anything else.

Yet, with the feverish pitch of activity, there were hours of relatively free time not exclusively given over to eating and sleeping. When tours changed, oil-town streets filled with people just off work and ready to unwind; some hours later, most workers would be either working or sleeping, and retail business would be slow. The stereotype of boomtown life notwithstanding, most people did not devote their spare time to illegal activities and vice. There was a ready market for harmless amusement, because there was vigorous activity to be had in clubs and organizations. What entertainment opportunities there were depended to some extent on the nature of the oil town; older established communities were likely to have a more varied range of available amusements than newly created towns. Most people's entertainment, however, was of a homely, domestic variety, simple amusements of the sort ordinarily encountered in a family setting. The ways in which boomtown residents used spare time were varied, if seldom sophisticated.

Among those who had oil-field jobs, spare time hung most heavily on the hands of unattached young men, the most mobile of all oil-field inhabitants. After a day's work, they had neither families nor homes to return to; if they slept in cot houses, they did not even have rooms to return to: and the beds they would eventually sleep in might well be occupied by other men until it came their turn to use them. With no immediate place to go once they were off work, young men in boomtowns did a lot of standing around. In a town like Snyder, where the center of activity was the courthouse square, young men gravitated to the sidewalks and grass around the square to talk, meet friends, swap jokes, and waste time. To one Snyder resident, it seemed like oil-field workers worked eight hours, slept eight hours, and sat on the northwest corner of the courthouse square eight hours each day; in that part of town it always looked "like there was a great exodus going on."[2] On a visit to Snyder in 1950, Bill Briggs saw two large, bored roughnecks on the street one evening bet twenty dollars on which of them could knock the timber support out from the wooden awning of the Dads and Lads Clothing Store with his bare shoulders: "[They would] just stand flat-footed with their toes against the post, a four-by-four post, and swing their shoulders into the post, like a mallet, to knock the post down. And it turned out to be a tie: it fractured both of their skulls as well as knocking down the porch of the store."[3] Making wagers on anything that could be bet upon was a common pastime among well-paid and bored young men. One Wink habitué, Hard Boiled Lewis, who worked as a roustabout when he was down on his gambling luck, took advantage of the popularity of betting by training his dog, Did-he-bite-you, to walk down a bar rail on four legs and back on two, a feat anyone would bet couldn't be done: Did-he-bite-you more than earned his keep.[4] For persons with somewhat more spare time, there were cock fights in McCamey and dog fights at the Odessa gravel pit, as well as more organized gambling enterprises.

Pranks and practical jokes were a common source of amusement at work as well as in town. Apart from amusement, practical joking allowed workers to let off steam. As one oil-field veteran explained, "You have to joke, kid around a little bit, to keep your mind off . . . [roughnecking work], because the physical labor as well as the danger is really tremendous on a drilling rig."[5] The "boll weevil," or novice oil worker, and the newcomer to West Texas alike were targets for conning into a state of confusion or alarm, to the infinite delight of all spectators. A driller would send a crew member new to the oil field to a neighboring rig to fetch a "maiden head" or some similar incongruous or imaginary item. An entire crew could be made to take to their heels in "boxing," as a former cable-tool hand recalled:

They would take a cigar box or some small box like that, nail the lid on it and nail a handle on it and crawl up on the belt house, and when the beam comes down, slip that box in under there and when the beam comes down on it [making a noise comparable to a cannon going off] the rig's fell in, no question about it, and they'll all take off. As soon as they quit running and get a chance to think, they'll know that somebody has boxed them.[6]

The unfamiliarity of newcomers with local wildlife of the nonhuman variety made it possible to terrorize them with tales of rattlesnakes, coyotes, and other creatures. One oil-field worker from Alabama was so alarmed at the stories he heard about vicious, man-eating coyotes that when he found himself alone at night in the oil field, he locked himself in an engine house and stayed there until daybreak: behavior that far surpassed the modest hope of tale-tellers to give him something to worry about.[7] Such amusements were always available, at no greater cost than that of the mental well-being of the butt of the joke.

Young men were not the only people to spend time standing around. Though members of families had many more varied ways of spending time than single men, it was a common family diversion in oil-field towns to climb into the family car and drive to the center of town, to park and watch people. This amusement also permitted oil-field workers to socialize with friends, often meeting people they had known in other oil fields. Men sat on the hoods of their cars, women sat in cars, and all gossiped to their hearts' content.[8] The evening's routine might be varied with a movie, or, for the men, with a few beers and some time in the pool hall, but the main entertainment was seeing and being seen.

Despite cramped quarters in tents and shacks, families not only socialized on main streets but in one another's homes. It was difficult to ignore one's neighbors when they lived in the tent fifty feet away, and most neighbors were in the habit of dropping in to see one another. As a former Wink resident recalled, "Wink was a place where you had to be at home because there was nothing much else to do."[9] Neighbors would get together for cards, and would cook fudge or pop popcorn, thus making their own quiet entertainment. Some families had windup Victrolas; young acquaintances with a fondness for popular music would buy the newest records and visit their friends to hear them played. On Saturday nights neighbors might move all the furniture out of a tent or shack and hold an impromptu dance, using records and live music of banjos, guitars, or the ever-popular ukelele. Radios were a welcome source of entertainment in oil fields near enough to broadcasting centers to pick up programs; it was many years, however, before radio reception was available to residents of Wink and similarly isolated towns.[10]

Those who lived in company camps or who worked in considerable number for a single company often got together to make their own fun, as former oil camp residents recall. Picnics, barbecues, socials, impromptu theatricals, and parties were common camp events. In Texon, as in many other oil-camp settlements, there was a community clubhouse for recreational events, but most often company employees would brave heat, wind, and clouds of sand to hold gatherings outdoors. Summing up company picnics, Alice Keene declares, "We ate enough sand."[11] But for all the natural drawbacks to such outings, they were pleasant, comfortable affairs. Company socials gave oil-field workers a chance to socialize, as with kinfolk back home, and get-togethers were as important to company employees in large towns as they were to those who lived in remote camps. A Midland couple, among those brought to town by professional work for the Honolulu Oil Company in the fifties, remember, "We entertained at home most of the time. If we did anything, it was at somebody's house. With the company, your friends were all the company people. We hardly knew anyone who wasn't in the company. At least once a month we went to one Honolulu affair or another and had a big party."[12]

Company employment thus offered not only an income but also a circle of friends: no one who worked for the company in a professional capacity was excluded.

Family socials could provide entertainment for children as well as adults. In new and isolated oil field communities as in crowded trailer parks, there were no parks or playgrounds, so children amused themselves as best they could in the dust out-of-doors. The favorite pastime of children in the new town of Crane in 1927 was rock-throwing: "They had no swimming pool, playground or park, no grass or trees, but they did have lots of rocks to throw."[13] Children in Wink sometimes congregated around the trash burners in company camps; with constant gas fires burning within them, trash burners were a favorite spot for marshmallow and wiener roasts. One man who grew up in a Wink oil camp recalls that the pipeyards and the substructure of an elevated icehouse were favorite places for play. Wherever they were, children drew what recreation they could from their surroundings. Tom Wilmeth, whose family lived in barracks apartments at Midland's air terminal in the late forties, recalls playing on the runways which, a few years before, had been used by bomber training flights: "I spent almost one whole summer dragging a dummy bomb from the caliche pit to the barracks. I mean, spent weeks. This thing weighed hundreds of pounds, and there were four or five of us. We dragged that thing to the barracks and got it up on the top floor and rolled it off. It took it about 1½ seconds to hit the ground."[14] Of all oil-field residents, children whose families lived in trailer parks were probably most disadvantaged in recreation, for the only space available for their play was that between parked trailers. Whether indoor or outdoors, they were in crowded quarters.

Once oil-field communities developed, more organized activities for children proliferated. Scouting, for example, found a ready following in Permian Basin oil-field towns. As small as it was, even Texon had its Boy Scout troop in the thirties. Some measure of the popularity of scouting can be taken by noting that Midland, a town of less than 22,000 in 1950, had forty-six girl scout troops containing eight hundred members. By the fifties, the YMCAs in Midland and Odessa offered recreational programs; there was no shortage of children's activities in either Midland or Odessa from the thirties onward.[15]

Since the population of oil-boom towns was a young population, it is not surprising that dancing, swimming, and sports in general were favorite amusements. In the late twenties, McCamey residents drove to a dance hall in Girvin, and Wink had at least three notable dance halls, a very respectable place in the heart of town as well as two platform dance halls outside the city limits. In Monahans, Jim Tubbs's dance hall drew large crowds in the thirties to hear big-name bands on tour.[16] Community barbecues were held by ranchers in Winkler and Midland counties; the whole community could and would turn out at these affairs.[17] Any opportunity for swimming was sure to attract crowds. McCamey residents both swam and fished in the Pecos River; when the new Yates Hotel in Rankin included a swimming pool and a dance pavilion, one former McCamey resident recalled that the Rankin Beach became "quite a Mecca for the oil field people." Wink residents went swimming in a pool at the Weeping Willow, a dairy near town, and in a concrete tank located southeast of town.[18] There were facilities for both swimming and baseball at Midland's privately owned Pagoda Park, a favorite resort of the thirties. With the understandable appeal of swimming in a hot, dusty region, it is not surprising that swimming eventually became a popular item in children's recreational programs in larger towns. Indeed, with its school construction well underway, one of the first nonemergency building projects taken on by the Snyder School Board of the early fifties was a modern swimming pool.[19]

Schools were not the only public institutions to promote swimming, as municipal and county governments in oil communities also provided swimming facilities. In 1939, after the small town of Monahans had enjoyed several years of prosperity as a local oil well servicing center, one civic leader ran a successful campaign for a city council seat on the "platform" that Monahans should have a public swimming pool: it had a pool, bathhouse, and park one year later. The cities of Midland and Odessa both built park wading pools for children in the thirties; by 1955 Odessa had four city-county pools, while Midland undertook construction of five city pools as part of a general parks construction program.[20] Swimming was perennially popular.

In southwestern oil towns far removed from big-city excitement, spectator sports always were crowd-pleasers. During the twenties and thirties, baseball was the reigning sport in oil communities; even small towns like Kiefer, Oklahoma, where there was little to do but drink, could boast of baseball games. In 1929, Midland, Texon, Big Spring, Thurber, Abilene, Coleman, and San Angelo all had West Texas League baseball teams; from time to time there were professional teams in McCamey, Wink, and Crane.[21] To have a professional baseball team was a sign that a boomtown had "arrived." Recognizing the importance of baseball in oil community amusement, many major oil companies sponsored West Texas League teams. Humble had a team at McCamey, and the Gulf Oilers played at Crane. Such sponsorship even included recruitment of players and managers. At Texon, for example, college baseball players were recruited for summer play and put on oil company payrolls; at Crane, Gulf hired a professional farm-team manager one summer for the company-sponsored team. One oil-field worker recalls being hired because he was a good ball player. Even the black community found a niche in the baseball world, as the Odessa Black Oilers team became important enough to play throughout the Southwest and Midwest. In the course of forty years Midland was the home of the Colts, the Cowboys, the Indians, and the Cubs baseball clubs. Midland city government licensed baseball clubs from the thirties on, and it provided lighted ball parks. In 1953, for example, the city took $80,000 from Midland's general funds to build a new ball park, the sum to be repaid from the sale of surplus city property.[22] To say that baseball was important in oil communities, then, is something of an understatement.

What school districts spent on the favorite oil field spectator sport, high school football, far surpassed what cities and oil companies spent on baseball. As school officials in oil-rich districts pumped great sums of money into high school athletic programs, football became both a community's entertainment and a source of community prestige. Always popular throughout the Southwest, there were a variety of reasons why high school football gained such overwhelming popularity in oil towns like those of the Permian Basin. In a region where ranching and farming long dominated rural economy, physical strength, coordination, and endurance found popular admiration. Rodeo was one outgrowth of the popularity of a display of strength and physical endurance. Football provided a showcase for the same sort of youthful prowess, except that boys took on boys rather than horses and steers. High school football also catered to another rural pastime, gambling; in Texas, where public gaming has been illegal, large sums were, and still are, surreptitiously placed on high school football contests. Football, then, fit in with these existing elements in regional culture.

More important in oil towns, football was one community activity in which a mobile family could readily find a part, because it was a school activity. The school was often the only institution to affect a family which moved every five or six months, and it did so because the law required parents to send children to school. An oil field student's mobility did not keep him from developing proficiency in athletics as it might have kept him behind in arithmetic. A boy who was a good football player in Gladewater could be a good football player in Wink: could be, and likely would be, if his father's company employer decided the Wink football team needed a shot in the arm. Oil companies not only hired men whose sons were promising high school athletes, but also transferred them to those towns in which the local football team needed immediate additional talent. So widespread was this practice that it eventually led to one-year residence requirements for high school athletes, a rule which then put pressure on oil-field families to let talented sons remain behind were the father of the family to decide to move.[23]

Wink, whose high school football teams achieved near-legendary area fame in the thirties, offers a good illustration of football's importance in Permian Basin oil communities. Wink's high school football program enjoyed not only ample funding but also recruitment aid from major oil companies active in the Wink area. During Wink's greatest days as a football power, high school students could continue on the team until they were 21, and, as a former football coach recalls, even beyond that if they understated their age.[24] Not surprisingly, the Wink football team was a notably burly lot, capable of intimidating teams from larger places. The whole of Wink turned out to see the team win home games and to enjoy community suppers thereafter. Great numbers traveled to watch the team when it played out of town.[25] Wherever the team played, the families whose children were in the game, or members of that necessary high school football accessory, the huge band, or simply spectators, could feel included in what amounted to a community effort. High school football gave everyone, transient or not, an immediate common interest, an immediate source of community pride. High school football was just as important in other Permian Basin communities, which vied with Wink and each other to put up expensive football stadiums and build high school athletic programs. Population may rise and fall with oil-field activity, but nothing has ever slowed down high school football in West Texas.

Because oil boomtowns were well supplied with young people making money, they offered a ready market for commercial entertainment. Before a boomtown was very old, it had its share of theaters, movie houses, pool halls, domino parlors, shooting galleries, skating rinks, and honky-tonks. As in the gold and silver boomtowns of the West, theaters were a favorite source of commercial entertainment in nineteenth-century oil boomtowns, but by the 1920s movies outstripped live drama in popularity and filled the place in boomtown life once enjoyed by theaters. The best patronized of all boomtown entertainment ventures, movie houses, even in remote and relatively small oil towns, often obtained first-run films. The Rig Theatre, the only masonry building apart from the school in Wink, often showed films simultaneously with theaters in Dallas and Fort Worth; by doing so, it attracted audiences not only from Wink but from surrounding counties. In 1929 McCamey had four movie theaters, Wink two, and Odessa two, the Palace and the Lyric; Midland could boast of four, the Yucca, the Ritz, the Palace, and the Grand. During its oil boom two decades later, Snyder acquired two new movie theaters and that entertainment innovation of the forties, the drive-in movie. Early fifties drive-in theaters in Midland and Odessa proved very popular.[26] A boomtown movie theater might be nothing more than a large tin building, or it might be as ornate as the Gothico-Egypto-Moorish Yucca in Midland. Oil boomtowns usually had at least one movie theater before anyone thought of paving the streets, and a town did not have to be especially large before a movie house appeared: even Crane, which did not grow to great size, had its own movie house at one time. The great popularity of movies in the late twenties brought some municipalities to attempt to regulate them, in response to church leaders' complaints that movies were competing with church services. The Odessa City Council decided not to allow Sunday evening shows before 9:00 P.M.; Midland city officials hedged at so hard-and-fast a policy, but told movie-house managers that Sunday shows would be prohibited if they continued to coincide with church times.[27] Municipal concern for public piety notwithstanding, it is unlikely that such regulations made much difference in either church or movie attendance.

During the twenties, Permian Basin municipalities demonstrated a similar concern for public behavior and morals in regulating tent shows, live entertainment that found ready audiences in boomtowns. Even isolated West Texas oil communities received circuses, wild animal shows, medicine shows, and traveling carnivals. McCamey, on a main railway line, was visited by no less than four tent shows during the spring and summer of 1929. One of the first acts of the McCamey Board of Aldermen was the passage of an ordinance requiring the licensing of tent shows and carnivals, and other municipal authorities followed suit. Both Odessa and Midland city governments barred tent shows from locating within municipal fire zones, a rule from which they seldom granted waivers. In Odessa, the new city council set a fee of seventy-five dollars for "police protection" for any show using a location within city limits. The Midland City Council flatly refused permission to the American Legion to bring a carnival into the city in 1929 "because of the evil influence accompanying such shows."[28] Skating rinks and shooting galleries also fell under municipal regulation in Midland and Odessa, though the two towns allowed the former to operate within city limits. With all these municipal attempts to regulate public entertainment, however, one municipality maintained an attitude of strict laissez faire with respect to entertainment ventures: the city fathers in Wink never troubled to regulate any commercial entertainment during boom days. In that respect, Wink was "wide open." Unfortunately for the entertainment entrepreneur, it was also somewhat off the beaten path.

Honky-tonks and roadhouses did a lucrative business in the oil fields. They catered to those who looked for something to drink and a good time; they also not uncommonly catered to those looking for racier diversion. For that reason, if municipal authorities tended to frown on loose night life, honky-tonk operators might follow the example of the proprietor of The Bucket of Blood, near McCamey, who set up business conveniently outside city limits. Location on a main oil-field road usually assured a honky-tonk of all the customers it needed. Thus Blacky Wilson's The Windmill, a lively gin mill located on the main road from Monahans to Wink, long did a thriving business. Two Monahans residents recall that during the thirties, the town had four honky-tonks: the Windmill to the north, the Flag Staff to the west, the Blue Moon to the south, and the Permain [sic] Club to the east.[29] After the end of prohibition, Ector County was wet; the legal sale of liquor and skyrocketing population growth from oil made Odessa a center for honky-tonk operators. Not only was there a thirsty population in Ector County, which was wet, but also an equally parched clientele from Midland County, which was dry. Midlanders in search of a high time, therefore, flocked to Odessa night spots like the Ace of Clubs; the probability of being snared by Odessa traffic patrolmen for drunken driving on the way back only marginally diminished the pleasure of an illicit evening away from home. Honky-tonks provided revenue in both the private and public sectors of Odessa's economy.

Prolonged growth and prosperity from oil permitted communities to develop public recreational facilities. In Odessa, where rapid growth was maintained from the mid-thirties through the fifties, county and city governments cooperated in an extensive development of parks and recreational facilities. Funds from a park tax, levied by the Ector County commissioners supported not only a county park with a swimming pool, bathhouse, auditorium, and playground equipment, but also acquisition of additional park land. The county and city cooperated in running summer recreational programs, and the city took over a considerable part of park maintenance. By 1957 there were ten county parks in Odessa, four with swimming pools; in addition to these facilities, the county built recreation halls at Goldsmith and Penwell

and a swimming pool at Goldsmith.[30] The combination of oil prosperity and a happy cooperation between government bodies brought
impressive results in recreational development.

In Midland the course of park development was not as smooth, in
part because city and county governments did not work readily together. Though there were a half dozen city parks in Midland in 1950,
the rapid outward development of the town created a pressing need for
additional park land. In June, 1951, Mayor Perry Pickett pointed out to
the city council that it should act quickly to provide new playgrounds
and recreational facilities; in September the Midland Jaycees told the
council it should build a new city pool; in May, 1952, the Parks Commission recommended that the city establish small parks throughout
town and supplement them with two larger parks. Clearly some comprehensive parks system would have been desirable in the growing city.
But when the city approached the county commissioners with a
suggestion that the two governmental bodies cooperate on a parks
system, the county officials vetoed the idea.[31]

That rejection left the city with the two options it had always had:
of developing a system on its own, or doing nothing at all. Therefore,
designs for a total system were shelved, and in 1953, the city passed a
$515,000 park bond issue; it provided for five new swimming pools, a
baseball stadium, twenty-one playgrounds, and a zoo. To meet immediate need, the city required that developers set aside 5 percent of
their tracts for park land. Shrewd developers discovered, however, that
such land could be dedicated in those low parts of their developments
which became "wet weather lakes." Indeed, the city started to pursue
one developer about a drainage problem only to discover that it had
somehow acquired the title to the land in need of drainage; the city
made the best of the situation by excavating one end of the property
and building a park on the other end.[32] It had better luck with its
expedient of park facilities on school grounds, jointly managed with
the school district. For the most part, however, it struggled alone, as
best it could, to provide parks for the growing community.

Though it was hard to build parks at the rate of town growth, it was
easy to subsidize private recreational facilities. In both Midland and
Odessa, private country clubs appeared in the late twenties. When oil
activity was off, of course, country clubs felt the pinch of recession, and
during the Great Depression, the cities subsidized the facilities. In
Midland, the city remitted all city taxes on the country club between
1931 and 1939, while in Odessa the city purchased the Bankhead

Highway Golf Club so that Reconstruction Finance Corporation funds could be used on the golf course; the latter facility later returned to private ownership. Even in good times, Midland indirectly subsidized private recreational organizations. In 1949 the Midland Women's Club built a clubhouse on city land, and in 1953 the city paved a road to and from the club building; in 1951 the city gave land to the Boy Scouts. In 1952 the city took over the tennis club's maintenance for five years. Piecemeal subsidy of private recreation did not require great budgetary outlay, and it broadened recreational facilities in the community.[33]

That public bodies were willing to subsidize private social and recreational organizations reflected the importance of organizational life in oil towns. The emergence of organizations—churches, lodges, civic clubs, social clubs, study groups, and charitable organizations—usually took place some months after the initial burst of boom activity. The most mobile elements of boomtown population, the young people who followed the opening of new areas and the drifters looking for whatever temporary work could be had, were not joiners of groups.[34] Oil company personnel, steadily employed workers, businessmen, and families settled into oil towns, by contrast, were enthusiastic group participants. For this reason, the great growth of churches and organizations usually occurred when communities gained substantial numbers of newcomers who could settle down for more than a few months. The one exception to this general rule was that universal phenomenon of the 1920s and 1930s, the ladies' bridge club, because it required only four ladies and a pack of cards. Most other organizations needed time to recruit members, find leaders, and acquire meeting places.

Churches were among the first organizations to grow with oil activity. In communities that predated the discovery of oil, newcomers swelled the ranks of existing congregations, making it necessary to undertake building programs and to establish new congregations in the most popular denominations. Since most newcomers were from the Southwest, those denominations strongest in the region were the first to grow rapidly; the coming of oil always meant the prompt enlargement of Baptist, Methodist, Christian, and Presbyterian denominations. During the peak of boom activity in Scurry County, for example, the First Christian Church of Snyder saw membership double in one year, after which planning started for a new church building. Feeling similar pressure of growth, the First Baptist Church of Snyder established missions in 1949 and 1951, but in the latter year it was nonetheless necessary to build a new sanctuary. By 1953, when a second

Methodist congregation was established in Snyder, the enlarged First Methodist Church had been overcrowded for many months.[35] Oil development also brought the establishment of denominations not previously represented in all small West Texas communities; Roman Catholic, Lutheran, Episcopal, Pentecostal, Church of Christ, and Church of Christ, Scientist congregations were among the churches that came to Midland and Odessa, along with oil. New congregations recruited members by newspaper advertisement or word of mouth; sometimes, as in the Episcopal Diocese of Northwest Texas, clergymen located potential church members through church records. New congregations met in homes and hotel dining rooms, as did Christian Scientists and Episcopalians during the first years of their existence in Midland; more often, however, space was borrowed from local schools for church services. During the growth of the fifties, thirty different congregations borrowed meeting facilities from the Midland Independent School District until they were able to build new or additional meeting rooms.[36] As different as some religious groups may have seemed to long-time residents, there appear to have been few incidents in which newcomers were not welcome; only the Jehovah's Witnesses, who were escorted out of Ector County by Sheriff Reeder Webb in 1939, seem to have encountered official discouragement.[37]

In remote new towns like McCamey and Wink, there were no existing church facilities. Before the coming of oil, residents of Winkler County could go to church only when an elderly preacher from New Mexico came to town, perhaps as often as once a month; they would then assemble in the courthouse and, as one Winkler County lady recalls, "He gave us that one sermon he had. We all got to where we knew, remembered, the sermon as well as he did."[38] For children who grew up on isolated ranches, such a gathering was enormously exciting: "These little girls, they'd never been to church. And they were so delighted over that. And they were asking me, how did you act at church, and did you get a partner like you were going to have a dance. One little girl who had been to church in Carlsbad, said 'Well, I've been to church once myself.' "[39] In thinly-settled counties church was no part of the daily life of either ranchers or the first oil-field workers; the oil-field workers, laboring twelve hours a day, seven days a week, would have found it difficult to attend church services in any location. But when families, businessmen, and professional people arrived in numbers in the new towns, they provided a population base for organized religion.

The first church services in new towns were of necessity community affairs, held without much notice in improvised settings. In McCamey a traveling clergyman held the town's first religious service on a street corner in December, 1925; there were no regular religious services until the following spring, when one lady organized a Sunday school which met in her back yard. The Sunday school relocated several times, to a shotgun shack behind the Burleson Hotel and an open-air theater, till it finally settled in the hastily constructed Westover School. Nondenominational religious services, like those in the Westover School and those held in Wink's first school building, were the first step toward the establishment of organized religion in new communities. A Baptist congregation, organized in July, 1926, was the first denomination to emerge in McCamey; it met in a wood and sheet-iron building that was used as a cot house nightly. Some six months later, McCamey Methodists organized a church. In Wink, as in McCamey, Baptists and Methodists were the first to organize their own congregations, but Presbyterians there also established a church at an early date. As one lady who attended Wink community church services recalls, "Suddenly there were churches all over the place," for six congregations grew from the original community church.[40] New congregations, however, often convened in rather primitive surroundings; a tent or simple frame building furnished with plank and nail-keg benches was all there was to many a boomtown church. But as Bessie Leonard, a former McCamey resident, summed it up, "Church was a tent, but it was still a church."[41]

A population with some roots in the community was necessary for the growth of religious and nonreligious organizations alike. Oil-field workers and families on the move had no time to be joiners, whether for religious, social, civic, or charitable purposes. As Martha Lyle recalls of the years her family lived in a trailer, "All I could do was keep house. I didn't do anything but [take care of] my home and my children, that's all I did. I didn't even participate in the PTA or anything like that . . . because there just wasn't time."[42] That most mobile oil-field workers knew they would not be spending a long time in any one community discouraged their joining organizations. Nor was that most stable element in West Texas population, the native rancher, much inclined to join lodges, clubs, and other groups; for ranchers, in so thinly settled an area as Winkler County, the travel necessary to get to any sort of meeting was no small matter. Those whose livelihood came from continuing production of an oil field, by contrast, were enthusiastic participants in all kinds of club life. When numbers of Humble management personnel arrived in McCamey in 1929, McCamey's first oil boom was over, but its boom in clubs was just beginning; in Snyder, similarly, the great growth in clubs and club membership came after the great years of oil discovery.

Midland offers the best illustration of the club growth which accompanied oil development. Excluding religious and bridge groups, in 1929, a joiner with the appropriate qualifications and sufficient income could have joined the American Legion; the Rotary, Lions, and Fine Arts clubs; the Midland Players, an amateur theater group; the Midland Bushers, an amateur baseball club, the Women's Wednesday Club; or Masonic groups. The Rotary and Lions clubs were only a year old. By 1950 a joiner's list could include the Jaycees, Kiwanis, Optimists, Knife and Fork Club, Civic Music Association, League of Women Voters, American Association of University Women, Business and Professional Women, Federated Women's clubs, Altrusa, Children's Service League, Daughters of the American Revolution, P.E.O. Sisterhood, Beta Sigma Phi, and the PTA of his or her children's school. Newcomers who had been members of national organizations in other communities introduced those organizations to Midland and other West Texas towns. The in-migration of educated and professional people, moreover, meant a rise in membership in such groups as the West Texas Geological Society and the American Association of University Women. Indeed, the establishment of a branch of the latter organization in Snyder came about as a result of boom growth that brought numbers of women with college degrees to what had formerly been a small farm market-town.[43] The in-migration of educated women also meant a proliferation of study clubs, book review clubs, and similar interest groups.

That clubs and organizations multiplied rapidly in towns like Midland indicates their importance to the people who came with oil and spent more than a few months in the community. Clubs were an easy means of socializing and meeting people in the newcomer's community; they were attractive even when joiners did not much care for the activity sponsored but simply wished for means of association. Clubs with a civic orientation offered the opportunity not only for contribution to, but for recognition in, the community, no ready commodities for a newcomer to town. Clubs also provided a means of focusing on community needs unanswered by governmental bodies. During the late thirties, for example, Odessa PTAs collected used clothing for needy children; they also cooperated with the Jaycees, Mothers' Clubs, Odessa Book Club, Odessa Study Club, Delphian Club, and American Legion Auxiliary to fund the distribution of milk and lunches to poor schoolchildren. In the course of the rapid growth of the fifties Midland PTAs gave schools audiovisual equipment and other substantial gifts, which removed some of the strain from hard-pressed school budgets.[44] Clubs also helped satisfy cultural hunger for theater, music, and fine arts; from theater groups emerged community theaters in Odessa and Midland, while community concerts and symphonic organizations grew from music appreciation groups. Such activity in Midland prompted one outside observer to note: "These people, intellectually isolated, must make their own social and cultural environment. They do it rather well."[45] Perhaps most important to the individual member, however, was the fact that such social participation in clubs offered psychological satisfactions. To belong was to enter the community. To belong to a lodge or sisterhood was to enter a circle of "brothers" and "sisters" when one was far away from kin. To belong to a national group was to bring one type of continuity to a life in which career advancement not uncommonly required moving to another locality. Belonging to clubs and organizations could, in other words, take the place of other types of belonging—to a family circle, to one's community of birth, to a circle of old and intimate friends. Clubs were interest groups: and much more.

Life in growing oil communities, then, did not consist entirely of working, eating, and sleeping, even though it may have seemed that way to those caught up in boom development. Apart from the general appeal of amusements for a youthful population, the diversions and pastimes that were most popular in an oil town depended on the sort of people who were most numerous at the moment. At the height of a boom, when there were many highly mobile workers in town, commercial entertainment of all sorts had a ready market. Because transient workers were not usually organizational joiners, organized ways of spending spare time, whether in religious, civic, or social groups, developed only when established production brought in families who settled down. Growth in churches and clubs, therefore, peaked after the greatest population growth was past. The more settled population, sustained by production, also got to use the public recreational facilities that communities took on once booms were underway; by the time such facilities were finished, the boomers and drifters were long gone. There were two diversions, however, which appealed equally to transients and settled residents in all Permian Basin oil towns: movies and high school football. At the movies one could use fantasy to escape from the hot, dusty reality of one's real life; at the football game one could feel a part of and proud of the community. Movies and football provided the heroics in everyday life: for other entertainment, the individual fell back on his own resources. Though oil boom life had its discomforts, hard work, and uncertainty, it left room for good times. Thus a Crane resident remembers the Saturday night parties in the family's two-room shotgun house: "We just had the best of times. You just can't imagine how much fun we had."[46]

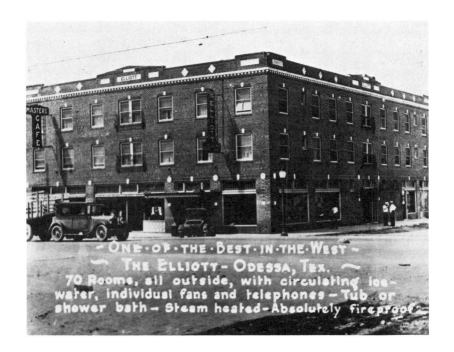

The new Elliott Hotel in Odessa, 1929.

8.
After the Boom

WERE ONE TO TRY TO SUM UP the feeling that prevailed in mineral booms in a phrase, "Make hay while the sun shines" would come closer than any other expression in describing the boom mentality. The excitement of headlong development and the hectic pace of boom life helped sustain both towering hopes for vast riches and more modest expectations of plentiful work and comfortable incomes. But behind the bouyant optimism of boom times there was always the apprehension that prosperity would be short-lived. Come what may, it was necessary to make the most of the opportunities of the moment and to move on when they started to dry up: for boom would be followed by bust. As one observer of the California gold rush noted, many newcomers regarded the territory "as a temporary home, a sort of huge goose, out of which a few feathers were to be plucked, and then forsaken."[1] During Odessa's growth from regional oil development in the late twenties, there were those local residents who predicted that the community "would slowly dwindle back to the sleepy cow town of some 300 population."[2] As oil activity in counties to the south brought people to town in 1927, the *Odessa News* reminded its readers of the ups and downs of Oklahoma oil towns, comparing local development to what was known of both good and bad results of oil activity in the neighboring state. Yet the paper tried to foster a degree of optimism: "One must remember Wink, Crane, and McCamey, and more recently Royalty and Van. They pop up over night, and many die out as soon, but some survive to make good towns."[3] Which towns would survive and which ones would not, however, remained a mystery to local observers and outside investors alike, and by 1930, as a decade of national speculation ended in economic disaster, oil towns had an undesirable reputation for failure among investors. Increased wariness of investors effectively dampened community development. The *Midland Reporter-Telegram* told its readers in February, 1930: "Under ordinary conditions Penwell would now be as large as Odessa, some oil men point out. But failures of other oil towns recently made the investor careful."[4] Yet, as the *Reporter-Telegram* noted, sales of townsite lots had begun to pick up in the Ector County settlement, so Penwell might, it thought, develop into a sizable town: "the producing fields indicate it certainly."[5]

As difficult as it was for those caught up in booming oil developments to see the course of the future, a pattern of community development tied to oil-field development does emerge from the history of Permian Basin oil-field towns. Once the misleading comparison of oil booms to natural cataclysms, events with an abrupt end in time, is put aside, it is easier to describe how booms wound down. Recollections of boomtown residents and public records alike show that in most Permian Basin communities the ending of the boom was a gradual process, a process whose beginning was barely perceptible and whose course varied considerably from community to community: booms did not simply end overnight.

Put in broadest terms, the boom was over for most oil towns once there had been a reasonably thorough definition of the economic possibilities of the area to which they were tied. That definition did not necessarily mean an immediate end to growth. The frenzied pace of development characteristic of boom times, however, came with the sort of speculation that ended once economic potential was more or less known. For most towns whose economies depended on oil-field exploration, then, the boom would begin to wane when the extent and character of area oil fields had been defined as well as existing technology allowed. Once the dimensions and nature of a field were fairly well known, drilling commonly slackened off. Once the principal pipelines and storage facilities were complete, the market for heavy labor dropped off. Increasing numbers of persons employed in some phase of exploration and initiation of production would thus move on to fresh areas of endeavor. Historically, declining production often followed decreased drilling activity, especially when fields brought to development had been in flush production. Flush production would not only rapidly exhaust small pools of oil, but the production of an enormous quantity of oil in a brief period predictably drove down prices, often to the point at which it was difficult to recoup operational expenses. Smaller operators in particular were hard pressed by such developments.

Once a field was in substantial production, problems involved in exploiting its oil might become more obvious than early wells indicated. The oil fields near Wink developed problems with water incursion before two years elapsed following their discovery. While there were technological solutions to these problems, it became evident that Winkler County oil would be more expensive to produce than oil in other areas. The large oil field discovered in East Texas, which insured that the price of oil would remain low, sealed the fate of Wink's boom. Production problems, East Texas oil, and national economic distress combined to put a period to Wink's startling growth.

When oil-field activity fell off, so, of course, did the rate of community growth. The job market for casual labor, however, sometimes tightened long before any great falling off in drilling activity. In Snyder, for example, the casual labor market contracted as early as February, 1950. The *Midland Reporter-Telegram* explained the lack of jobs for laborers as the result of oil company personnel policies: "Most of the new firms, oil drilling companies, etc., bring their own crews."[6] In contrast to the on-the-spot, no-questions-asked hiring characteristic of early twentieth-century booms, oil companies by mid-century preferred to move crews of experienced, skilled workers from operation to operation. Company personnel policies thus tended to phase out the old-fashioned boomers and drifters, as those who looked in vain for jobs in Scurry County soon learned. Company decisions, however, were not the sole influence upon the movement of oil-field workers. While a closing out of company operations would mean that most employees would move on, there were always some workers who preferred a change of employer, or even of work, to moving on.[7] A plethora of individual decisions governed the movement of persons in and out of boomtowns, and for that reason, McCamey, Wink, Midland, Odessa, and Snyder did not experience an overnight exodus of population.

When the extent and nature of an oil field appeared to be reasonably well defined, when extensive production had taken place and price levels had stabilized, when labor no longer enjoyed a seller's market, the boom phase of development had ended. But precisely what the economic implications of the end of the boom were varied with individual communities.

During most oil booms, especially in those taking place in remote areas, small settlements sprang up with drilling activity. Consisting of a grocery store or two, a saloon, several filling stations and cafés, and an assortment of tent and shack shelters, such mushroom settlements existed solely to meet the day-to-day needs of oil-field workers in the immediate area. As drilling, pipelining, tank building, and similar oil-field employment brought in workers, Winkler County settlements like Tulsa and Cheyenne thrived on meeting newcomers' immediate needs. Not all immediate needs to be met were entirely lawful. Settlements like Best and Crossett, near McCamey, supplied immediate needs for gambling, women, and bootleg liquor, rather than for groceries and gas. But all these towns depended for their existence on the large, transient population brought in with extensive exploration. Their economies were not diversified; oil-field supplies came from elsewhere, and there were no refineries in them. Such settlements undertaken by townsite companies, as in the example of Crossett, were often examples of pure real estate speculation. Guesswork determined their locations, and, as in the Permian Basin's Crossett and Tulsa, wrong guesses meant the speculation was a failure. In any event, these small towns, booming because of activity in the immediate area and nothing else, could not outlast exploration. For them, the end of the boom meant extinction: as their buildings were moved away to other sites, they quite literally vanished.

Most oil-field communities were not so narrowly tied to exploration in their immediate areas. McCamey, for example, developed initially in response to exploration and production in Upton County. But because McCamey was both convenient to oil fields in Crane and Pecos counties, and because it was located on a railroad line, it made a good base of regional operations for a number of oil-field supply and service companies; while oil-field activity in adjoining counties was lively, McCamey prospered as a modest-sized regional supply center. Humble Oil's decision to move management offices from San Angelo to McCamey and to construct a refinery there further broadened the base of McCamey's economy. Thus, by 1929, McCamey prospered not only from oil development in Upton County but more generally from development and production in the southern Permian Basin. When exploration activity moved to the northwestern parts of the Basin, McCamey lost its geographical advantage to Odessa. The town's development sustained severe blows in the 1930s when Humble moved its regional offices to Midland and closed down its refinery as well. These setbacks wrote an end to McCamey's hopes for continued development. Still, McCamey's growth had been based broadly enough to prevent sudden extinction or even precipitous decline. It had developed as a retailing center. Like many other oil-field towns, moreover, McCamey continued to benefit from continued production in surrounding oil fields, serving as the home base of operations of area production workers.

In a similar fashion, oil production sustained Wink after the drilling boom ended. Wink, too, had developed during its boom as a modest retailing center. Its isolation, however, meant that it was far less attractive than McCamey as a base of regional operations; unlike McCamey, no major company ever built extensive offices or plants in Wink. The unsavory reputation of Wink's early government, moreover, was no asset to promoting growth. Wink's economy, less diversified than that of McCamey, emerged from its first boom quite narrowly tied to production.

The greater the extent to which a town's economy diversified beyond dependence on oil activity in its immediate area, then, the greater the likelihood that it would continue to endure after boom days. Economic diversification meant that a leveling off of growth and the emergence of a relatively stable local economy followed the end of the boom. Towns like Snyder, which had had a long existence as farm market centers before the coming of oil, continued as more prosperous farm market towns after the excitement of the boom died down. Because some production personnel continued to be based in Snyder, the town's population never dropped to pre-boom levels. Snyder, like Kermit and Monahans, had the additional survival advantage of being the county seat. Economic diversification, taken with agribusiness activity predating oil, cushioned the impact of the end of the boom in towns like Snyder. They were quieter but still very much alive after the boom passed.

In oil booms, as in other mineral booms, those towns which continued to grow after the boom were important regional economic centers. The regions they served were wide enough so that even modest and unconcentrated activity supported their economies. They attracted new industries and became retailing and financial centers. They were thus in a position to weather highly localized downturns in the fortunes of the mineral industry with which they were associated and to maintain their growth. San Francisco and Denver were among the regional centers growing out of the extraction of hard minerals; among the regional centers for oil development have been Tulsa, Wichita Falls, Tyler, Midland, and Odessa.

Location played an important part in a town's emergence as an enduring regional center. Wichita Falls and Tyler, for example, were well situated respectively to serve the North Texas and East Texas oil fields. Given its location near the middle of the Permian Basin, Odessa emerged as the leading area oil-field supply and service center. But a town's development prior to the discovery of oil also played a part in shaping its growth with oil. Like Fort Worth, to which it was tied financially, Midland was the financial hub of a wide region; when oil development took place in that region, Midland grew as a financial center. Midland was located on a main railroad line. For a long time it was the retail center for the western half of the Permian Basin, and it had medical and legal professionals among its residents. All this enhanced Midland's attractiveness as a center for management.

In the late twenties, entrepreneurs like Dr. John B. Thomas, T.S. Hogan, and Clarence Scharbauer built office and hotel accommodations in Midland; to a company looking for a management base, the availability of office and hotel space made Midland a desirable location. Odessa could not offer as extensive facilities for management operations, but thanks to ambitious road building undertaken by the Ector County commissioners when it began to develop as an oil-field supply center, Odessa's ready access to regional oil fields promoted its position as a supply and industrial center. Odessa civic leaders, moreover, never lost sight of the dependence of the community on continued regional development, and they did all they could to attract as much industry as possible to the area. The town's modern petrochemical complex, developed during the 1950s and 1960s, was the fruit of their endeavors. Energetic local leadership, then, could do much both to build a small community into a regional center and to keep a town growing when oil activity was slack.

In few industries have science and technology had as much impact as in the petroleum industry. Scientific and technological progress had led to ever deeper drilling and tapping of ever deeper reservoirs of oil, as well as to greatly improved methods of recovery in older oil fields. For this reason, in many oil field communities the first boom, while likely the most spectacular in terms of growth, was not the last. After its initial boom, for example, McCamey experienced subsequent periods of rapid growth; situated amid rich oil fields, McCamey benefited from the continued scientific progress of the oil industry, as new pay zones were opened and new recovery techniques were applied in area oil fields. Similarly, the exploitation of the oil fields near Kermit created at least limited spill-over prosperity for Wink. When the high oil prices of the mid-seventies made it profitable to reenter older fields and undertake relatively new and expensive recovery processes, the economic vitality of many Permian Basin oil communities revived afresh. Once a town grew with oil, it was not as likely, as pessimists feared, to revert to the sleepy cow town or farm-market town it had once been.

The historical experience of Permian Basin oil communities not only demonstrates the characteristic pattern of development that oil booms follow, but also illustrates the kind of short-run problems common with rapid development. Oil booms always created sudden and pressing problems in housing and public services. Shortages of adequate housing forced workers into makeshift accommodations, a situation eased only by the availability of cheap mobile homes. While trailers were an improvement, they were no panacea, for, like tents and shotgun houses before them, they were crowded housing. The immediate problems communities faced with overcrowded water and sewer systems, like problems with crowded schools, varied in acuteness with the peculiar timing of population movement during oil booms. Permian Basin communities demonstrate that greatest pressure on water and sewer systems came soon after the onset of the boom; school crowding hit a peak somewhat later. Though these difficulties were predictable, communities could not plan ahead for them; they usually completed new water mains, sewers, and schools only when the boom was weakening.

Crime was one problem accompanying oil booms that was much less serious than authors have long described it. The thousands of workers and their families who came to the Permian Basin oil towns between 1920 and 1960 did not find those towns especially perilous. Occasionally, where there were inept or corrupt lawmen, underworld factions warred among themselves for the proceeds of victimless crime, a staple element in boomtown life. But when local civic leaders were determined to limit gambling, prostitution, and bootlegging, they generally succeeded in keeping the lid on shady enterprise. Oil boomtowns were always somewhat rowdy, but rarely bloody.

The short-term problems of oil booms were less important in Permian Basin communities than real economic gains from petroleum development. The continued production of oil, even in unspectacular quantities, generated wealth and jobs in oil communities long after boom days. Royalties and lease monies gave an often much-needed boost to agriculture, as oil income in farming country like Scurry County generally found its way into improvements of stock, plant, and equipment.[8] Lease money from oil operators enabled ranchers in

Winkler, Ector, Crane, and other counties to get through the hard dry years of the early twenties and the Great Depression of the next decade. While ranchers often granted oil leases for sums that were very low, the importance of lease and royalty money to hard-pressed farmers and ranchers was great indeed: it pulled many families through hard times and paid for substantial agricultural improvements thereafter.[9] As local ranchers observe, cattle seem to grow fatter when they have an oil well or two to scratch their backs on.

Economic gains from oil development showed not only in a community's agricultural income but also in the tax rolls of its public bodies. While the total taxable value of property declined after an oil boom ended, there nonetheless remained income-producing oil property to yield local revenue. Counties were most often beneficiaries from taxes on oil property, but depending on boundary lines, school districts and city governments might share in tax revenues resulting from oil development. Tax revenues from oil property enabled communities to fund lasting improvements for good roads, modern schools, and efficient public services; and oil development provided not only the income but also the impetus for communities to undertake improvement. While noticing a one-time boomtown's vacant lots and abandoned buildings, past chroniclers of oil booms tended to overlook such solid if prosaic improvements as water mains and street lights. Yet in many communities these improvements came only with oil.

If oil development brought real and lasting gains to communities, it was also a means of advancement for many thousands of individuals. The great twentieth-century movement of population from oil field to oil field was part of a far larger, more deeply reaching movement of Americans away from the farm in general, and declining, submarginal farms in particular. Men, women, and children entered oil-field life. Its hard work and primitive living conditions were like those on the farms left behind; its noisy, crowded settlements were a foretaste of urban life. Oil-field life had its discomforts and uncertainties, but it opened up a new horizon of economic promise to those who found but a bleak future on the small farm. The economic promise created by oil, moreover, was broad enough to include all who wanted work in its scope; women and members of racial and ethnic minority groups did not often work in the oil fields themselves, but they found a myriad of other job opportunities in bustling boomtowns. Boomtown jobs, moreover, paid better wages than the same work elsewhere.

As startling as were the changes oil booms brought to communities, the end results of petroleum development were, by and large, positive. Booms always created community problems, but they also created community benefits. Not infrequently, they created new communities. Much has been written of the fortunes made and lost in oil booms, of the wild speculation that accompanied boom times. That speculation, though a colorful part of any oil boom, occupied but a small number of persons. The vast majority of those who came to oil boomtowns were speculating on their own futures and those of their families. For them, oil booms did not mean social chaos: oil booms meant personal economic gains. Boomers, mobile workers, women, and members of racial and ethnic minority groups all accepted discomfort and uncertainty in the hope of getting ahead in life. Oil booms offered them the chance to realize that hope, to prosper in the present and to secure comfort in the future.

Top: Boomtown in the making:
Goldsmith, Ector County, Texas, in 1937.

Bottom: Lion Oil Company camp near
Snyder in 1949, when it was new.

Appendixes

APPENDIX A: The Origins of Labor, 1927–30 (Percentages)

	No. of Workers	TX	OK	AR	LA	PA	NM	KY
Promoter	5	40						20
Management, oil	57	47	9	2	7	9		2
Drillers	34	18		3	6	38		6
Tool dressers	25	60	8	8	4		8	8
Rig builders	11	46		9	9			
Truckers	49	69	12					2
Pumpers	19	47	10	5		5		
Oil-field workers	355	49	10	11	7	1	1	1
Engineers	8	50		25				
Bankers	4	100						
Ministers	3	33						
Lawyers	5	60						
Merchants	24	54	4	8				
Salesmen	33	70	9					3
Clerks	22	60		10				5
Waiters, waitresses	20	55	5	10	5			
Barbers	8	75		13				
Cooks	14	57	29	7				
Hotel workers	7	14	29					
Laundry workers	5	40	20	40				
Dairymen	4			25				
Carpenters	25	72	8	12				
Painters	5			40				
Electricians	8	25			13			
Plumbers	3	67				33		
Plasterers	2							
Maintenance	4	75		25				
Laborers	71	47	8	6	1			1

SOURCE: Workers were identified in death records of Ector, Midland, Upton, and Winkler counties for 1926 through 1930. Birth records of the same counties usually

TN	MS	AL	GA	WV	OH	IN	IL	KS	MO	CA	Other
							20				20
	4	5						5	4		7
		3	6	6				3	3	6	3
	4							4	4		
9				21							6
2	4	2	4			2		2	2		
	20								10		3.3
1	5	2	2	1	.3	1	.3	2	2	.3	1.8
								13	13		
33									33		
20											20
4	4							4	8		12
	3		9								6
5						5		10	5		5
5								5	5		10
											13
	7										
	14					14			29		
25		50									
4			4								
			20					40			
13			13					13			25
											100
1	1								3		32*

included occupations and birthplaces of fathers of children born within the jurisdictions, and were consulted for the period 1926 through 1930.   * Mexico: 30%

APPENDIX B: Estimates of the Relatively Permanent
Population and of Gain or Loss through Migration

Year	Midland	Odessa	McCamey	Wink	Snyder
1920	1,795	760			
1921	1,853	718			
	(+29)	(−59)			
1922	1,940	631			
	(+76)	(−91)			
1923	1,911	629			
	(−51)	(−21)			
1924	1,995	624			
	(+58)	(−14)			
1925	2,140	609			
	(+13)	(−21)			
1926	2,187	655			
	(+13)	(+22)			
1927	2,671	1,187	1,775	11	
	(+453)	(+522)			
1928	3,989	1,760	2,546	2,517	
	(+1,259)	(+539)	(+778)	(+2,502)	
1929	4,425	2,052	2,775	3,969	
	(+383)	(+237)	(+113)	(+1,464)	
1930	5,484	2,406	3,468	3,938	
	(+972)	(+310)	(+592)	(−69)	
1931	5,112	1,851	3,373	3,101	
	(−479)	(−590)	(−174)	(−876)	
1932	4,706	1,490	3,268	2,359	
	(−508)	(−420)	)−171)	(−776)	
1933	5,085	1,548	2,326	2,223	
	(+259)	(+8)	(−1,022)	(−176)	
1934	4,961	1,681	2,270	2,170	
	(−221)	(+110)	(−94)	(−99)	
1935	5,823	2,090	2,280	2,182	
	(+756)	(+360)	(−36)	(−110)	
1936	6,036	2,620	2,331	3,341	
	(+98)	(+457)	(+8)	(+1,073)	
1937	7,240	5,003	2,790	3,398	
	(+1,082)	(+2,306)	(+432)	(−10)	

Year	Midland	Odessa	McCamey	Wink	Snyder
1938	8,164	8,306	2,981	3,101	
	(+829)	(+3,189)	(+150)	(−387)	
1939	8,822	9,178	2,777	2,488	
	(+518)	(+666)	(−254)	(−703)	
1940	9,352	9,573	2,595	1,945	11,545
	(+368)	(+119)	(−232)	(−623)	
1941	9,188	9,187	2,402	1,570	10,108
	(−367)	(−647)	(−245)	(−419)	(−1,596)
1942	10,588	9,760	2,397	1,413	9,860
	(+1,251)	(+295)	(−40)	(−207)	(−391)
1943	10,325	9,123	2,128	1,462	8,371
	(−502)	(−925)	(−312)	(+19)	(−1,621)
1944	10,830	10,255	2,370	1,415	8,482
	(+244)	(+806)	(+218)	(−92)	(−21)
1945	12,377	12,692	2,693	1,547	8,041
	(+1,167)	(+2,038)	(+295)	(+95)	(−575)
1946	13,383	15,078	2,909	1,766	7,603
	(+626)	(+1,844)	(+187)	(+184)	(−542)
1947	14,456	18,160	2,941	1,675	7,565
	(+720)	(+2,540)	(−3)	(−156)	(−200)
1948	16,443	22,016	3,063	1,865	7,689
	(+1,570)	(+3,132)	(+45)	(+118)	(−228)
1949	18,712	25,408	3,220	1,720	11,411
	(+1,834)	(+2,442)	(+97)	(−235)	(+3,544)
1950	21,713	29,495	3,121	1,521	22,779
	(+2,384)	(+2,525)	(−165)	(−277)	(+11,144)
1951	26,417	33,754	3,107	1,375	25,313
	(+4,174)	(+3,139)	(−37)	(−236)	(+2,278)
1952	32,677	39,025	3,727	1,383	24,750
	(+5,290)	(+3,885)	(+532)	(−81)	(−1,133)
1953	37,436	45,059	3,679	1,287	22,025
	(+3,432)	(+4,355)	(−173)	(−294)	(−3,231)
1954	35,567	44,756	3,372	1,299	20,893
	(−3,076)	(−1,867)	(−368)	(−127)	(−1,403)
1955	37,333	49,532	3,308	1,395	21,167
	(+525)	(+3,263)	(−27)	(−82)	(−40)

Year	Midland	Odessa	McCamey	Wink	Snyder
1956	45,151	56,606	3,340	1,369	21,965
	(+6,449)	(+5,384)	(+48)	(−180)	(+432)
1957	50,060	66,318	3,558	1,490	21,916
	(+3,570)	(+7,705)	(+135)	(+34)	(−469)
1958	52,558	72,041	3,474	1,640	20,976
	(+1,074)	(+3,618)	(+163)	(+67)	(−1,317)
1959	57,525	77,446	3,474	1,760	21,713
	(+3,599)	(+3,555)	(−84)	(+26)	(+499)
1960	62,625	80,338	1,863	3,381	20,369
	(+3,714)	(+694)	(−144)	(0)	(−1,639)

Source: Our estimates of relatively permanent population were reached by determining the ratios of school population to census count population for censual years; the ratio was then used to project populations during intercensual periods, with the variation in the ratio from one census to the next distributed equally over intervening years. The net gain or loss by migration for a specific year was computed by subtracting the natural increase from this figure. The population data are from decennial census reports, and school population is listed in biennial reports and public school directories of the Texas State Department of Education, 1921–60. The natural increase was computed from the birth and death records of Ector, Midland, Scurry, Upton, and Winkler counties. For census data see: United States Department of Commerce, Bureau of the Census, *Fourteenth Census of the United States, 1920: Population,* vol. 3, part 2, pp. 955, 996, 1006, 1112; *Fifteenth Census of the United States, 1930: Population,* vol. 3, part 2, pp. 955, 1012, 1013; *Sixteenth Census of the United States, 1940: Population,* vol. 2, part 6, pp. 993, 999, 1000, 1002; *Seventeenth Census of the United States. 1950: Population,* vol. 2, part 43 (Texas), pp. 12, 30, 32. *Eighteenth Census of the United States, 1960: Population,* vol. 1, part 45 (Texas), pp. 23, 38, 40.

Notes

INTRODUCTION

1. For a common definition of the term, see *The Oxford English Dictionary*, Supplement, vol. 1 (Oxford: Oxford University Press, 1972), p. 326. For general descriptions of urban growth, see Asa Briggs, *Victorian Cities* (New York: Harper and Row, 1965) and Blake McKelvey, *The Emergence of Metropolitan America, 1915–1966* (New Brunswick: Rutgers University Press, 1968). A general account of defense industry relocations is given by Richard Polenberg, *War and Society: The United States, 1941–1945* (Philadelphia: J.B. Lippincott, 1972). On western mining camps, see William S. Greever, *The Bonanza West: The Story of Western Mining Rushes, 1848–1900* (Norman: University of Oklahoma Press, 1963) and Duane A. Smith, *Rocky Mountain Mining Camps: The Urban Frontier* (Bloomington: Indiana University Press, 1967).

2. Greever, *Bonanza West*, p. 166; Smith, *Rocky Mountain Mining Camps*, p. 10; for the general history of Pennsylvania oil developments to 1870, see Paul H. Giddens, *The Birth of the Oil Industry* (New York: Macmillan Company, 1938). The most recent study of Pithole, a spectacular but short-lived Pennsylvania oil town, is William Culp Darrah, *Pithole: The Vanished City* (n.p., 1972).

3. Franklin D. Scott, *Sweden: The Nation's History* (Minneapolis: University of Minnesota Press, 1977), pp. 448–51; David Wharton, *The Alaska Gold Rush* (Bloomington: Indiana University Press, 1972); Harold D. Roberts, *Salt Creek, Wyoming: The Story of a Great Oil Field* (Denver: Midwest Oil Corporation, 1956); *Business Week*, September 12, 1959, pp. 164–65; *Newsweek*, January 6, 1964, pp. 56–57; *Time*, February 21, 1964, p. 84; and November 30, 1970, p. 74.

4. Max W. Ball, *This Fascinating Oil Business* (New York: Bobbs-Merrill Company, 1940), pp. 7–21, 138–52; Robert T. Wheeler and Maurine Whited, *Oil: From Prospect to Pipeline*, 3d ed. (Houston: Gulf Publishing Company, 1975), p. 77.

5. Ball, *This Fascinating Oil Business*, pp. 15, 141, 144–45.

6. *Index to Oil and Gas Leases*, Winkler County, vol. 1; Kendall Beaton, *Enterprise in Oil: A History of Shell in the United States* (New York: Appleton-Century-Crofts, 1957), pp. 333–35; Charles D. Vertrees, interviewed by S.D. Myres, June 9, 1970, Midland, Texas. All of the interviews by S.D. Myres cited

are in the Abell-Hanger Collection, the Permian Basin Petroleum Museum, Library, and Hall of Fame, Midland, Texas.

7. Albert Raymond Parker, "Life and Labor in the Mid-Continent Oil Fields, 1859–1945," (Ph.D. diss., University of Oklahoma, 1951), pp. 29, 203, 204; Henrietta M. Larson and Kenneth W. Porter, *The History of the Humble Oil and Refining Company* (New York: Harper & Brothers, 1949), p. 122; D.E.L. Byers, *The Lone Gambler* (Casper, Wyo.: n.p., n.d.), p. 5; S.O. Cooper, interviewed by S.D. Myres, May 13, 1970, Midland, Texas; P.O. Sill, interviewed by S.D. Myres, May 12, 1970, Midland, Texas.

8. Charles B. Carpenter and H.B. Hill, *Report of Investigations: Petroleum Engineering Report, Big Spring Field and Other Fields in West Texas and Southeastern New Mexico* (Washington, D.C.: U.S. Bureau of Mines, November, 1936), pp. 127–30; Ora Lee Bowles, "Cushing, An Oklahoma Oil Boom Town," (M.A. thesis, University of Oklahoma, 1949), pp. 31–32.

9. Carpenter and Hill, *Report of Investigations*, pp. 104–7, 127–30, 140–43.

10. Gilbert L. Robinson, "A History of the Healdton Oil Field," (M.A. thesis, University of Oklahoma, 1937), pp. 7–8; *Odessa American*, March 12, 1972.

11. Carpenter and Hill, *Report of Investigations*, pp. 126–31; Bowles, "Cushing," pp. 34–40; Ray V. Hennen and R.J. Metcalf, "Yates Oil Pool, Pecos County Texas," *Bulletin*, American Association of Petroleum Geologists, December, 1929, pp. 1527–43. Hereafter this publication is cited as *Bulletin*, AAPG.

12. Bowles, "Cushing," p. 17; W.H. Collyns, interviewed by Roger M. Olien, December 12, 1978. The interviews by Roger M. and Diana Davids Olien are in the Permian Historical Society Collection at the University of Texas of the Permian Basin, Odessa, Texas.

13. The 1976 production of the Yates Field was 27,447,765 barrels of crude oil and 5,837,933 thousand cubic feet of gas. The Railroad Commission of Texas, *Annual Report of the Oil and Gas Division: 1976* (Austin, 1977), p. 276.

14. *Odessa News-Times*, March 28, 1930; *Midland Reporter-Telegram*, February 26, 1950; *West Texas Today*, August, 1929, p. 11.

15. Hans Peter Nielson Gammell, comp., *The Laws of Texas, 1822–1897* (Austin: Gammell Book Company, 1898), 9:644. United States Department of Commerce, Bureau of the Census, *Fourteenth Census of the United States, 1920: Population*, vol. 2, pp. 14–18.

16. *Fourteenth Census of the United States, 1920: Agriculture*, vol. 6, pp. 120–30; John Howard Griffin, *Land of the High Sky* (Midland: First National Bank of Midland, 1959), p. 77.

17. *Fourteenth Census of the United States, 1920: Manufactures:* vol. 19, p. 244. Griffin, *Land of the High Sky*, pp. 86–87; Mrs. Tom Linebery, interviewed by Roger M. and Diana Davids Olien, June 15, 1978, Midland, Texas.

18. *Fourteenth Census of the United States, 1920: Population*, vol. 2, p. 25; vol. 3, p. 1006.

19. *West Texas Today,* August, 1929, p. 11.

20. George T. Schmitt, "Genesis and Depositional History of The Spraberry Formation, Midland Basin, Texas," *Bulletin,* AAPG, September, 1954, pp. 1957–58; Russell Owen, "New Boom Town," *New York Times,* April 15, 1971; *Baltimore Sun,* February 15, 1948; *New York Times,* April 24, 1978.

21. Margaret Ann Price, "From Rails to Rigs: The Early History of Ector County, Texas, 1881–1927," (M.A. thesis, University of Texas of the Permian Basin, 1977); *Fourteenth Census of the United States, 1920: Population,* vol. 2, pp. 14–18; vol. 3, p. 996.

22. Byers, *The Lone Gambler,* p. 44; *Odessa News-Times,* March 28, 1930; William Paul Moss, *Rough and Tumble* (New York: Vantage Press, 1954), p. 94.

23. Samuel D. Myres, *The Permian Basin: The Era of Discovery* (El Paso: Permian Press, 1973), pp. 381–82; N. Ethie Eagleton, *On the Last Frontier: A History of Upton County, Texas* (El Paso: Texas Western Press, 1971), pp. 12–20, 26, 27; Robert McCamey, interviewed by S. D. Myres, February 8, 1971, Fort Worth, Texas; Mr. Walter Wingo, interviewed by Roger M. Olien, April 7, 1978, Midland, Texas; Claude B. Pennington, interviewed by Suzanne Agnew Pennington, September 19, 1959, Corpus Christi, Texas: Pioneers of Texas Oil Collection, Barker Texas History Center, University of Texas at Austin; hereafter referred to as PTO Collection. Cullin Akins, interviewed by S. D. Myres, June 17, 1970, Odessa, Texas; *El Paso Evening Post,* October 29, 1929; *Fourteenth Census of the United States, 1920: Population,* vol. 2, pp. 14–18.

24. *Fourteenth Census of the United States, 1920: Population,* vol. 2, pp. 17–18; Linebery interview; Clyde Barton, interviewed by Roger M. Olien, March 15, 1978, Kermit, Texas.

25. S. A. Parker, interviewed by Ann Smith, January 16, 1974, Wink, Texas: Permian Historical Society Collection; Clyde Barton, interviewed by S. D. Myres, July 15, 1970, Kermit, Texas; J. S. Peebles, interviewed by S. D. Myres, July 16, 1970, Wink, Texas. *Odessa Times,* November 4, 1927; *Pecos Enterprise and Gusher,* July 23, 1926; Clarence Pope, *An Oil Scout in the Permian Basin* (El Paso: Permian Press, 1972), p. 63.

26. *Odessa American,* March 2, 1969; Clyde Barton, interviewed by Roger M. Olien.

27. Myres, *The Permian Basin: The Era of Discovery,* p. 524.

28. Hugh Boren, interviewed by Roger M. Olien, February 21, 1978, Snyder, Texas; Robbie Knoy, "The Oil Boom in Snyder, Texas," (M.A. thesis, Hardin-Simmons University, August, 1950), pp. 1–7; Hooper Shelton, comp., *From Buffalo . . . to Oil: A History of Scurry County, Texas* (Snyder, Tex.: Feather Press, 1973), pp. 31, 48, 55, 59, 108, 119.

29. *Oil and Gas Journal,* February 26, 1950, March 9, 1950; *Midland Reporter-Telegram,* February 26, 1950: Hugh Boren interview.

30. Mrs. Wayne Boren, interviewed by Diana Davids Olien, February 23, 1978, Snyder, Texas; *Eighteenth Census of the United States, 1960: Population,* vol. 1, part 45 (Texas), pp. 23, 48.

CHAPTER ONE

1. David T. Day, "Petroleum," *Mineral Resources of the United States, 1910* (Washington, D.C.: Government Printing Office, 1911), pp. 336; David T. Day, "Petroleum," *Mineral Resources of the United States, 1913* (Washington, D.C.: Government Printing Office, 1914), p. 949; John D. Northrup, "Petroleum," *Mineral Resources of the United States, 1914* (Washington, D.C.: Government Printing Office, 1916), p. 371; John D. Northrup, "Petroleum," *Mineral Resources of the United States, 1915* (Washington, D.C.: Government Printing Office, 1917), p. 579; John D. Northrup, "Petroleum," *Mineral Resources of the United States, 1916* (Washington, D.C.: Government Printing Office, 1919), p. 698; E. Russell Lloyd, "Petroleum," *Mineral Resources of the United States, 1918* (Washington, D.C.: Government Printing Office, 1921), p. 982; G. B. Richardson, "Petroleum," *Mineral Resources of the United States, 1921* (Washington, D.C.: Government Printing Office, 1922), p. 413. For the Permian Basin, see Ralph U. Fitting, Jr., "Developments in West Texas Oil fields during 1947," in *Statistics of Oil and Gas Development* (New York: American Institute of Mechanical Engineers, 1948), p. 76 (hereafter, cited as *Statistics*, AIME); Ralph U. Fitting, Jr., "Developments in West Texas Oil Fields during 1948," *Statistics*, AIME, 1949, p. 30; Leonard H. Thawley, "Oil and Gas Developments and Production Covering 1949," *Statistics*, AIME, 1950, pp. 293, 302–3; Raymond E. Howard et al., "Oil and Gas Development in West Texas during 1950," *Statistics*, AIME, 1951, p. 417.

2. *Oil Weekly*, July 30, 1926, p. 88; Clarence H. Dunaway, interviewed by Roger M. Olien, April 30, 1980, Odessa, Texas; all of the interviews by Roger M. and Diana Davids Olien are in the Permian Historical Society Collection at the University of Texas of the Permian Basin, Odessa, Texas.

3. O. C. Profitt, interviewed by Roger M. Olien, October 20, 1978, Odessa, Texas.

4. J. S. Peebles, interviewed by Roger M. Olien, May 15, 1978, Wink, Texas.

5. L. V. Gill, interviewed by Roger M. Olien, May 15, 1978, Wink, Texas.

6. Hoke Tehee, interviewed by Roger M. Olien and J. Conrad Dunagan, October 11, 1979, Monahans, Texas.

7. John Swendig, interviewed by Roger M. Olien, May 28, 1979, Midland, Texas.

8. Arvin L. Eady, interviewed by Roger M. Olien, October 27, 1979, Midland, Texas.

9. W. H. Bond, interviewed by Roger M. Olien, October 12, 1979, Midland, Texas.

10. E. L. Frazier, interviewed by Roger M. Olien, October 27, 1979, Midland Texas; Lewis Gray, interviewed by Roger M. Olien, May 22, 1979, Kermit, Texas.

11. J. R. Wright, interviewed by Roger M. Olien, October 9, 1979, Mid-

land, Texas; Bond interview; Jack Steele, interviewed by Roger M. Olien, February 19, 1980, Midland, Texas; Albert Raymond Parker, "Life and Labor in the Mid-Continent Oil Fields, 1859–1945" (Ph.D. diss., University of Oklahoma, 1951), pp. 78–79.

12. Captain Robert R. Vincent, S.A., interviewed by Roger M. Olien, February 8, 1980, Midland, Texas; Steele interview; J. Ray Reid, interviewed by Diana Davids Olien, February 12, 1980, Odessa, Texas; L. E. Windham, interviewed by S. D. Myres, February 11, 1970, Rankin, Texas; all of the Myres interviews are in the Abell-Hanger Collection at the Permian Basin Petroleum Museum, Library, and Hall of Fame, Midland, Texas.

13. George Montgomery, interviewed by Roger M. Olien, February 19, 1980, Odessa, Texas; William C. Smith, interviewed by Roger M. Olien, February 21, 1980, Midland, Texas; Reid interview; Francis C. Stickney, interviewed by Roger M. Olien, February 5, 1980, Midland, Texas; Windham interview; Clyde Barton, interviewed by Roger M. Olien, March 15, 1978, Kermit, Texas.

14. Carleton H. Parker, *The Casual Laborer and Other Essays* (New York: Harcourt, Brace and Howe, 1920; reprint ed./Seattle: University of Washington Press, 1972), pp. 70–73; Peter Alexander Speek, "The Psychology of Floating Workers," *The Annals of the American Academy of Political and Social Sciences* 69 (January, 1917): 72–78; Eric Hoffer, "The Role of the Undesirables," *Harper's Magazine*, 205, no. 1231 (December, 1952); 79–84.

15. Walter Wingo, interviewed by Roger M. Olien, April 7, 1978, Midland, Texas.

16. For Humble, see Henrietta M. Larson and Kenneth W. Porter, *History of Humble Oil and Refining Company* (New York: Harper & Brothers, 1959), p. 382; Shell "farmed out" its acreage for exploration; see Kendall Beaton, *Enterprise in Oil: Shell* (New York: Appleton-Century-Crofts, 1957), pp. 364–65.

17. Steele, Stickney, Montgomery, and Smith interviews.

18. Mrs. Fred Leonard, interviewed by Diana Davids Olien, May 19, 1978, Midland, Texas.

19. S. A. Parker, interviewed by Ann Smith, January 16, 1974, Wink, Texas, Permian Historical Society Collection; P. O. Sill, interviewed by S. D. Myres, May 12, 1970, Midland, Texas; Sue Sanders, *Our Common Herd* (Garden City, N.Y.: Country Life Press, 1939), p. 78; E. N. Beane, interviewed by S. D. Myres, June 19, 1970, Crane, Texas; Ruth Allen, *Chapters in the History of Organized Labor in Texas* (Austin: Bureau of Research in the Social Sciences, University of Texas, 1941), p. 223; Wingo interview; Hood V. May, interviewed by Roger M. Olien, April 19, 1978, Monahans, Texas; George T. Abell, interviewed by S. D. Myres, November 24, 1971, Midland, Texas.

20. United States Department of Commerce, Bureau of the Census, *Fourteenth Census of the United States, 1920: Population,* vol. 3, pp. 985, 996; *Fifteenth Census of the United States, 1930: Population,* vol. 3, part 2, pp. 942, 971;

Sixteenth Census of the United States, 1940: Population, vol. 2, part 6, pp. 763, 1000; *Seventeenth Census of the United States, 1950; Population,* vol. 2 part 43 (Texas), pp. 63, 104.

21. The Reverend Horace F. Doyle, interviewed by Diana Davids Olien and Mrs. Willsie Lee McKinney, April 5, 1978, Midland, Texas; Mrs. Barbara Bass Lane, interviewed by Diana Davids Olien, January 21, 1978, Midland, Texas.

22. Luis Saenz Ramos, interviewed by Roger M. Olien with Mrs. Severo Hinojosa, June 28, 1978, Midland, Texas; Mike Gonzales, "Barrio, 1934" (unpublished essay, June 10, 1976.)

23. *Fourteenth Census of the United States, 1920: Population,* vol. 3, pp. 984, 996; *Fifteenth Census of the United States, 1930: Population,* vol. 3, part 2, pp. 763, 941; *Sixteenth Census of the United States, 1940: Population,* vol. 2, part 6, pp. 762, 1000; *Seventeenth Census of the United States, 1950: Population,* vol. 2, part 43 (Texas), pp. 63, 104.

24. *Odessa News-Times,* July 5, 1935; Charles W. Chancellor, interviewed by S. D. Myres, October 29, 1971, Midland, Texas; Burton F. Weekley, interviewed by S. D. Myres, October 29, 1971, Fort Worth, Texas; Orville Myers, interviewed by S. D. Myres, October 17, 1971, Midland, Texas.

25. *Midland Reporter-Telegram,* February 28, 1930.

26. See, for example, Ford Chapman, interviewed by Roger M. Olien, May 27, 1980, Midland, Texas.

27. Maria Spencer, interviewed by Diana Davids Olien, January 25, 1978, Midland, Texas.

28. Miss Allie V. Scott, interviewed by Diana Davids Olien, March 23, 1978, McCamey, Texas.

29. Upton County Medical Register, 1913–1927. Before 1926 only two physicians had registered in Upton County.

30. H. P. Redwine, M.D., interviewed by Diana Davids Olien, February 24, 1978, Snyder, Texas.

31. Edna Brown Hibbitts, "Patterns of Transiency and Population Growth in Midland, Texas, 1950 to 1975" (unpublished paper, April 20, 1976); Henry S. Shryock, *Population Mobility Within the United States* (Chicago: Community and Family Study Center, 1964), pp. 135, 167–68; *Seventeenth Census of the United States, 1950: Special Report, Mobility,* p. 244; the region surveyed did not include Upton, Scurry, Pecos, Reeves, Ward, and Mitchell counties.

32. Mrs. Fred Keene, interviewed by Diana Davids Olien, March 21, 1978, Wink, Texas; Mr. and Mrs. Ewell McKnight, interviewed by S. D. Myres, June 10, 1970, Odessa, Texas.

33. A. H. Blackiston, "Desdemona the Fair," *Sunset,* June, 1920, p. 46. The first issue of the *Pithole Daily Record,* on September 25, 1865, puffed up that settlement's population to "some eight or ten thousand or even more." See William C. Darrah, *Pithole, the Vanished City* (n.p., 1972), p. 4.

34. The *Pecos Enterprise and Gusher,* October 23, 1927; "Wink Townsite," published by the townsite company in 1927, personal files.

35. Midland City Council, *Minutes,* vol. 13, p. 302; Odessa City Council *Minutes,* vol. 11, p. 123; *San Angelo Standard-Times,* August 24, 1954; Robbie Knoy, "The Oil Boom in Snyder, Texas" (M.A. thesis, Hardin-Simmons University, August, 1950), p. 9; James G. Dunn, "History of the Oil Industry in Navarro County" (M.A. thesis, Baylor University, 1967), pp. 63–65; *Midland Reporter-Telegram,* March 2, 1930.

36. Our method, the Census Bureau's Migration-and-Natural Increase Method II, is described fully in Shryock, *Population Mobility,* p. 17.

37. Hibbitts, "Patterns of Transiency," p. 5.

CHAPTER TWO

1. C. P. Bowie, "Oil-Camp Sanitation," Bureau of Mines Technical Paper 261 (Washington, D.C.: Government Printing Office, 1921), p. 6.

2. See, for example, Charles E. Coons, *13 Months in an Oil Field and 23 Hours in Jail* (Pioneer, Tex., n.p., 1922), p. 47.

3. E. N. Beane, interviewed by Robbie Goodwin, April 17, 1970, Crane, Texas, Permian Historical Society Collection, University of Texas of the Permian Basin, Odessa, Texas; anonymous interviewee.

4. *Pecos Enterprise and Gusher,* October 23, 1927; *Midland Reporter-Telegram,* February 7, 16, 1950; *Odessa American,* August 14, 1949; *Odessa News,* October 14, 30, 1927; William T. Briggs, interviewed by Roger M. and Diana Davids Olien, August 20, 1977, Midland, Texas; Homer Johnson, M.D., interviewed by Diana Davids Olien, January 30, 1978, Midland, Texas. All of the interviews by Roger M. and Diana Davids Olien are in the Permian Historical Society Collection, University of Texas of the Permian Basin, Odessa, Texas.

5. Hood V. May, interviewed by Roger M. Olien and J. Conrad Dunagan, April 19, 1978, Monahans, Texas; E. N. Beane, interviewed by S. D. Myres, June 19, 1970, Crane, Texas; all of the interviews by S. D. Myres are in the Abell-Hanger Collection at the Permian Basin Petroleum Museum, Library, and Hall of Fame, Midland, Texas.

6. W. W. Allman, interviewed by S. D. Myres, June 19, 1970, Crane, Texas; Beane interviewed by Myres; P. F. Bridgewater, interviewed by Roger M. Olien, May 17, 1978, Midland, Texas; H. A. Hedberg, interviewed by S. D. Myres, June 26, 1970, Fort Worth, Texas; *San Angelo Standard-Times,* June 19, 1927; *Winkler County News,* July 19, 1960.

7. William Franklin Ash, interviewed by Roger M. Olien, March 2, 1979, Hobbs, New Mexico; May interview; Dr. and Mrs. H. P. Redwine, interviewed by Diana Davids Olien, February 24, 1978, Snyder, Texas.

8. *Oil and Gas Journal,* March 1, 1918; Mrs. M. A. Harrison, interviewed

by Carol Soderberg, July 5, 1974, Odessa, Texas, Permian Historical Society Collection.

9. D. O. Bowen, interviewed by Virginia White, April 7, 1974, Odessa, Texas, Permian Historical Society Collection; Martin Yates III, interviewed by S. D. Myres, January 21, 1970, Artesia, New Mexico; L. V. Gill, interviewed by Roger M. Olien, May 15, 1978, Wink, Texas; Walter Wingo, interviewed by Roger M. Olien, April 7, 1978, Midland, Texas; J. S. Peebles, interviewed by Roger M. Olien, May 15, 1978, Wink, Texas.

10. Hugh Boren, interviewed by Roger M. Olien, February 21, 1978, Snyder, Texas; Joel Hamlett, interviewed by Roger M. Olien, February 24, 1978, Snyder, Texas; Bridgewater interview; Albert Raymond Parker, "Life and Labor in the Mid-Continent Oil Fields, 1859–1945" (Ph.D. diss., University of Oklahoma, 1951), p. 170; James L. Horlacher, *A Year in the Oil Fields* (Lexington: Kentucky Kernal Press, 1929), p. 20.

11. Kendall Beaton, *Enterprise in Oil: A History of Shell in the United States* (New York: Appleton-Century-Crofts, 1957), pp. 74–75.

12. Mrs. Fred Leonard, interviewed by Diana Davids Olien, May 19, 1978, Midland, Texas; Dr. Merle Montgomery, interviewed by Diana Davids Olien, February 4, 1978, by telephone from Midland to New York, N.Y.; perhaps the Marland Oil Company went the furthest in providing fringe benefits, including medical and dental clinics in its camps and by subsidizing polo teams. See J. J. Mathews, *Life and Death of an Oil Man* (Norman: University of Oklahoma Press, 1951), pp. 154, 178.

13. Montgomery interview.

14. Mrs. Clifford Lyle, Mrs. John Hendrix, and Mr. Tom Wilmeth, interviewed by Diana Davids Olien, October 26, 1978, Midland, Texas; Mrs. Robert Boykin, interviewed by Diana Davids Olien, January 27, 1978, Midland, Texas.

15. Clell Reed, interviewed by Betty Fields, April 3, 1974, Odessa, Texas, Permian Historical Society Collection; Charles Vertrees, interviewed by Roger M. Olien, January 22, 1978, Midland, Texas; W. H. Collyns, interviewed by Roger M. Olien, May 9, 1979, Midland, Texas.

16. Carey McWilliams, *Ill Fares the Land: Migrants and Migratory Labor in the United States* (Boston: Little, Brown and Company, 1942), p. 63; Carl Burgess Glasscock, *Then Came Oil* (Indianapolis: Bobbs-Merrill Company, 1938), p. 21; Ruth Godwin, interviewed by Roger M. Olien, March 16, 1978, Kermit, Texas.

17. Horlacher, *A Year in the Oil Fields*, p. 41; Godwin interview; Mrs. Fred Keene, interviewed by Diana Davids Olien, March 21, 1978, Wink, Texas.

18. Keene interview; Leonard interview; Godwin interview; Bill Heaton, interviewed by Mary Horne, May 15, 1974, Jal, New Mexico, Permian Historical Society Collection; Mr. and Mrs. James Williams, interviewed by S. D. Myres, September 15, 1971, San Angelo, Texas.

19. Godwin interview.

20. Mr. and Mrs. R. V. Melton, interviewed by S. D. Myres, June 10, 1970, Crane, Texas.

21. D. E. L. Byers, *The Lone Gambler* (Casper, Wyo.: n.p., [1973?]), p. 38.

22. Sylvia Ann Grider, "The Shotgun House in Oil Boom Towns in the Texas Panhandle," *Pioneer America* 7 (1975): 51–53; Johnson interview; J. Conrad Dunagan, interviewed by Roger M. Olien, April 19, 1978, Monahans, Texas.

23. Michael N. Miller, "Victory Village" (unpublished essay, May, 1976).

24. Lyle-Hendrix-Wilmeth interview.

25. Ibid.

26. Hamlett interview.

27. United States Department of Commerce, Bureau of the Census, *Seventeenth Census of the United States, 1950: Housing*, vol. 1, part 6, p. 36.

28. *Fifteenth Census of the United States, 1930: Population*, vol. 6, pp. 1322–24; *Sixteenth Census of the United States, 1940: Housing*, vol. 2, part 6, pp. 323, 346; *Seventeenth Census of the United States, 1950: Housing*, vol. 1, part 6, pp. 30, 43–45, 70, 135, 141, 145, 146.

29. *Sixteenth Census of the United States, 1940: Housing*, vol. 2, part 5, pp. 323, 346; *Seventeenth Census of the United States, 1950: Housing*, vol. 1, part 6, pp. 36–38, 51–52.

30. *Sixteenth Census of the United States, 1940: Housing*, vol. 2, part 5, pp. 323, 346; *Seventeenth Census of the United States, 1950: Housing*, vol. 1, part 6, pp. 36–38, 51–52.

31. Building permits, Midland and Odessa; *Sixteenth Census of the United States, 1940: Housing*, vol. 2, part 5, pp. 323, 346; *Seventeenth Census of the United States, 1950: Housing*, vol. 1, part 6, pp. 43–44; *Eighteenth Census of the United States, 1960: Housing*, vol. 1, part 8, pp. 47, 48; *Fifteenth Census of the United States, 1930: Population*, vol. 3, pp. 1322–24.

32. *Sixteenth Census of the United States, 1940: Housing*, vol. 2, part, 5, p. 323; *Seventeenth Census of the United States, 1950: Housing*, vol. 1, part 6, p. 44; *Eighteenth Census of the United States, 1960: Housing*, vol. 1, part 8, pp. 47, 48.

33. *Seventeenth Census of the United States, 1950: Housing* vol. 1, part 6, pp. 45, 52; Hugh Boren interview; Hamlett interview; Briggs interview.

34. *Midland Reporter-Telegram*, February 7 and 16, 1950; *Odessa American*, February 7, 1950; Hugh Boren interview.

35. Briggs interview; *Odessa American*, January 3, 1955.

CHAPTER THREE

1. Midland Independent School District, *Board Minutes*, September 14, 1931. The Midland Independent School District will be identified hereafter as MISD.

2. On Humble's miscalculated venture into Eastland County, see Henrietta M. Larson and Kenneth Wiggins Porter, *History of Humble Oil & Refining Company: A Study in Industrial Growth* (New York: Harper & Brothers, 1959), pp.

126–27; see also Mrs. Jimmie Wagner, "The Ranger Oil Boom" (M.A. thesis, Southern Methodist University, August, 1935).

3. William Culp Darrah, *Pithole, The Vanished City* (n.p., 1972), p. 32; Frank M. Clark, "The Theatre of Pithole, Pennsylvania, Oil Boom Town," *Western Pennsylvania Historical Magazine* 56 (January, 1973): 42; Marilyn Diane Stodghill Trevey, "The Social and Economic Impact of the Spindletop Boom on Beaumont in 1901" (M.A. thesis, Lamar University, 1974), pp. 107–8; James A. Clark and Michel T. Halbouty, *Spindletop* (New York: Random House, 1952), p. 85; Ora Lee Bowles, "Cushing, An Oklahoma Oil Boom Town" (M.A. thesis, University of Oklahoma, 1949), p. 50; Carl Burgess Glasscock, *Then Came Oil* (Indianapolis: The Bobbs-Merrill Company, 1938), p. 223; Sue Sanders, *Our Common Herd* (Garden City, N.Y.: Country Life Press, 1939); Mary Rogers, interviewed by Diana Davids Olien, May 21, 1980, Midland, Texas.

4. R. C. Bowles, interviewed by S. D. Myres and Berte R. Haigh, October 7, 1970, Houston, Texas; all interviews by S. D. Myres are in the Abell-Hanger Collection of the Permian Basin Petroleum Museum, Library, and Hall of Fame, Midland, Texas; Miss Allie V. Scott, interviewed by Diana Davids Olien, March 23, 1978, McCamey, Texas; Mrs. Fred Leonard, interviewed by Diana Davids Olien, May 19, 1978, Midland, Texas; J. Ben Carsey, interviewed by S. D. Myres and Berte R. Haigh, October 9, 1970, Houston, Texas; Mr. and Mrs. R. V. Wilson, interviewed by S. D. Myres, June 16, 1970, Odessa, Texas; George W. Ramer, interviewed by S. D. Myres, February 12, 1970; all of the interviews by Roger M. and Diana Davids Olien are in the Permian Historical Society Collection at the University of Texas of the Permian Basin, Odessa, Texas.

5. Leonard interview; Dr. Merle Montgomery, interviewed by Diana Davids Olien, February 4, 1978, by telephone from Midland to New York, N.Y.

6. Upton County Commissioners Court, *Minutes,* vol. 1, pp. 620–21, 624; McCamey Board of City Aldermen, *Minutes,* vol. 1, February 18, 21, 28, 1927.

7. McCamey Board of City Aldermen, *Minutes,* vol. 1, March 19, 24, April 30, May 4, 9, 21, 27, 28, July 18, 1927, June 4, 1928, May 20, October 7, 1929; S. D. Myres, *The Permian Basin: The Era of Discovery* (El Paso: The Permian Press, 1973), p. 389.

8. A doubling or tripling of school enrollment was a usual feature in a booming oil community. In Seminole, Oklahoma, for example, where the entire population in 1926 amounted to under 900 persons, there were nearly 2,300 school-age children alone in 1927. Similarly, before the discovery of oil in 1931, the Gladewater Independent School District in East Texas served some 300 pupils. Within a year it had to teach 1,100 students, with only nine classrooms available. See Albert Raymond Parker, "Life and Labor in the Mid-Continent Oil Fields, 1859–1945" (Ph.D. diss., University of Oklahoma, 1951), pp. 218, 231–32.

9. Scott interview; A. C. Copeland, "History of Rankin Public Schools, Upton County," *The Permian Historical Annual,* December, 1972, pp. 21–23;

Upton County Commissioners Court, *Minutes*, vol. 2, pp. 18–19; McCamey Independent School District, *Board Minutes*, April 10, 1928, September 10, 20, November 6, 1929. The McCamey Independent School District will hereafter be identified as McISD.

10. McISD, *Board Minutes*, February 21, November 8, 1928, March 12, October 24, 1929, February 19, 1930.

11. McISD, *Board Minutes*, September 20, 1929.

12. McISD, *Board Minutes*, February 18, July 1, 1929.

13. McISD, *Board Minutes*, February 19, 1930, April 10, 1928, September 10, 20, October 21, 24, November 6, 1929, August 26, 1930, October 1, 1931.

14. Winkler County Commissioners Court, *Minutes*, vol. 2, pp. 45–47, 534; Wink Board of Commissioners, *Minutes*, vol. 1, pp. 1–3, 11, 27, 29–33.

15. Wink Board of Commissioners, *Minutes*, vol. 1, pp. 1–3, 39, 41, 55–59; J. S. Peebles, interviewed by Roger M. Olien, May 15, 1978, Wink, Texas; F. Ellis Summers, interviewed by Roger M. Olien and George Mitchell, May 22, 1979, Kermit, Texas; Wendell E. Cook, "The Wink Oil Boom," *The Permian Historical Annual* 6 (December, 1966): 18–19.

16. Wink Board of Commissioners, *Minutes*, vol. 1, pp. 44–46, 53, 67, 3, 62.

17. Wink Board of Commissioners, *Minutes*, vol. 1, pp. , 24, 68.

18. In the absence of reliable statistics on the general incidence of contagious disease, these rates must be used with a certain amount of caution. Taken on a small statistical base, they are indicative of type and relative extent of health problems rather than absolute measures of health with respect to national standards. Because of statistical distortion from working with a small base, the composition of which was not a cross section of the national population, mortality rates make oil boomtowns look much more unhealthy than they probably were. Much the same problem arises in working with crime rates. Death records, moreover, reflect the human fallibility of those who wrote down data. Doctors were not universally meticulous in their diagnoses, and clerks struggling to translate medical scrawls occasionally resorted to guesswork, producing such entries on cause of death as "serenity" and "horrible." Comparison of local with state mortality records reveals discrepancies between the two sources; figures which follow in this chapter are based on local sources.

19. Winkler County Death Records, 1929; *The Statistical History of the United States from Colonial Times to the Present* (Stamford, Conn.: Fairfield Publishers, 1965), p. 26; Bureau of Business Research, College of Business Administration, University of Texas, *An Economic Survey of Ector County Prepared for the Texas and Pacific Railroad Company* (Austin: University of Texas Press, 1949), table 14; Ector County Death Records, 1934–38, 1946–52; Midland County Death Records, 1950–53; *Midland Reporter-Telegram*, August 4, 5, 6, 11, 18, 1952. On the spread of gastrointestinal infections, see Sir Macfarlane Burnet and David C. White, *Natural History of Infectious Diseases*, 4th ed. (Cambridge: Cambridge University Press, 1972), pp. 105–7.

20. In 1927, deaths by such misadventures as auto accidents, burns, gunshot wounds, and stabbing accounted for 24.2 percent of Upton County deaths; in 1929 such deaths by misadventure accounted for 23.4 percent of Winkler County deaths. Upton County Death Records, 1927–30; Winkler County Death Records, 1928–30.

21. Cook, "The Wink Oil Boom," p. 9; Mrs. Neva Campbell, interviewed by Diana Davids Olien, March 20, 1978, Kermit, Texas; Mrs. Ruth Godwin, interviewed by Roger M. Olien, March 16, 1978, Kermit, Texas; Calvin A. Stewart, interviewed by Edd Cox, March 24, 1978, San Saba, Texas; Winkler County Commissioners Court, *Minutes*, vol. 2, pp. 26–27, 55.

22. Wink Independent School District, *Board Minutes*, May 1, 3, 17, June 9, August 9, 20, 31, 1928, October 9, 1929. The Wink Independent School District will be identified hereafter as WISD.

23. WISD, *Board Minutes*, June 14, September 10, 1928; A. E. Lang to the *Winkler County News*, August 29, 1960; Cook, "The Wink Oil Boom," p. 9; Godwin interview.

24. WISD, *Board Minutes*, May 2, 1929. The board had hired Thomas Y. Pickett to do oil valuations on January 3, 1929.

25. WISD, *Board Minutes*, August 31, 1928, February 18, 1929.

26. WISD, *Board Minutes*, May 1, June 13, 14, 1928, May 2, September 3, November 4, 1929, April 4, June 5, 1930.

27. WISD, *Board Minutes*, October 9, 18, 1929.

28. WISD, *Tax Rolls*, 1928–32; *Board Minutes*, February 17, June 12, October 13, 1930, April 13, July 31, October 12, 1931; Mrs. Fred Keene, interviewed by Diana Davids Olien, March 21, 1978, Wink, Texas.

29. On the early efforts of major oil companies to build a steady corps of reliable workers, see Larson and Porter, *History of Humble Oil,* pp. 101–2; Gerald T. White, *Formative Years in the Far West: Standard Oil Company of California through 1919* (New York: Appleton-Century-Crofts, 1962), pp. 522–23; George S. Gibb and Evelyn H. Knowlton, *History of Standard Oil Company, 1911–1927* (New York: Harper & Brothers, 1956), p. 577; and Henrietta M. Larson, Evelyn H. Knowlton, and Charles S. Popple, *New Horizons, 1927–1956: History of Standard Oil Company (New Jersey)* (New York: Harper & Row, 1971), p. 352. W. H. Collyns, interviewed by Roger M. Olien, May 9, 1979, Midland, Texas; Henry A. Meadows, interviewed by Roger M. Olien, May 17, 1978, Midland, Texas.

30. Odessa City Council, *Minutes,* vol. 1, pp. 2–3, 50, 53, 69–73.

31. City of Midland, "Building Code," June 19, 1928; Midland City Council, *Minutes,* vol. 3A, p. 42; Bowles, "Cushing," p. 68; John Derwin Palmer, "A History of the Desdemona Oil Boom" (M.A. thesis, Hardin-Simmons University, 1938), pp. 107–10. Darrah stressed the importance of devastating fires in the decline of Pithole; Darrah, *Pithole,* pp. 161–71.

32. Odessa City Council, *Minutes,* vol. 2, p. 252.

33. Odessa City Council, *Minutes,* vol. 2, pp. 260, 266–72.

34. Odessa City Council, *Minutes*, vol. 1, pp. 26–29, 82; vol. 2, p. 11; vol. 4, p. 114, vol. 5, p. 195; vol. 6, pp. 262–63; vol. 8, pp. 31, 46; vol. 9, pp. 208–9; *Odessa American*, January 1, 1948, September 17, 1961.

35. Odessa City Council, *Minutes*, vol. 8, pp. 76–78; vol. 11, p. 105.

36. Odessa City Council, *Minutes*, vol. 7, pp. 147, 236; *Odessa American*, January 28, 1949, January 2, 1953, January 1, 1954, September 17, 1961; Ector County Death Records, 1950–52.

37. Ector County Commissioners Court, *Minutes*, vol. 4, p. 104; Ector County Independent School District, *Board Minutes*, November 1, 1937, March 24, 1939; Odessa City Council, *Minutes*, vol. 3, p. 3; *Odessa News-Times*, March 24, 26, 1939; *Odessa American*, September 14, 1941. The Ector County Independent School District will hereafter be identified as ECISD.

38. ECISD, *Board Minutes*, September 22, 1922, November 1, December 26, 1926, April 18, 1928.

39. ECISD, *Board Minutes*, May 17, 1948; Gail Smith, interviewed by Betty Clary, n.d., Odessa, Texas, Permian Historical Society Collection.

40. ECISD, *Board Minutes*, April 5, August 11, 25, 1930, September 9, 1937, May 16, 1940.

41. ECISD, *Board Minutes*, August 9, 1937, June 9, November 13, 1948, June 9, 1960.

42. ECISD, *Board Minutes*, February 19, October 29, 1951, January 10, March 13, September 22, October 7, December 11, 1952, January 21, 1953, May 13, 1936, April 12, 1939, April 22, 1950, March 10, 1951, October 13, 1952, February 1, 1954, July 16, 1942, June 19, 1945, August 11, 23, 1955, and *passim*.

43. Cope Routh, "The Design of the City," *Objectives for Midland* (Midland: Midland Chamber of Commerce, 1967), p. 11.

44. *Midland Reporter-Telegram*, May 13, 1943; Midland City Council, *Minutes*, vol. 4, p. 662; vol. 5, p. 136; vol. 8, p. 857; vol. 9A, p. 907; vol. 11, p. 19.

45. Midland City Council, *Minutes*, vol. 7, pp. 828, 838, 840; vol. 8, p. 899; vol. 9B, p. 23; vol. 10, pp. 218–19, 375–77, 461; Perry D. Pickett, interviewed by Roger M. Olien, May 18, 1978, Midland, Texas; P.F. Bridgewater, interviewed by Roger M. Olien, May 17, 1978, Midland, Texas. Joining the water district in the early fifties would have put considerable strain on city finances, which were already hard pressed by development, and this, too, may have induced city government to avoid regional activity. But continued problems with summertime water supply went unresolved by development of city water-fields, and Midland ultimately joined the Colorado River Municipal Water Authority.

46. *Midland Reporter-Telegram*, July 10, 14, August 4, 5, 6, 11, 17, 18, 24, 1952; Midland City Council, *Minutes*, vol. 11, pp. 106, 138–39, 144, 164, 332, 489, 590; Pickett interview; Mrs. Helen Steck, interviewed by Diana Davids Olien, April 7, 1978, Midland, Texas; Midland County Death Records, 1952.

47. Midland City Council, *Minutes*, vol. 11, pp. 53, 85; vol. 10, p. 213; vol. 12, pp. 389–91; vol. 14, p. 153.

48. Midland City Council, *Minutes*, vol. 11, p. 313.

49. Midland County Commissioners Court, *Minutes*, vol. 5, p. 391; vol. 7, p. 58; Midland City Council, *Minutes*, vol. 11, pp. 92–93; vol. 15, pp. 137, 169. In January, 1953, the Midland County Commissioners voted to pay the County Health Officer a salary of $37.50 a month; they also agreed to pay the Cattle Protective Association $110 a month; *Minutes*, vol. 7, p. 93.

50. Midland City Council, *Minutes*, vol. 9C, p. 932; vol. 15, p. 297; "The Midland City Plan" (Midland, 1950).

51. Ione Moran, "Housing," in *Objectives for Midland*; Meadows interview; Bridgewater interview; Midland City Council, *Minutes*, vol. 11, pp. 335, 340; vol. 14, p. 26; vol. 16, pp. 278–79.

52. *Midland Reporter-Telegram*, January 1, 1960; MISD, *Board Minutes*, January 11, 1949, May 9, October 10, December 14, 1950, January 9, March 15, April 13, 1951, September 19, 1952, September 14, 1954, and *passim*.

53. MISD, *Board Minutes*, September 26, 1954, February 28, April 10, 1956.

54. MISD, *Board Minutes*, May 13, July 8, 1958.

55. MISD, *Board Minutes*, September 23, 1957, April 18, 1956.

56. MISD, *Board Minutes*, April 19, 1956. The experts predicted an enrollment for 1960–61 of 21,691. Actual enrollment was 16,442.

57. Dr. and Mrs. H.P. Redwine, interviewed by Diana Davids Olien, February 24, 1978, Snyder, Texas; Joel Hamlett, interviewed by Roger M. Olien, February 24, 1978, Snyder, Texas; Mrs. Wayne Boren, interviewed by Diana Davids Olien, February 23, 1978, Snyder, Texas; Snyder City Council, *Minutes*, vol. 5, pp. 61, 63, 65.

58. Robbie Knoy, "The Oil Boom in Snyder, Texas," (M.A. thesis, Hardin-Simmons University, August, 1950), p. 15; Redwine interview; Hugh Boren, interviewed by Roger M. Olien, February 21, 1978, Snyder, Texas; Hamlett interview; Snyder City Council, *Minutes*, vol. 5, p. 71.

59. Snyder City Council, *Minutes*, vol. 5, pp. 86–87, 160; Knoy, "The Oil Boom in Snyder, Texas," pp. 16–17, 27; *Fort Worth Star-Telegram*, February 21, 1954.

60. Snyder Independent School District, *Board Minutes*, September 19, November 1, 1949, January 26, 1950; "Good Schools Exist for the Children" (Snyder, 1953). The Snyder Independent School District will hereafter be identified as SISD.

61. "Good Schools Exist for the Children"; Humble Oil's K. L. Sappington was a member of the school boards of both McCamey and Wink.

62. SISD, Board Minutes, September 26, 1950, May 8, 1951. Similarly, in 1937, Gulf Oil loaned the Ector County Independent School District $50,000 at 4 percent interest, to cover costs of construction and operations; the prevailing rate at the time was 6 percent. ECISD, *Board Minutes*, July 28, 1937; Board of Equalization, *Minutes*, June 23, 1937.

63. SISD, *Board Minutes,* November 21, 1950, January 23, March 20, August 14, 1951, June 30, July 13, 1953.

CHAPTER FOUR

1. Carl Coke Rister, *Oil! Titan of the Southwest* (Norman: University of Oklahoma Press, 1949), p. 247; Carl Burgess Glasscock, *Then Came Oil* (Indianapolis: The Bobbs-Merrill Company, 1938), p. 223.

2. Rister, *Oil!,* pp. 167, 155. For an extended portrait of a boomtown bad woman, see John P. ("Slim") Jones, *Borger, The Little Oklahoma* (n.p., n.d.), part 2, which contains the "true" story of a "well educated" girl whose fondness for opium led her to prostitution and an early death.

3. United States Department of Commerce, Bureau of the Census, *Fourteenth Census of the United States, 1920: Population,* vol. 3, table 9; *Fifteenth Census of the United States, 1930: Population,* vol. 3, part 2, pp. 955, 985, 989, 990; *Sixteenth Census of the United States, 1940: Population,* vol. 2, part 6, p. 1002; *Seventeenth Census of the United States, 1950: Population,* vol. 2, part 43 (Texas), p. 23.

4. Sue Sanders, *Our Common Herd* (Garden City, N.Y.: Country Life Press, 1939), pp. 74, 115–17; Hood V. May, interviewed by Roger M. Olien, April 19, 1978, Monahans, Texas; Mrs. Fred Leonard, interviewed by Diana Davids Olien, May 19, 1978, Midland, Texas; Allie V. Scott, interviewed by Diana Davids Olien, March 23, 1978, McCamey, Texas; Ruth Godwin, interviewed by Roger M. Olien, March 16, 1978, Kermit, Texas.

5. John P. ("Slim") Jones, "Ten Years in the Oil Fields," in Borger, *The Little Oklahoma,* part 1, p. 154; Sanders, *Our Common Herd,* p. 133.

6. *Fourteenth Census of the United States, 1920: Detailed Statistics for Mining Industries:* 1919, table 7, p. 263. Albert Raymond Parker, "Life and Labor in the Mid-Continent Oil Fields, 1859–1945" (Ph.D. diss., University of Oklahoma, 1951), p. 256. Similarly, there were women oil operators and lease brokers, but they were extremely few in number; again, the perception of the oil fields as a place for men and the oil business as a man's business may explain this. The financial transactions involved in both independent oil and lease brokerage were a type of activity in which women did not commonly take part.

7. *Sixteenth Census of the United States, 1940: Population,* vol. 2, part 6, pp. 866, 878, 883, 886, 999, 1000; *Seventeenth Census of the United States, 1950: Population,* vol. 2, part *43* (Texas), pp. 114, 115, 117. *Eighteenth Census of the United States, 1960: Population,* vol. 1, part 45 (Texas), p. 389.

8. Miss Maria Spencer, interviewed by Diana Davids Olien, January 25, 1978, Midland, Texas.

9. Ibid.

10. Mrs. Charles Vertrees, interviewed by Diana Davids Olien, January 22, 1978, Midland, Texas; Spencer interview; West Texas Geological Society,

Membership Directories, 1946–58; *Midland Reporter-Telegram,* February 27, 1949, March 24, 1963. The directories of the West Texas Geological Society record the following numbers of women members: 15 in 1946, 11 in 1948, 14 in 1950, 12 in 1951, 16 in 1952, 20 in 1953, 16 in 1954, 14 in 1955, and 11 in 1958. To some degree these figures reflect overall oil activity in the Permian Basin, but the dip in membership in 1951, during the Spraberry boom, indicates that the level of oil activity alone cannot be used to explain women's membership. The number of women members in the Society changed relatively little compared to rapid growth of male membership; it must be remembered that far more men than women set out to pursue careers in geosciences.

11. Mrs. Hoke Tehee, interviewed by Roger M. Olien and J. Conrad Dunagan, October 11, 1979, Monahans, Texas; Leonard interview; J. S. Peebles, interviewed by Roger M. Olien, May 15, 1978, Wink, Texas; Niles B. Winter, interviewed by S. D. Myres, May 11, 1970, Midland, Texas; S. A. Parker, interviewed by Ann Smith, January 16, 1974, Wink, Texas, Permian Historical Society Collection; James L. Horlacher, *A Year in the Oil Fields* (Lexington: Kentucky Kernal Press, 1929), pp. 19–20; Sanders, *Our Common Herd,* p. 133.

12. Peebles interview; Mrs. Ruth Godwin, interviewed by Roger M. Olien, March 16, 1978, Kermit, Texas.

13. Mrs. Fred Keene, interviewed by Diana Davids Olien, March 21, 1978, Wink, Texas.

14. *Fifteenth Census of the United States, 1930: Population,* vol. 1, p. 1050; *Seventeenth Census of the United States, 1950: Population,* vol. 1, part 43 (Texas), p. 117. In 1950, 10.7 percent of the Odessa female work force was employed in eating and drinking places.

15. Mrs. L. V. Gill's father would not permit her to look for a teaching position in Wink; L. V. Gill, interviewed by Roger M. Olien, May 15, 1978, Wink, Texas.

16. Scott interview; McCamey Independent School District, *Board Minutes,* May 4, 1928, May 17, 27, 1929; Ector County Independent School District, *Board Minutes,* July 28, 1932, May 27, 1935, June 10, 1943; Midland Independent School District, *Board Minutes,* April 23, 1932, April 24, 1937, August 26, 1942.

17. Midland Independent School District, *Board Minutes,* April 20, 1929; Wink Independent School District *Board Minutes,* August 9, 1928; Scott interview.

18. Wink Independent School District, *Board Minutes,* April 9, 1930.

19. Scott interview.

20. Ector County Independent School District, *Board Minutes,* June 19, 1934; Godwin interview.

21. Scott interview.

22. Parker, "Life and Labor," p. 389.

23. Dr. Tom C. Bobo, interviewed by S. D. Myres, June 22, 1970, Mid-

land, Texas; Dr. Homer Johnson, interviewed by Diana Davids Olien, January 30, 1978, Midland, Texas; Mrs. Jno. P. Butler, interviewed by Diana Davids Olien, January 30, 1978, Midland, Texas.

24. Keene interview.

25. Gill interview.

26. *Odessa News-Times,* September 25, 1936.

27. Clell Reed, interviewed by Betty Fields, April, 1974, Wink, Texas, Permian Historical Society Collection; Bobo interview; Dr. Merle Montgomery, interviewed by Diana Davids Olien, February 4, 1978, by telephone from Midland to New York, N.Y.

28. Keene interview; W. C. Hayes, interviewed by S. D. Myres, February 12, 1970, McCamey, Texas.

29. Montgomery interview; Mr. and Mrs. R. V. Melton, interviewed by S. D. Myres, June 10, 1970, Crane, Texas.

30. Mrs. H. N. Phillips, interviewed by Roger M. and Diana Davids Olien, November 1, 1977, Midland, Texas; Mrs. Jno. P. Butler interview; Mrs. Charles Vertrees interview; Leonard interview; Keene interview; Godwin interview.

31. Keene interview; Godwin interview; Bill Heaton, interviewed by Mary Horne, May 15, 1974, Jal, New Mexico.

32. Mrs. Clifford Lyle, Mrs. John Hendrix, and Mr. Tom Wilmeth, interviewed by Diana Davids Olien, October 26, 1978, Midland, Texas.

33. Such an event pushed one young Midland wife beyond her endurance of West Texas. After seeing her clothesline of freshly washed diapers turn red from dust, she took the night train to Dallas and stayed with her sister for the remainder of her husband's tour of duty in the Permian Basin. Confidential source.

34. Mr. and Mrs. W. W. Allman, interviewed by S. D. Myres, June 19, 1970, Crane, Texas; Scott interview.

35. Mrs. Jno. P. Butler interview.

36. Montgomery interview.

37. Godwin interview; Mrs. Mary Adams, interviewed by Diana Davids Olien, March 22, 1978, McCamey, Texas; Mr. and Mrs. R. V. Wilson, interviewed by S. D. Myres, June 16, 1970, Odessa, Texas.

38. Scott interview.

39. Leonard interview.

40. Lucy Conoly Foster Miller, "Memories of a Happy Childhood" (unpublished essay, 1977), pp. 18–19.

41. Allman interview.

42. Ibid.

43. Miller, "Memories of a Happy Childhood," p. 19; May interview; J. S. Peebles, interviewed by Roger M. Olien; William T. Briggs, interviewed by Roger M. and Diana Davids Olien, August 20, 1977, Midland, Texas; Ernest W. Burgess, Harvey J. Locke, and Mary Margaret Thomas, *The Family from*

Institution to Companionship, 3d ed. (New York: American Book Company, 1963), pp. 38–39.

44. Don W. Dittman, interviewed by Roger M. Olien, with George Mitchell and Clyde Barton, April 6, 1979, Kermit, Texas.

45. Briggs interview.

46. Hugh Boren, interviewed by Roger M. Olien, February 21, 1978, Snyder, Texas. Not surprisingly, some oil people recall that "The old-timers didn't take to the oil people too well"; Mrs. Gladys Kindlesparger, interviewed by Karen Lozano, 1975, Odessa, Texas, Permian Historical Society Collection.

47. Mrs. Jno. P. Butler interview; Mrs. Charles Vertrees interview.

48. Mrs. Wayne Boren, interviewed by Diana Davids Olien, February 23, 1978, Snyder, Texas.

49. Wendell E. Cook, "The Wink Oil Boom," *The Permian Historical Annual* 6 (December, 1966): 7; Briggs interview; Cullen Akins, interviewed by Jo McGuire, April, 1974, McCamey, Texas, Permian Historical Society Collection; Charles Stroder, interviewed by S. D. Myres, June 18, 1970, Crane, Texas.

50. Leonard interview; Keene interview.

51. Wilson interview.

52. Godwin interview; Reed interview; W. H. Collyns, interviewed by Roger M. Olien, May 9, 1979, Midland, Texas.

53. Keene interview; Reed interview. One sociologist describes such casting of friends in family roles as the creation of "pseudo-kin": Robert O. Blood, Jr., *The Family* (New York: Free Press, 1972), p. 255.

54. D. E. L. Byers, *The Lone Gambler* (Casper, Wyo.: n.p., n.d.), p. 70.

55. Horlacher, *A Year in the Oil Fields,* pp. 59–60, 53–54.

56. Ibid., p. 58.

57. Leonard interview. Christiane Fischer quotes a woman writing to her sister from California in 1853: "It is all the go here for ladys to leave there husbands two out of three do it." *Let Them Speak for Themselves: Women in the American West* (Hamden, Conn.: Archon Books, 1977), p. 52. Sarah Royce deplored marital instability in Gold Rush days in San Francisco: Sarah Royce, *A Frontier Lady: Recollections of the Gold Rush and Early California,* ed. Ralph Henry Gabriel (Lincoln: University of Nebraska Press, 1977), pp. 116–19.

58. *Odessa Times,* December 30, 1927.

59. Lyle, Hendrix, Wilmeth interview. Some sociologists have maintained that families who move with mobile homes may not participate in community life but, by the same token, have a great degree of association with family members, thus promoting family unity: Burgess, Locke, and Thomas, *The Family,* p. 379. See also Ruth Chaskell, "Effect of Mobility on Family Life," *Social Work* 9: 85, 89.

60. Burgess, Locke, and Thomas are among those who note that to highly organized families, such problems need not be disunifying: *The Family,* pp. 376–7. See also Reuben Hill, "Generic Features of Families Under Stress," *Social Casework* 39:139–50.

61. Aaron Damron, interviewed by Sue Ann Damron, December 29, 1973, Big Spring, Texas, Permian Historical Society Collection; Adams interview; C. L. McKinney, interviewed by S. D. Myres, September 23, 1971, Midland, Texas; George R. Bentley, interviewed by S. D. Myres, May 20, 1970, Monahans, Texas; Melton interview.

62. To explain why divorce rates have long been higher on the Pacific Coast than in other regions, Henry Pang and Sue Marie Hanson cite the proportion of population in that region which is young, mobile, and not tied to the more conservative religious denominations: "Highest Divorce Rates in Western United States," *Sociology and Social Research* 52:228–38.

63. David K. Workman, interviewed by Louise Workman, March 30, 1975, Stanton, Texas, Permian Historical Society Collection.

64. Leonard interview.

65. Ibid.; W. H. Measures, interviewed by Roger M. Olien, February 16, 1979, Midland, Texas; Mrs. I. L. Edwards, interviewed by Diana Davids Olien, May 30, 1979, Midland, Texas.

66. Montgomery interview.

67. Leonard interview.

68. Burgess, Locke, and Thomas, *The Family,* p. 29.

69. Lucille Glasscock, *A Texas Wildcatter: A Fascinating Saga of O* (San Antonio: The Naylor Press, 1952), pp. 55–56.

70. Parker, "Life and Labor," p. 167.

71. Keene interview.

72. Ibid.

CHAPTER FIVE

1. *Odessa News,* November 1, 1927.

2. Rudolph M. Lapp, *Blacks in Gold Rush California* (N᾽ Haven: Yale University Press, 1977), pp. 49, 64.

3. Mrs. Tom Linebery, interviewed by Roger M. ᵈ Diana Davids Olien, June 15, 1978, Midland, Texas; Luis Saenz Raᵣ᾽ interviewed by Roger M. Olien, with Mrs. Severo Hinojosa, June 28, 197ᴵidland, Texas; J. Conrad Dunagan and Edd Cox, interviewed by Roger Mᵉⁿ, April 19, 1978, Monahans, Texas; Dr. and Mrs. H. P. Redwine, intervᵉᵈ by Diana Davids Olien, February 24, 1978, Snyder, Texas.

4. While the Census commonly undercounᵗᵉmbers of minority groups, recollections of long-time residents of thesᵘⁿties support Census reports.

5. Department of Commerce, Bureau of thᵉˢᵘˢ, *Fourteenth Census of the United States, 1920: Population,* vol. 3, pp. 50, 6⟨ 66, 69; *Fifteenth Census of the United States, 1930:* Population, vol. 3, part 2,ᵏ95, 1012–13; Department of Commerce, Bureau of the Census, *Negroᵉ ᴵhe United States, 1920-32,*

prepared by Charles E. Hall (1935; reprint ed., New York: Arno Press, 1969), pp. 816–17, 822, 824, 826.

6. Midland County Death Records; Ector County Death Records; *Sixteenth Census of the United States, 1940: Population,* vol. 2, part 6, pp. 795, 801, 804–6, 999–1000; *Seventeenth Census of the United States, 1950: Population,* vol. 2, part 42 (Texas), p. 102; *Eighteenth Census of the United States, 1960: Population,* vol. 45, part 1 (Texas), p. 114.

7. Midland County Death Records; Ector County Death Records. One Odessa resident who attended an all-black school in the fifties recalls that none of his classmates had been born in Odessa: Willie Hammond, Jr., interviewed by Rosalind McFarland, July 7, 1974, Odessa, Texas, Permian Historical Society Collection.

8. *Eighteenth Census of the United States, 1960: Population,* vol. 1, part 45 (Texas), p. 448; Ector County Birth and Death Records; Midland County Birth and Death Records; Midland Independent School District, *Board Minutes,* April 16, 1930, October 12, 1948, June 13, 1950.

9. Ector County Birth Records, 1949. Texas had lost 10.9 percent of its 1940 black population by 1950, as compared with a decade's loss of 32.4 percent in Arkansas, 31.5 percent in Oklahoma, and 30.2 percent in Mississippi: Henry S. Shryock, Jr., *Population Mobility Within the United States* (Chicago: Center for Community and Family Study, 1964), p. 111.

10. Ector County Birth Records, 1928–31, 1949. During the 1950s the *bracero* program brought in Mexican nationals for agricultural labor in West Texas counties where cotton was important, but those persons were, in theory, visitors rather than immigrants.

11. Mrs. Willsie Lee McKinney, interviewed by Diana Davids Olien, January 11, 1978, Midland, Texas.

12. Mrs. Barbara Bass Lane, interviewed by Diana Davids Olien, January 21, 1978, Midland, Texas.

13. McKinney interview.

14. Orah Lillie Corrales, interviewed by Diana Davids Olien, January 28, 1978, Midland, Texas.

15. Lane interview.

16. Corrales interview; McKinney interview. The Midland Independent School District at schools in 1950 so deviated school days in the black and Mexican-American schools in 1950 so that farmers could recruit children for the cotton harvest: *Board Minutes,* October 20, November 14, 1950; *Midland Reporter-Telegram,* December 31, 1950. The oil fields themselves child labor was uncommon, for the physical demand of oil work were generally beyond a child's capacity.

17. *Seventeenth Census of the United States, 1950: Population,* vol. 2, part 43 (Texas), pp. 123, 124; Ector County Death Records, Midland County Death Records.

18. Ector County Birth Records, 1949; Midland County Birth Records, 1951; Wink Board of Commissioners, *Minutes,* vol. 1, pp. 13–14; Ector County

Commissioners Court, *Minutes,* vol. 2, p. 266; Midland County Commissioners Court, *Minutes,* vol. 4, p. 73; Midland City Council, *Minutes,* vol. 3C, p. 535; vol. 4 p. 691.

19. *Negroes in the United States,* pp. 287, 309; W. Sherman Savage, *Blacks in the West* (Westport, Conn.: Greenwood Press, 1976), p. 87; Kenneth Wiggins Porter, *The Negro on the American Frontier* (New York: Arno Press, 1971), pp. 495, 503, 515; Lapp, *Blacks in Gold Rush California,* p. 96.

20. Ramos interview. For additional information on Mexican-American employment, see Matt S. Meier and Feliciano Rivera, eds., *Readings on La Raza: The Twentieth Century* (New York: Hill and Wang, 1974), pp. 13–15, 24, 33–34.

21. Corrales interview; P. F. Bridgewater, interviewed by Roger M. Olien, May 17, 1978, Midland, Texas; Midland Independent School District, *Board Minutes,* October 9, 1939, September 10, 1946.

22. A useful picture of the Mexican-American community in Midland during the 1930s may be found in Mike Gonzales, "Barrio, 1934" (unpublished essay, 1976).

23. Midland City Council, *Minutes,* vol. 5, p. 752. Still, the Midland City Council denied a 1959 request by the Yellow-Checker Cab Company for an exclusive franchise to serve the Anglo population: vol. 16, pp. 108–9.

24. Mr. and Mrs. Allan Patterson, interviewed by Diana Davids Olien, October 27, 1979, Midland, Texas; Mrs. Fred Leonard, interviewed by Diana Davids Olien, May 19, 1978, Midland, Texas; McKinney interview; Mrs. Fred Keene, interviewed by Diana Davids Olien, March 21, 1978, Wink, Texas; J. S. Peebles, interviewed by Roger M. Olien, May 15, 1978, Wink, Texas.

25. Lee O. White, interviewed by S. D. Myres and Berte R. Haigh, February 17, 1970, Fort Stockton, Texas; Samuel D. Myres, *The Permian Basin: Era of Discovery* (El Paso: Permian Press, 1973), p. 487; Sue Sanders, *Our Common Herd* (Garden City, N.Y.: Country Life Press, 1939), p. 159. The 1930 Census recorded such employment under black employment on oil and gas wells.

26. C. J. ("Red") Davidson, interviewed by S. D. Myres and Berte R. Haigh, March 19, 1971, Fort Worth, Texas; Claude B. Pennington, interviewed by Suzanne Agnew Pennington, September 19, 1959, Corpus Christi, Texas, Pioneers of Texas Oil Collection, Barker History Center, University of Texas at Austin; Mr. and Mrs. R. V. Wilson, interviewed by S. D. Myres, June 16, 1970, Odessa, Texas; John P. ("Slim") Jones, *Borger, The Little Oklahoma* (n.p., n.d.), part 1, p. 170; Carl Steffey, interviewed by Charles Wheeler, April 24, 1975, Odessa, Texas, Permian Historical Society Collection; Keene interview; S. A. Parker, interviewed by Ann Smith, January 16, 1974, Wink, Texas; Permian Historical Society Collection; J. S. Peebles, interviewed by Roger M. Olien.

27. J. Rudolph Wright, interviewed by Roger M. Olien, October 9, 1979, Midland, Texas; W. H. Bond, interviewed by Roger M. Olien, October 12, 1979, Midland, Texas; On April 22, 1929, the *Midland Reporter-Telegram* noted that "S. E. Perez, Mexican," was bringing suit against the Southern Casualty

Company for an injury sustained while using dynamite in pipeline work.

28. Ector County Birth Records, 1945, 1946, 1949.

29. Midland County Commissioners Court, *Minutes,* vol. 5, p. 37; Corrales interview; McKinney interview; Lane interview; Doc Rand, interviewed by Glen Ragsdale, June 29, 1974, Odessa, Texas, Permian Historical Society Collection; Allie V. Scott, interviewed by Diana Davids Olien, March 23, 1978, McCamey, Texas; Leonard interview; Keene interview.

30. The expansion of minority neighborhoods into areas previously Anglo met with resistance from Midland Anglos both in the 1940s and early 1960s: Midland City Council, *Minutes,* vol. 3A, p. 515; vol. 3B, p. 323; vol. 4, pp. 567, 597; vol. 10, p. 60; Corrales interview; McKinney interview.

31. McKinney interview; Rand interview; Corrales interview; The Reverend Horace F. Doyle, interviewed by Diana Davids Olien, with Willsie Lee McKinney, April 5, 1978, Midland, Texas.

32. McKinney interview; Doyle interview.

33. Rand interview; Doyle interview.

34. McKinney interview; Lane interview; Rand interview.

35. Midland City Council, *Minutes,* vol. 3B, p. 281; vol. 4, p. 662; vol. 11, p. 19; Odessa City Council, *Minutes,* vol. 3, p. 200; *Midland Reporter-Telegram,* May 13, 1932. In several instances of threatened epidemic during the thirties, the Midland City Council extended limited water service in black and Mexican-American neighborhoods following the sealing of contaminated wells: Marion Martin Nordeman, "Midland, Texas During the Depression, 1929–1933" (M.A. thesis, University of Texas at Austin, 1967), p. 130; Lane interview.

36. Midland City Council, *Minutes,* vol. 6, p. 795; vol. 8, p. 869.

37. Ector County Commissioners Court, *Minutes,* vol. 4, p. 144; *Odessa American,* January 1, 1949.

38. McCamey Independent School District, *Board Minutes,* July 1, 31, August 15, September 10, 1929, May 29, 1930; *McCamey News,* June 24, 1965; Scott interview; Texas, State Department of Education, "Public School Directory, 1931–1932," (Austin, 1931), p. 87.

39. Wink Independent School District, *Board Minutes,* June 5, August 12, August 26, 1930.

40. Prior to 1952, black students who wished a high school education attended out-of-town schools at which the Snyder Independent School District paid their tuition: Snyder Independent School District, *Board Minutes,* April 19, 1949, August 7, 1951, August 25, 1952, October 11, 1953; Hooper Shelton, comp., *From Buffalo . . . to Oil, History of Scurry County, Texas* (Snyder, Tex.: Feather Press, 1973), p. 122; *Snyder Daily News,* March 11, 1956.

41. Ector County Independent School District, *Board Minutes,* September 26, 1929, August 3, 1931, November 29, 1932, May 22, 1947, January 13, 1949, December 11, 1952; Rosalind O. McFarland, "Blackshear: A School of Growth" (unpublished essay, 1974).

42. Ector County Independent School District, *Board Minutes,* May 25, 1923, June 15, 1923; Redwine interview.

43. Midland Independent School District, *Board Minutes,* May 15, 1920, April 25, 1921, April 16, 1929, April 16, 1930, January 9, 1931, October 9, 1939, September 10, 1946, December 12, 1950; Bridgewater interview; Corrales interview.

44. *Seventeenth Census of the United States, 1950: Population,* vol. 1, part 43 (Texas), p. 130; McKinney interview.

45. Lane interview.

46. Ramos interview.

CHAPTER SIX

1. Earle Gray, *The Impact of Oil: The Development of Canada's Oil Resources* (Toronto: The Ryerson Press/Maclean Hunter, 1969), p. 93. For current appraisals of cattle and mining town violence, see Odie B. Faulk, *Dodge City* (New York: Oxford University Press, 1977); Robert B. Dykstra, *The Cattle Towns* (New York: Alfred Knopf, 1968); William S. Greever, *The Bonanza West: The Story of Western Mining Rushes, 1844–1900* (Norman: University of Oklahoma Press, 1963); and Duane A. Smith, *Rocky Mountain Mining Camps: The Urban Frontier* (Bloomington: Indiana University Press, 1967).

2. Sam T. Mallison, *The Great Wildcatter* (Charleston, W. Va.: Education Foundation of West Virginia, 1953), p. 345; Reagan County Death Records.

3. Carl Burgess Glasscock, *Then Came Oil* (Indianapolis: Bobbs-Merrill Company, 1938), p. 21.

4. Boyce House, *Oil Boom* (Caldwell, Ida.: Caxton Printers, 1941), p. 70; John Derwin Palmer, "A History of the Desdemona Oil Boom" (M.A. thesis, Hardin-Simmons University, 1938), pp. 96–97.

5. E. E. Brackens, interviewed by S. D. Myres, July 16, 1970, Wink, Texas; Philip S. Owen, interviewed by S. D. Myres, n.d., n.p. The Myres interviews are in the Abell-Hanger Collection at the Permian Basin Petroleum Museum, Library, and Hall of Fame, Midland, Texas; Death Records, Winkler County, vol. 1.

6. William Franklin Ash, interviewed by Roger M. Olien, March 2, 1979, Hobbs, New Mexico; the interviews by Roger M. and Diana Davids Olien are in the Permian Historical Society Collection at the University of Texas of the Permian Basin, Odessa, Texas.

7. Edward Gould Buffum, *Six Months in the Gold Mines* (Philadelphia: Lea and Blanchard, 1950), p. 133; Ovando J. Hollister, *The Mines of Colorado* (Springfield, Mass.: Samuel Bowles and Company, 1867), p. 84; Franklin Street, *California in 1850* (Cincinnati: R. E. Edwards and Company, 1851), pp. 46–47; James L. Horlacher, *A Year in the Oil Fields* (Lexington: Kentucky Kernal

Press, 1929), p. 60; Charlie Jeffries, "Reminiscences of Sour Lake," *Southwestern Historical Quarterly,* July, 1946, p. 35.

8. Mrs. F. J. Hawkins, interviewed by Bobbye Hill, November 23, 1974, Odessa, Texas, Permian Historical Society Collection; William T. Briggs, interviewed by Roger M. and Diana Davids Olien, August 20, 1977, Midland, Texas; Ash interview; Lewis Gray, interviewed by Roger M. Olien, May 22, 1979, Kermit, Texas.

9. Edd Cox, interviewed by Roger M. Olien, April 19, 1978, Monahans, Texas; Gray interview.

10. Clarence H. Dunaway, interviewed by Roger M. Olien, April 30, 1980, Odessa, Texas; John Jackson, interviewed by Roger M. Olien, April 30, 1980, Odessa, Texas; George Luck, interviewed by Roger M. Olien, May 2, 1980, Odesa, Texas; V. L. Cox, interviewed by Roger M. Olien, April 25, 1980, Odessa, Texas.

11. Briggs interview; Dunaway interview.

12. Hood V. May, interviewed by Roger M. Olien and J. Conrad Dunagan, April 19, 1978, Monahans, Texas.

13. F. Ellis Summers, interviewed by Roger M. Olien and George Mitchell, April 22, 1979, Kermit, Texas; May interview; J. S. Peebles, interviewed by Roger M. Olien, May 15, 1978, Wink, Texas.

14. Mary Lougan Bailey, "Crime, Punishment, and Legal Procedure in Howard County, Texas, from 1882 through 1901" (M.A. thesis, Texas Tech University, 1966), p. 14; Faulk, *Dodge City,* pp. 69, 150, 154.

15. Charles W. Chancellor, interviewed by S. D. Myres, October 29, 1971, Midland, Texas; Fannie Bess Taylor, interviewed by S. D. Myres, March 12, 1970, Midland, Texas; Snyder *Reporter-News,* October 18, 1964.

16. J. M. Flanigan, interviewed by S. D. Myres, May 15, 1970, Midland, Texas; Chancellor interview; Taylor interview; Hawkins interview; Dr. and Mrs. H. P. Redwine, interviewed by Diana Davids Olien, February 24, 1978, Snyder, Texas.

17. May interview; Peebles interview; L. V. Gill, interviewed by Roger M. Olien, May 15, 1978, Wink, Texas; Summers interview; Mrs. Fred Keene, interviewed by Diana Davids Olien, March 21, 1978, Wink, Texas; Mrs. Fred Leonard, interviewed by Diana Davids Olien, May 19, 1978, Midland, Texas.

18. James G. Dunn, "History of the Oil Industry in Navarro County" (M.A. thesis, Baylor University, 1967), pp. 69–70; Upton County Commissioners Court, *Minutes,* vol. 2, p. 52; Wink Board of Commissioners, *Minutes,* vol. 1, p. 38; Cullen Akins, interviewed by S. D. Myres, June 17, 1970, Odessa, Texas.

19. Wendell E. Cook, "The Wink Oil Boom," *The Permian Historical Annual* 6 (December, 1966): 12–13; Mr. and Mrs. W. W. Allman, interviewed by S. D. Myres, June 19, 1970, Crane, Texas; Akins interview; Upton County Commissioners Court, *Minutes,* vol. 1, p. 581; Cal Smith, interviewed by S. D. Myres, May 1, 1970, Odessa, Texas; R. C. Bowles, interviewed by S. D. Myres and

Berte R. Haigh, October 7, 1970, Houston, Texas; Mr. and Mrs. R. V. Wilson, interviewed by S. D. Myres, June 16, 1970, Odessa, Texas.

20. *Report of the Adjutant General of the State of Texas for the Fiscal Year, September 1, 1929 to August 31, 1930*, pp. 51–52.

21. *Pecos Enterprise and Gusher*, April 15, 1927; Calvin A. Stewart, interviewed by Edd Cox, March 24, 1978, San Saba, Texas; Peebles interview; Summers interview; Clyde Barton, interviewed by Roger M. Olien, April 6, 1979, Kermit, Texas.

22. *Winkler County News*, July 23, 1951; 109th District Court, *Criminal Minutes*, vol. 1, p. 38; Winkler County Commissioners Court, *Minutes*, vol. 2, pp. 4, 161; *Pecos Enterprise and Gusher*, May 13, 1928; Cook, "The Wink Oil Boom," p. 11–12.

23. Summers interview; Stewart interview.

24. 109th District Court, *Criminal Minutes*, vol. 1, pp. 38–39, and June, 1931 (no pagination); Barton interview; Stewart interview; Charles L. Klapproth, interviewed by S. D. Myres, September 16, 1970, Midland, Texas.

25. Stewart interview; Summers interview; Ash interview; Gray interview.

26. Justice of the Peace, Precinct 1, Winkler County, *Criminal Docket*, 1929; Winkler County Court, *Criminal Trial Docket*, 1921–30; 109th District Court, *Criminal Docket*, vols. 1 and 2; 109th District Court, *Criminal Minutes*, June, 1930 (no pagination).

27. Summers interview; Stewart interview; Ash interview; Gray interview; C. P. Laughlin, interviewed by Roger M. Olien, April 6, 1979, Wink, Texas.

28. Stewart interview; Barton interview; Summers interview; Laughlin interview; Ash interview; Gray interview.

29. Summers interview; Ash interview, Gray interview; Laughlin interview; John Williams, interviewed by Roger M. Olien and Clyde Barton, April 17, 1980, Kermit, Texas.

30. Gray interview; Laughlin interview; Williams interview; Ash interview; Keene interview; Cook, "The Wink Oil Boom," p. 13; Wink Board of Commissioners, *Minutes*, vol. 1, pp. 1, 3; Winkler County Death Records.

31. Ash interview; Laughlin interview; Summers interview.

32. Peebles interview; Keene interview; Summers interview; Laughlin interview; Ash interview; Williams interview; Wink Board of Commissioners, *Minutes*, vol. 1, pp. 35, 39, 55–59, 109, 110, 121.

33. Keene interview; Laughlin interview; Stewart interview; Summers interview; Ash interview; Keene interview; Winkler County Death Records.

34. Peebles interview; Wink Board of Commissioners, *Minutes*, vol. 1, pp. 13–15, 24; *Midland Reporter-Telegram*, April 4, 1929.

35. Upton County Death Records; Ector County Death Records; Midland County Death Records; Winkler County Death Records.

36. 142nd District Court, *Criminal File Docket*, vol. 1.

37. 142nd District Court, *Criminal File Docket,* vol. 1, nos. 2824 through 5024.

38. Ed Darnell, interviewed by Roger M. Olien, November 8, 1977, Midland, Texas; 142nd District, *Criminal File Docket,* vols. 1–4; *Midland Reporter-Telegram,* August 4, 1952; *San Angelo Standard-Times,* August 8, 1926.

39. Darnell interview.

40. Leonard interview.

CHAPTER SEVEN

1. D. D. Bowden, interviewed by Virginia White, April 7, 1974, Odessa, Texas, Permian Historical Society Collection.

2. Claude B. Pennington, interviewed by Suzanne Agnew Pennington, September 19, 1959, Corpus Christi, Texas, Pioneers of Texas Oil Collection, Barker History Center, University of Texas at Austin; Dr. and Mrs. H. P. Redwine, interviewed by Diana Davids Olien, February 24, 1978. The interviews by Roger M. and Diana Davids Olien are in the Permian Historical Society Collection at the University of Texas of the Permian Basin, Odessa, Texas.

3. William T. Briggs, interviewed by Roger M. and Diana Davids Olien, August 20, 1977, Midland, Texas.

4. George Mitchell and Clyde Barton, interviewed by Roger M. Olien, March 15, 1978, Kermit, Texas.

5. Jack Masters, interviewed by Bob Masters, July 1, 1979, Odessa, Texas. Permian Historical Society Collection.

6. Arthur Stout and Joseph W. Graybeal, interviewed by S. D. Myres, n.d., n.p. Interviews by S. D. Myres are in the Abell-Hanger Collection of the Permian Basin Petroleum Museum, Library, and Hall of Fame.

7. Charles Stroder, interviewed by S. D. Myres, June 18, 1970, Crane, Texas.

8. Mrs. Fred Keene, interviewed by Diana Davids Olien, March 21, 1978, Wink, Texas; Stroder interview.

9. Clell Reed, interviewed by Betty Fields, April, 1974, Wink, Texas. Permian Historical Society Collection.

10. Keene interview; Dr. Homer Johnson, interviewed by Diana Davids Olien, January 30, 1978, Midland, Texas; Mr. and Mrs. R. V. Wilson, interviewed by S. D. Myres, June 16, 1970, Odessa, Texas; Stroder interview.

11. Mrs. Robert Boykin, interviewed by Diana Davids Olien, January 27, 1978, Midland, Texas; Ruth Godwin, interviewed by Roger M. Olien, March 16, 1978, Kermit, Texas; David K. Workman, interviewed by Louise Workman, March 30, 1975, Stanton, Texas; Permian Historical Society Collection; Keene interview; Ralph W. Hidy and Muriel E. Hidy, *Pioneering in Big Business, 1882–1911: History of Standard Oil Company (New Jersey)* (New York: Harper & Brothers, 1955), p. 590; Gerald T. White, *Formative Years in the Far West: A*

History of Standard Oil Company of California and Predecessors through 1919 (New York: Appleton-Century-Crofts, 1962), p. 532.

12. Reed interview; Mr. and Mrs. L. G. Byerley, interviewed by Roger M. and Diana Davids Olien, October 16, 1977, Midland, Texas.

13. *Crane News,* September 6, 1962.

14. Godwin interview; Stroder interview; Mrs. Clifford Lyle, Mrs. John Hendrix, and Mr. Tom Wilmeth, interviewed by Diana Davids Olien, October 26, 1978, Midland, Texas.

15. Godwin interview; Workman interview; *Midland Reporter-Telegram,* February 16, 1950.

16. Mrs. Fred Leonard, interviewed by Diana Davids Olien, May 19, 1978, Midland, Texas; Godwin interview; Mr. and Mrs. J. S. Peebles, interviewed by S. D. Myres, July 16, 1970, Wink, Texas; Mr. and Mrs. J. M. Horner, interviewed by S. D. Myres, July 13, 1970, Wink, Texas; J. Conrad Dunagan and Edd Cox, interviewed by Roger M. Olien, April 19, 1978, Monahans, Texas.

17. Keene interview; Jess W. Massingill, interviewed by S. D. Myres, July 17, 1970, Mentone, Texas. On the tradition of this type of entertainment in Upton County, see N. Ethie Eagleton, *On the Last Frontier: A History of Upton County, Texas* (El Paso: Texas Western Press, 1971), p. 21.

18. Leonard interview; Mrs. Mary Adams, interviewed by Diana Davids Olien, March 22, 1978, McCamey, Texas; Cullen Akins, interviewed by S. D. Myres, June 17, 1970, Odessa, Texas; Godwin interview.

19. Snyder Independent School District, *Board Minutes,* March 10, 1951.

20. J. Conrad Dunagan, interviewed by Roger M. Olien, April 19, 1978, Monahans, Texas; Perry D. Pickett, interviewed by Roger M. Olien, May 18, 1978, Midland, Texas; Midland City Council, *Minutes,* vol. 2, p. 151; Odessa City Council, *Minutes,* vol. 2, p. 167; Ector County Commissioners Court, *Minutes,* vol. 4, p. 519.

21. Albert Raymond Parker, "Life and Labor in the Mid-Continent Oil Fields, 1859–1945" (Ph.D. diss., University of Oklahoma, 1951), p. 46; *Midland Reporter-Telegram,* March 12, 1929.

22. Cullen Akins, interviewed by S. D. Myres; W. H. Collyns, interviewed by Charlene Ramsey, July 3, 1974, Midland, Texas, Permian Historical Society Collection; Hood V. May, interviewed by Roger M. Olien, April 19, 1978, Monahans, Texas; Midland City Council, *Minutes,* vol. 11, p. 445.

23. Clark Storm, interviewed by Diana Davids Olien, September 7, 1978, Midland, Texas; Anne Swendig, interviewed by Diana Davids Olien, May 31, 1979, Midland, Texas.

24. Storm interview.

25. Godwin interview; Reed interview.

26. Dunagan interview; Godwin interview; Redwine interview; Mrs. F. J. Hawkins, interviewed by Bobbye Hill, November 23, 1974, Odessa, Texas, Permian Historical Society Collection; *Midland Reporter-Telegram,* February 26, 1950.

27. Odessa City Council, *Minutes,* vol. 1, p. 248; Midland City Council, *Minutes,* vol. 3A, pp. 42, 121. In 1945, the Midland Civic Righteousness Committee tried to bring the Midland City Council to close pool halls "as a testimony to our faith in the 'Higher Things' of Life," but the city took no action: *Minutes,* vol. 5, p. 767.

28. McCamey Board of Aldermen, *Minutes,* April 7, 1927; Odessa City Council, *Minutes,* vol. 1, p. 72; Midland City Council, *Minutes,* vol. 3A, p. 162; vol. 3B, p. 300.

29. Dunagan, Cox interview.

30. Ector County Commissioners Court, *Minutes,* vol. 3, pp. 190–91, 221, 335, 439; vol. 4, pp. 110, 137, 338–39, 454, 595, 601; vol. 5, pp. 14, 238.

31. Midland City Council, *Minutes,* vol. 10, pp. 343, 347, 405; vol. 11, pp. 69, 74.

32. Midland City Council, *Minutes,* vol. 16, pp. 377, 386; Henry A. Meadows, interviewed by Roger M. Olien, May 17, 1978, Midland, Texas; Pickett interview.

33. Odessa City Council, *Minutes,* vol. 2, pp. 80–81; Midland City Council, *Minutes,* vol. 3C, p. 486; vol. 10, p. 91; vol. 12, p. 34; vol. 10, p. 321; vol. 11, p. 19.

34. One sociologist has noted that when "rootedness" is disturbed, there may be a decreased tendency to social participation; W. G. Steglich, "Participation of Migrants in Urban Associations," *Proceedings of the Southwestern Sociological Association,* vol. 15, pp. 89–93.

35. Hooper Shelton, comp., *From Buffalo . . . to Oil, History of Scurry County, Texas* (Snyder, Tex.: Feather Press, 1973), pp. 125–26, 134, 139; Robbie Knoy, "The Oil Boom in Snyder, Texas" (M.A. thesis, Hardin-Simmons University, 1950), pp. 10–11.

36. Mrs. Jno. P. Butler, interviewed by Diana Davids Olien, January 30, 1978, Midland, Texas; *Midland Reporter-Telegram,* March 10, 1929; *Odessa American,* September 17, 1961; Midland Independent School District, *Board Minutes,* February 14, 1951, December 11, 1951, July 8, 1952, August 12, 1952, September 9, 1952, and *passim.*

37. *Odessa Bulletin,* n.d. (1939).

38. Mrs. Neva Campbell, interviewed by Diana Davids Olien, March 20, 1978, Kermit, Texas.

39. Campbell interview.

40. *McCamey News,* June 24, 1965; Mrs. R. Russell Heaner, "Church History of Upton County," in the McCamey Woman's Study Club, *Footprints on the Sands: A History of Upton County* (McCamey, n.p., 1963); Dr. Merle Montgomery, interviewed by Diana Davids Olien, February 4, 1978, by telephone from Midland to New York, N.Y.; Allie V. Scott, interviewed by Diana Davids Olien, March 23, 1978, McCamey, Texas; Godwin interview; Samuel D. Myres, *The Permian Basin: Era of Discovery* (El Paso: Permian Press, 1973), p. 317.

41. Leonard interview.

42. Lyle-Hendrix-Wilmeth interview.

43. Mrs. Jno. P. Butler interview; Mrs. H. N. Phillips, interviewed by Roger M. and Diana Davids Olien, November 11, 1977, Midland, Texas; Mrs. Wayne Boren, interviewed by Diana Davids Olien, February 23, 1978, Snyder, Texas; Hugh Boren, interviewed by Roger M. Olien, February 21, 1978, Snyder, Texas; P. F. Bridgewater, interviewed by Roger M. Olien, May 17, 1978, Midland, Texas; Maria Spencer, interviewed by Diana Davids Olien, January 25, 1978, Midland, Texas; *Midland Reporter-Telegram*, February 26, 1950.

44. *Odessa News-Times,* November 2, 1938; *Midland Reporter-Telegram,* February 26, 1950; Midland Independent School District, *Board Minutes,* April 12, October 10, 1950; January 9, April 10, 1951; February 12, March 12, 1952; and *passim.*

45. *New York Times,* April 15, 1951.

46. Wilson interview.

CHAPTER EIGHT

1. Edward Gould Buffum, *Six Months in the Gold Mines* (Philadelphia: Lea and Blanchard, 1850), p. 136.

2. *Odessa News-Times,* March 28, 1930.

3. *Odessa News,* September 9, 1927.

4. *Midland Reporter-Telegram,* February 23, 1930.

5. *Midland Reporter-Telegram,* February 23, 1930.

6. *Midland Reporter-Telegram,* February 26, 1950.

7. Mrs. M. A. Harrison, interviewed by Carol Soderberg, July 5, 1974, Odessa, Texas. Permian Historical Society Collection, University of Texas of the Permian Basin.

8. Mrs. Wayne Boren, interviewed by Diana Davids Olien, February 23, 1978, Snyder, Texas; Hugh Boren, interviewed by Roger M. Olien, February 21, 1978, Snyder, Texas; Permian Historical Society Collection.

9. Mrs. Tom Linebery, interviewed by Roger M. and Diana Davids Olien, June 15, 1978, Midland, Texas; Mrs. Earl Vest, interviewed by Roger M. Olien, May 15, 1978, Kermit, Texas; Permian Historical Society Collection.

Top: West Texas mud: Avenue R, Snyder, in 1949.

Bottom: Bus apartments for rent in Snyder, 1949.

Bibliographical Note

FROM TITUSVILLE TO ANCHORAGE, the fast-paced and dramatic action of oil booms has had an enduring attraction for popular writers. Scores of magazine and newspaper articles thrilled readers with colorful tales of oil boom bustle and commotion. Using many of the same literary expressions as their predecessors who wrote of the goldfields of the American West, the journalists who described new oil towns developed a highly colored stereotypical portrayal of oil town growth. Oil boomtowns were "wide open," populated by brawling workers, conniving promoters, profiteering merchants, vicious criminals, and, on rare occasions, hard-bitten lawmen. Oil booms, in short, created anarchic hell holes.

The works of Boyce House best illustrate the mud and blood school of popular writing on oil booms. A newspaper columnist, House built a career and reputation as the chronicler of the "Rip-Roaring Days in the Oil Fields." In *Were You in Ranger?* (Dallas: Tardy Publishing Co., 1935); *Oil Boom* (Caldwell, Ida.: Caxton Printers, 1941); *Roaring Ranger: The World's Biggest Boom* (San Antonio: Naylor Company, 1951); and *Oil Field Fury* (San Antonio: Naylor Company, 1954), House gave his readers a spectacular and horrifying view of the oil boomtown, whose muddy streets were strewn with murdered workers: a picture so violently colorful that it was far more entertaining than reality. Like the teller of tales of the Spanish Main, Boyce House painted a scene of danger and derring-do which was considerably larger than life.

If authors like House at least gave their readers good entertainment, the same cannot be said of the scholars who uncritically adopted the mud and blood view of oil booms. Carl Coke Rister's *Oil! Titan of the Southwest* (Norman: University of Oklahoma Press, 1949), is typical of academic writing that falls back on the hackneyed stereotype of oil booms as sources of hellish disorder. It is ironic that, while unpublished work available to Rister reflected a thoughtful sifting of primary source material and offered convincing alternatives to popular sensationalism, he was less analytical and more negative than his predecessors in writing about settlements that expanded in response to the development of petroleum resources. He summed up his feelings toward oil development in communities with the term "social chaos," seeing it wherever oil booms occurred. Thus Seminole City was typical of Rister's boomtowns: "Its every expression was disorder." Borger, Texas, was "a wild, rootin'-tootin', snortin', hell-raisin' place," reminiscent of "Dawson's Klondike gold-rush days." The latter quotation shows Rister at double exaggeration, for as David B. Wharton indicated in *The Alaska Gold Rush* (Bloomington: University of Indiana Press, 1972), the Canadian government maintained good order in Dawson. Rister never tried to explain why oil boomtowns developed as they did; he merely added scholarly veneer and embellishments of personal prejudice to the popular sensational portrayal of oil towns.

The few academic histories of oil-field activity and related community development that have appeared since Rister's work have not advanced the study of oil booms. Robert L. Martin's *The City Moves West: Economic and Industrial Growth in Central West Texas* (Austin: University of Texas Press, 1969), followed in Rister's path; drawing in large part on secondary sources, Martin covered a century's history of an area larger than New England in less than two hundred pages of text, ignoring new oil boomtowns like Best, McCamey, and Wink. More may have been promised but less delivered by Richard R. Moore's *West Texas After the Discovery of Oil* (Austin: Pemberton Press, 1971), which drew on House, Rister, and other secondary sources. Moore left the story of oil booms where he found it, in the worn tracks of House and Rister. Samuel D. Myres worked far more diligently than either Martin or Moore to assemble information for his two encyclopedic volumes on oil development in the Permian Basin, *The Permian Basin: Petroleum Empire of the Southwest* (El Paso: Permian Press, 1973, 1977), but oil booms and their effect on community development were not the focus of his interest; nor did he reinterpret what he found. The most recent commentary on oil development is James Presley's *A Saga of Wealth: The Rise of the Texas Oilman* (New York: G. P. Putnam's Sons, 1978), which produces the usual tired tales of Ranger's iniquities to demonstrate that the Eastland County boom was "a classic illustration of the basic pattern" of an oil boom, whose sequence ran through "leasing, drilling, trading, carousing, gambling, letting blood." Selecting colorful material from Boyce House and other secondary sources, and the Pioneers of Texas Oil Oral History Collection at the University of Texas at Austin, Presley offers up familiar old yarns like the demonstrably false story that dead bodies were so common in Ranger's streets that they caused little excitement.

To arrive at a reasonable understanding of petroleum development and how it affected persons and communities, then, the serious reader has to go beyond the House-Rister school of florid journalism with academic flourishes. There are a few popular works that are helpful even though their principal focus is neither oil booms nor oil towns. Two pictorial surveys of the opening of regional oil fields, Paul H. Giddens's *Early Days of Oil: A Pictorial History of the Beginnings of the Industry in Pennsylvania* (Princeton, N.J.: Princeton University Press, 1948) and William Rintoul's *Spudding In: Recollections of Pioneer Days in the California Oil Fields* (Fresno, Calif.: Valley Publishers, for the California Historical Society, 1978) avoid the excesses of the mud and blood school and present useful accounts of the development of Pennsylvania and California oil fields. Giddens's first work on oil, *The Birth of the Oil Industry* (New York: Macmillan Company, 1938), is still useful, though it was drawn largely from newspaper accounts of events.

A number of solid scholarly works contain incidental information on the topic: Henrietta M. Larson and Kenneth W. Porter, *History of Humble Oil and Refining Company* (New York: Harper & Brothers, 1959); Ralph W. and Muriel E. Hidy, *Pioneering in Big Business, 1882–1911: History of Standard Oil Company (New Jersey)* (New York: Harper & Brothers, 1955); George S. Gibbs and Evelyn H. Knowlton, *The Resurgent Years: History of Standard Oil Company (New Jersey), 1911–1927* (New York: Harper & Brothers, 1956); Henrietta M. Larson, Evelyn H. Knowlton, and Charles S. Popple, *New Horizons, 1927–1950: History of Standard Oil Company (New Jersey)* (New York: Harper & Row, 1971); Kendall Beaton, *Enterprise in Oil: A History of Shell in the United States* (New York: Appleton-Century-Crofts, 1957); Gerald T. White, *Formative Years in the Far West: A History of Standard Oil Company of California and Predecessors through 1919* (New York: Appleton-Century-Crofts, 1962). Though these scholars were necessarily more concerned with corporate strategies and growth than with the social consequences of business activity, they included useful information on personnel policies, the effect of economic and market conditions on the labor force, the operation of company camps, and the sequence of field development. The organization of their work around the histories of companies, however, precluded extensive consideration of social conditions.

Most of the important data for this study have been obtained from the U.S. Census reports for 1920 through 1960, from the directories and reports of the Texas State Department of Education, and from county birth and death records. Additional documents, in the form of minutes of city councils, commissioners' courts, and school boards were also useful. Local court and death records provided data to test the prevalent belief that death and mayhem were commonplaces of life in oil boomtowns. Local newspapers, such as the *Pecos Enterprise and Gusher* and the *Midland Reporter-Telegram*, reflected local reactions to boom conditions. But, for a human perspective on oil booms, it was necessary to leave the archives and listen to men and women who lived and worked in the oil fields. In the absence of letters, diaries, and other personal memorabilia so useful to historians in constructing the human dimensions of earlier times, oral recollections are of great value to the historian of relatively recent events, and we are indebted to those persons who so generously gave us their time in interviews. Taken with hard data like statistics, ordinances, indictments, and certificates of birth and death, oral material permits a fuller reconstruction of what happened in oil booms and what social and individual consequences followed from petroleum development.

The following people most generously gave us their time in interviews for this study. We have added a brief note indicating each interviewee's occupation or status at the time his or her community experienced boom growth.

Mrs. Mary Adams was a schoolgirl in McCamey.

William Franklin Ash was a friend and associate of Heavy Brackeen in Wink.

Clyde Barton, a Kermit businessman, served on the Winkler County grand jury.

W. H. Bond was a paymaster and supervisor in pipeline construction in the Permian Basin.

Hugh Boren was in the insurance and real estate business in Snyder.

Mrs. Wayne Boren was a leader in women's organizations in Snyder.

Mrs. Robert Boykin lived in an oil-field camp near Royalty and was a librarian in Midland during the Spraberry boom.

Percy F. Bridgewater was a banker, civic leader, and school board member in Midland.

William T. Briggs was a regional investigator for Dun and Bradstreet in the Permian Basin in the 1950s.

Kenneth Burroughs owned a drugstore in Kermit.

Jno. P. Butler was a banker and civic leader in Midland.

Mrs. Jno. P. Butler was a leader in women's and civic organizations in Midland.

Mr. and Mrs. Leo G. Byerley came to Midland in the early 1950s when Mr. Byerley's employer, Honolulu Oil Company, was active in the Permian Basin.

Mrs. Neva Campbell was the wife of a Winkler County rancher and county commissioner.

Floyd L. Carney was an oil-field worker and a bartender at the City Cafe, Wink.

William H. Collyns worked for Humble in McCamey and was later a newspaper editor in Midland.

Mrs. Oralia Corrales was a schoolgirl in Midland.

Edd Cox worked in the Ward County oil fields and was a rancher.

V. L. Cox built rigs in the Odessa area.

Ed Darnell was sheriff of Midland County.

Dr. Carl Dillaha practiced medicine in Snyder.

Don Dittman worked on his father's drilling rigs near McCamey.

Reverend Horace F. Doyle was a civic leader and pastor of the Macedonia Baptist Church in Midland.

J. Conrad Dunagan managed a Coca-Cola bottling plant in Monahans and delivered soft drinks to Wink.

Clarence Dunaway built rigs in Hobbs and Odessa.

Arvin D. Eady worked for Humble in various Permian Basin towns.

Mr. and Mrs. I. L. Edwards lived in McCamey, where Mr. Edwards worked for Humble.

E. L. Frazier worked for Humble as a teamster near Wink.

L. V. Gill worked as a pumper near Wink.

Lewis Gray ran the Dew Drop Inn in Wink.

Mrs. Ruth Godwin was a schoolgirl in Wink.

Joel Hamlett was a letter carrier in Snyder.

Mrs. John Hendrix attended school in Odessa and Midland.

John Jackson built rigs near Odessa.

Dr. Homer Johnson practiced medicine in Midland.

Mrs. Fred Keene was a homemaker in Wink.

Tom King was a schoolboy in Snyder.

W. Porter King owned an appliance store in Snyder.

Mrs. Barbara Jean Bass Lane was a schoolgirl in Midland.

C. P. Laughlin repaired autos in Wink.

Stanley Leavitt was a Midland businessman.

Mrs. Fred Leonard was a homemaker, nurse, and boardinghouse assistant in McCamey.

Mrs. Tom Linebery was a rancher's daughter in Winkler County.

Mrs. Clifford Lyle was a homemaker in Odessa and Midland.

George Luck built rigs near Odessa.

Mrs. John R. McKinley attended school and was later a homemaker in Midland.

Mrs. Willsie Lee McKinney taught at George Washington Carver School in Midland.

Hood V. May was an oil-field worker near Wink.

Henry A. Meadows was a member of the zoning commission in Midland.

William H. Measures worked in pipelining and later for the water department of the City of Midland.

George Mitchell was a schoolboy in Winkler County.

George P. Mitchell was a rancher and tax assessor-collector for Winkler County.

Dr. Merle Montgomery was a homemaker in McCamey.

Tom H. Neel was an attorney in Pyote and Monahans.

Mr. and Mrs. Allen Patterson worked for Humble in McCamey.

J. S. Peebles dressed tools and owned a boardinghouse in Wink.

Mrs. H. N. Phillips was partner in an electrical supply and service business and a Midland homemaker.

Perry D. Pickett was a mayor of Midland.

O. C. Profitt was a driller in the Permian Basin.

Colin Puckett was a schoolboy in Big Lake.

Luis Saenz Ramos was a labor and trucking contractor in Midland and in Winkler County.

Dr. and Mrs. H. P. Redwine resided in Snyder, where he practiced medicine.

Dr. C. A. Robinson practiced medicine in Kermit.

Dr. L. Rose Robinson practiced medicine in Kermit.

Mrs. Mary Rogers was a homemaker in Burkburnett.

William Sanders was a tool dresser and driller near Wink.

Miss Allie V. Scott taught school in McCamey.

Thomas Sealy practiced law and was a civic leader in Midland.

Miss Maria Spencer was a geologist in Midland.

Mrs. Helen Steck was a nurse in Midland.

Calvin A. Stewart (interviewed by Edd Cox) was deputy sheriff of Winkler County.

Clark Storm taught school and worked for a drilling company in New Mexico.

F. Ellis Summers was deputy sheriff and later sheriff of Winkler County.

Mr. and Mrs. Hoke Tehee made various Oklahoma and Texas booms and settled in Monahans.

Mr. and Mrs. Charles Vertrees were geologists in Midland.

Mrs. Earl Vest was the daughter of a rancher and county judge of Winkler County.

Captain Robert R. Vincent was head of Midland's Salvation Army center in 1980.

Tony Wilburn was a barber in Wink and Snyder.

Jack Williams owned cafés in McCamey and Wink.

Tom Wilmeth was a schoolboy in Odessa and Midland.

Ben Wilson was owner of an auto supply store in Snyder.

Walter Wingo worked for Texas Electric Service in Wink and did oil-field work.

J. Rudolph Wright was employed by the pipeline division of the Mobil Oil Company in various Permian Basin communities.

Exhausted crew of Ohio Company's Yates Number 30A in 1929.
The well came in at 200,000 barrels per day.

Index